STUDY GUIDE

Jill Austin

Middle Tennessee State University

MANAGEMENT

FOURTH EDITION

Stephen P. Robbins

San Diego State University

PRENTICE HALL

Englewood Cliffs, New Jersey 07632

Production Editor: *Naomi Nishi*
Acquisitions Editor: *Natalie Anderson*
Assistant Editor: *Lisamarie Brassini*
Production Coordinator: *Trudy Pisciotti*

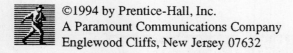©1994 by Prentice-Hall, Inc.
A Paramount Communications Company
Englewood Cliffs, New Jersey 07632

Printed in the United States of America

10   9   8   7   6   5   4   3   2   1

ISBN 0-13-085804-8

Prentice-Hall International (UK) Limited, *London*
Prentice-Hall of Australia Pty. Limited, *Sydney*
Prentice-Hall Canada Inc., *Toronto*
Prentice-Hall Hispanoamericana, S.A., *Mexico*
Prentice-Hall of India Private Limited, *New Delhi*
Prentice-Hall of Japan, Inc., *Tokyo*
Simon & Schuster Asia Pte. Ltd., *Singapore*
Editora Prentice-Hall do Brasil, Ltda., *Rio de Janeiro*

This Study Guide is dedicated to the memory
of JorjAnne, a special little girl who
enriched the lives of all who knew her.

CONTENTS

PREFACE

This Student Study Guide has been designed to supplement <u>Management,</u> fourth edition, by Stephen Robbins. The purpose of this Student Study Guide is to aid in your understanding of the text material.

Each chapter of the Student Study Guide contains an outline and corresponding learning objectives, a summary, key terms and definitions. In addition, three types of questions are included to help you understand the basic management concepts more fully.

These question types include:

        true/false questions
        multiple choice questions
        application cases

SUGGESTED STUDY APPROACH

You should read the main text material first, paying particular attention to the learning objectives and end of chapter questions. Then review the definitions and chapter summary from the Student Study Guide. After you feel that you have mastered the chapter concepts, answer the questions in the Student Study Guide for "self test" and review. You should then check the correct answers to the Student Study Guide questions and review any necessary text sections. This process should allow for a thorough understanding of the material in the textbook. The application case sections will help you relate text material to things you know about and this should aid in your understanding of management concepts.

For those of you who are using this Study Guide on your own and would like some suggested answers to the Application Cases in it, they can be found in the instructor's Applications Pack. Please request them from your instructor.

Chapter 1

Managers and Management

CHAPTER OUTLINE	CORRESPONDING LEARNING OBJECTIVES
I. Who are Managers?	1. Differentiate managers from operatives.
II. What is Management and What Do Managers Do?	
A. Defining Management	2. Define management.
	3. Distinguish between effectiveness and efficiency.
B. Management Functions	
C. Management Roles	
1. Interpersonal Roles	4. Identify the roles performed by managers.
2. Informational Roles	
3. Decisional Roles	
D. Are Effective Managers Also Successful?	5. Differentiate the activities of successful managers from effective ones.
E. Is the Manager's Job Universal?	
1. Organizational Level	6. Explain whether the manager's job is generic.
2. Organizational Type	
3. Organizational Size	
4. Cross-National Transferability	

CHAPTER OVERVIEW	CORRESPONDING LEARNING OBJECTIVES

III. The Value the Marketplace Puts on Managers

IV. Why Study Management?

7. Explain the value of studying management.

CHAPTER OVERVIEW

Managers work in organizations that are set up to accomplish specific purposes. Groups are considered to be organizations if they have three characteristics:

1. a distinct purpose

2. composed of people

3. a structure that defines and limits group behavior

Organizations can be profit or nonprofit; social or business; large or small.

Managers who work at the lowest level of management are called first-line managers. Middle managers are usually department heads, district managers, or division managers. Top managers consist of vice-presidents, directors, chief operating officers, or the chairman of the board. Operatives are employees who work directly on a job and do not have any managerial or supervisory responsibility.

Management can be defined as a process of getting things done through other people. Managers are concerned with achieving efficiency and effectiveness. Efficiency means improving the relationships between inputs and outputs. Managers are also concerned with effectiveness or getting things done. It is possible for organizations to be efficient, but not effective and for organizations to be effective, but not efficient. However, managers are concerned with achieving both effective and efficient operations.

In the early 1900's, Henri Fayol discussed management as a set of functions. The four basic management functions include: planning, organizing, leading, and controlling.

1. Planning includes defining an organization's goals and developing plans to coordinate activities.

2. Organizing includes determining what tasks are to be done and how work is to be organized.

3. The leading function involves motivation of workers and directing the activities of others.

4. Controlling is monitoring work and making corrections as they are needed.

When Henry Mintzberg studied managerial work in the late 1960's, he discussed ten roles performed by managers. These roles are divided into three categories:

1. Interpersonal - Figurehead, Leader, Liaison

2. Informational - Monitor, Disseminator, Spokesperson

3. Decisional - Entrepreneur, Disturbance Handler, Resource Allocator, Negotiator

Research indicates that different management roles are emphasized at different levels of the organization. For example, the figurehead role and the negotiator role are more important at higher levels in the organization than they are at lower organization levels. These ten roles do seem to clearly indicate activities related to managerial work, but nothing new is really learned using the role approach to explain managerial work. This is true because each of the roles can be explained by one of the four management functions. For example, the three interpersonal roles are part of the leading function.

In another research study, Fred Luthans suggested that managers engage in four activities: traditional management, communication, human resource management, and networking. Results indicate that on average, managers use between twenty and thirty percent of their time for each of the four activities. However, successful managers do not allocate their time the same way that effective managers allocate their time. Successful managers seem to spend more of their time networking while effective managers spend more of their time communicating.

If management is a generic discipline, the manager's tasks should be the same regardless of level in the organization, profit or nonprofit status, small or large size, or location in the United States or internationally. Managers in different organizations do have different managerial tasks to perform. The tasks are not different in function, but they are different in degree of importance. For example, all managers plan, but planning becomes more important as the manager move up in the hierarchy.

Good managerial skills are important for the success of organizations. Managers who possess these skills usually are paid well for their expertise.

The two primary reasons that students can benefit from a course in management include the following:

1. Everyone has a vested interest in improving the way organizations are managed. (We interact with them every day of our lives.)

2. Every worker will either be managed or will be a manager. (Employees can benefit from knowledge about management because this knowledge aids in understanding how a boss behaves.)

KEY TERMS AND DEFINITIONS

1. organization - A systematic arrangement of people to accomplish some specific purpose.

2. operatives - People who work directly on a job or task and have no responsibility for overseeing the work of others.

3. managers - Individuals in an organization who direct the activities or others.

4. first-line managers - Supervisors; the lowest level of management.

5. management - The process of getting activities completed efficiently through other people.

6. efficiency - The relationship between inputs and outputs: seeks to minimize resource costs.

7. effectiveness - Goal attainment.

8. management functions - Planning, organizing, leading, and controlling.

9. planning - Includes defining goals, establishing strategy, and developing plans to coordinate activities.

10. organizing - Determining what tasks are to be done, who is to do them, how the tasks are to be grouped, who reports to who, and where decisions are to be made.

11. leading - Includes motivating subordinates, directing others selecting the most effective communication channels, and resolving conflicts.

12. controlling - Monitoring activities to ensure that they are being accomplished as planned and correcting any significant deviations.

13. management roles - Specific categories of managerial behavior.

14. interpersonal roles - Roles that include figurehead, leadership, and liaison activities.

15. informational roles - Roles that include monitoring, disseminating, and spokesperson roles.

16. decisional roles - Roles that include those of entrepreneur, disturbance handler, resource allocator, and negotiator.

17. small business - An independently owned and operated profit-seeking enterprise having fewer than 500 employees.

TRUE/FALSE QUESTIONS

1. T F First-line managers are usually called supervisors.

2. T F Management is a process of getting activities completed efficiently with and through other people.

4

3.   T   F   It is enough for managers to simply be efficient in carrying out their duties.

4.   T   F   Controlling is a process used to make sure organization actions are consistent with plans.

5.   T   F   It is usually not necessary for managers to perform all four management functions in carrying out their jobs.

6.   T   F   Mintzberg's ten roles are different enough from the four management functions that the roles illustrate managerial actions not covered in the functions.

7.   T   F   The informational roles of managers include monitor, disturbance handler, and disseminator.

8.   T   F   Managers have different orientations toward planning at different levels of the organization.

9.   T   F   Since management is a generic activity, a manager's work is the same regardless of what he/she manages.

10.   T   F   The roles of small and large business managers are basically the same.

11.   T   F   Management concepts are not generically transferable to international settings.

12.   T   F   One reason that management is an important topic of study for students is because every worker will either manage or be managed.

MULTIPLE CHOICE QUESTIONS

13.   Which is not a characteristic of an organization?

   a.   An organization has a distinct purpose.
   b.   An organization is composed of people.
   c.   An organization always seeks to earn a profit.
   d.   An organization has a structure that defines and limits people.

14.   Operatives are:

   a.   people who manage others
   b.   first-line supervisors
   c.   middle managers
   d.   people who work directly on a job and have no managerial responsibility

15.   Which level of management works directly with operatives?

   a.   first-line supervisors
   b.   middle managers
   c.   top managers
   d.   all of the above

16. Which is not true for efficiency?

    a. There is a relationship between efficiency and effectiveness.
    b. If the number of outputs increases, efficiency increases.
    c. If more outputs can be obtained for a given input, there is an increase in efficiency.
    d. If less outputs are obtained for a given input, there is a decrease in efficiency.

17. A manager who provides incentives to improve productivity in workers is:

    a. planning
    b. organizing
    c. leading
    d. controlling

18. A manager who checks the quality of goods produced to make sure the products have the desired quality standards is:

    a. planning
    b. organizing
    c. leading
    d. controlling

19. A manager who determines goals for efficiency or profits is:

    a. planning
    b. organizing
    c. leading
    d. controlling

20. Behavior associated with transmitting information received from outsiders to organization members:

    a. interpersonal role
    b. leader role
    c disseminator role
    d. decisional role

21. A manager allocating supplies and administrative dollars to departments is performing this role:

    a. resource allocator
    b. monitor
    c. disseminator
    d. leader

22. When Sears opened a new store, the CEO attended a ribbon cutting. What role did he perform?

    a. informational role
    b. figurehead role
    c. spokesperson role
    d. negotiator role

23. An example of this role is when Jim Burke of Johnson & Johnson announced to the public that several people had died from poisoned Tylenol capsules:

    a. spokesperson
    b. figurehead
    c. monitor
    d. leader

24. The managerial role that involves searching the organization and the external environment for new project ideas:

    a. leader role
    b. informational role
    c. disseminator role
    d. entrepreneur role

25. The functional approach to management:

    a. corresponds with Mintzberg's roles
    b. includes three functions-- planning, organizing, and controlling
    c. is a less accepted way of explaining managerial work than the role approach
    d. is a more elaborate explanation of managerial work than the role approach

26. Managerial actions that Fred Luthans found all managers engage in include:

    a. traditional management, communication, human resource management, and networking
    b. traditional management, communication, human resource management, and negotiating
    c. traditional management, spokesperson, human resources management, and disseminating
    d. planning, organizing, leading, and controlling

27. Which is true for the way managers spend their time?

    a. Successful managers spend more time on human resource management than other activities.
    b. Average managers spend more time on human resource management than other activities.
    c. Effective managers spend more time communicating than other activities.
    d. Average managers spend less time making decisions, planning, and controlling than other activities.

28. Differences in the Dow Chemical research lab supervisor and the top manager are differences in degree and emphasis, not in function. This illustrates:

   a. differences because of organization type
   b. differences because of organization level
   c. differences because of organization size
   d. differences because of cross-national transferability

29. In regard to a manager's pay:

   a. Operatives tend to be more highly paid than managers.
   b. Managerial salaries are independent of supply and demand.
   c. Managers tend to be more highly paid than operatives.
   d. There is not a relationship between the amount of authority and pay.

30. Why should students study management?

   a. All people must interact with business throughout their lives and should be interested in improving the way organizations are managed.
   b. Every worker will either be a manager or will be managed.
   c. Studying management will allow students to more fully understand the way bosses behave.
   d. All of the above are good reasons to study management.

1 - 1 APPLICATION CASE

IDENTIFYING MANAGERIAL ROLES

Read the two memos and identify the managerial roles that J. Abbott performs in his job.

MEMO 1

TO: J. Abbott, Plant Manager

FROM: Mary Higgins, Production Supervisor

SUBJECT: Conference for Production Supervisors

Again this year we are pleased to have the opportunity to send a representative to the Chicago conference on supervision. I know from personal experience that this conference has developed such a prestigious reputation that it is considered an important form of recognition for those who are selected to attend.

I have reviewed our staff carefully and I have narrowed the choice to a few individuals who I feel are qualified to attend: Mike Carter and Kathy Bell. Unfortunately, we can only send one person.

I have enclosed specific information related to each candidate's work abilities and performance record in our company. I look forward to hearing your selection for conference representative.

1.   Which interpersonal roles is J. Abbott performing?
      (Explain why you select each role.)

2. Which informational roles is J. Abbott performing?
    (Explain why you select each role.)

3. Which decisional roles is J. Abbott performing?
    (Explain why you select each role.)

MEMO 2

TO: Scott Anderson, Marketing Director

FROM: J. Abbott, Plant Manager

SUBJECT: New Product Idea

I am very pleased that you and your staff have been working to improve our Model XT Exercise Machine. Your ideas sound very good. I am particularly interested in maintaining our competitive edge in this area.

You can be assured that production is willing to help with design changes for the equipment. In addition, our two groups could meet to discuss our ideas and try to decide how to integrate the design changes for next year's models.

If you would like me to discuss this matter with the company president, I will be glad to do so. Also, our two groups should probably work on publicity for the product jointly since the design changes will require that customers understand some technical information related to the new version of the XT.

Let's try to work out specific budget needs and allocate production time for the new product design so that we can begin production by May.

We appreciate your hard work on this project!

1.   Which interpersonal roles is J. Abbott performing?
      (Explain why you select each role.)

2. Which informational roles is J. Abbott performing?
   (Explain why you select each role.)

3. Which decisional roles is J. Abbott performing?
   (Explain why you select each role.)

1 - 2 APPLICATION CASE

IDENTIFYING MANAGEMENT FUNCTIONS

Consider a specific manager you know about and determine what activities he/she does related to each of the four management functions. (If you do not have any work experience or knowledge of managerial work, you can observe a manager from a fast food organization like McDonald's or Burger King.)

1. Planning

2. Organizing

3. Leading

4. Controlling

1 - 3 APPLICATION CASE

UNDERSTANDING DIFFERENCES IN MANAGERS' JOBS

Describe how an organization you know about is different from another organization in terms of: type, size, and international operations.

1. Compare your university with another university in your area that is a different size from your university. How do managers (vice presidents, deans, department chairmen) act differently because of size? How do they act similarly? Do both groups perform the four functions of management?

2. Compare a locally owned, small business with a similar company that operates internationally. How do managers act differently because of scope of operations? How do they act similarly? Do both groups perform the four functions of management?

3. Compare a nonprofit organization such as Girl Scouts, United Way, or your city's water department with a for profit company. How do managers act differently because of their orientation toward profit? How do they act similarly? Do both groups perform the four functions of management?

Chapter 2

The Evolution of Management

CHAPTER OUTLINE	CORRESPONDING LEARNING OBJECTIVES
I. Historical Background	1. Explain the value of studying management history.
	2. Identify some major pre-twentieth-century contributions to management.
II. The Period of Diversity	3. Explain why the first half of this century is described as a period of diversity.
A. Scientific Management	4. Define Frederick Taylor's principles of scientific management.
1. Frederick Taylor	
2. Frank and Lillian Gilbreth	
3. Henry Gantt	
4. Putting Scientific Management into Perspective	5. Summarize scientific management's contribution to management.
B. General Administrative Theorists	
1. Henri Fayol	6. Identify Henri Fayol's contributions to management.
2. Max Weber	7. Define Max Weber's ideal bureaucracy.
3. Putting the General Administrative Theorists into Perspective	

CHAPTER OUTLINE	CORRESPONDING LEARNING OBJECTIVES
C. The Human Resources Approach	
1. Early Advocates	
2. The Hawthorne Studies	8. Explain the Hawthorne studies' contributions to management.
3. The Human Relations Movement	9. Contrast the approaches taken by human relations' advocates and the behavioral science theorists.
4. Behavioral Science Theorists	
5. Putting the Behavioral Contributors into Perspective	
D. The Quantitative Approach	
III. Recent Years: Toward Integration	
A. The Process Approach	
B. The Systems Approach	10. Distinguish between the process, systems, and contingency approaches.
C. The Contingency Approach	
IV. Current Trends and Issues: The Changing Face of Management Practice	
A. Globalization	11. Define work force diversity.
B. Work Force Diversity	
C. Ethics	12. Describe why managers have become increasingly concerned with stimulating innovation and change.
D. Stimulating Innovation and Change	

CHAPTER OVERVIEW	CORRESPONDING LEARNING OBJECTIVES
E. Total Quality Management	13. Define the five primary components of TQM.
F. Empowerment	
G. The Bi-Modal Work force	

CHAPTER OVERVIEW

The purpose of this chapter is to illustrate how management theories and practices have evolved over time. Understanding how management thinking has evolved over time should help in your understanding of current management practice. As a body of knowledge, management is still evolving. New ideas and theories are tested, modified, and retested and this new knowledge is then added to current management theories.

The history of management can be traced to the Egyptian Pyramids and the Great Wall of China. Even though overseers of these projects were probably not called managers, they did managerial work. For example, someone had to plan what was to be done, organize people and materials to do the work, direct the workers, and control activities to ensure that activities were completed as they had been planned. Other examples of managerial activities come from the Bible and from the historical operation of the Catholic Church.

Probably the most important pre-twentieth-century influence on management was the industrial revolution. The introduction of machine power allowed for division of labor and production became more efficient. However, it was not until the early 1900's that the first major step toward developing formal management theory occurred.

Early management theory was very diverse. Some theorists concentrated on scientific process and efficiency, others concentrated on human elements of work, and still others concentrated on developing quantitative models for management. These diverse approaches include: the scientific management approach, the general administration approach, the human resources approach, and the quantitative approach. Following is a brief discussion of major contributors for each approach to management.

1. Scientific Management is the use of scientific methods to define the "one best way" for a job to be done. Frederick Taylor studied worker output at the Midvale and Bethlehem Steel companies and tried to improve efficiency of work by studying the way workers completed their jobs.

Taylor wanted to create a "mental revolution" among both the workers and managers by defining clear guidelines for improving productivity. He developed four principles of scientific management:

- Develop a science for work.
- Scientifically, select and train workers.
- Cooperate with workers to ensure that work is done.
- Divide work equally between managers and workers.

Two examples that illustrate the usefulness of Taylor's scientific management theories are the pig iron experiment (loading pig iron onto rail cars) and the shovel experiment (the correct size for different types of shoveling jobs). Taylor believed that an incentive wage system was the best approach for compensating workers who tried his "one best way" to complete their jobs.

Frank and Lillian Gilbreth also worked to determine more efficient approaches to work by studying jobs. One of the most famous experiments conducted by Frank Gilbreth is the bricklaying study where he significantly reduced the motions involved in the job. This reduction in motions increased the productivity of the bricklayer. In their time and motion studies, the Gilbreths developed therbligs (classifications for basic hand motions used in completing work.) Henry Gantt was an associate of Taylor's at the Bethlehem Steel plant. He shared most of Taylor's ideas. Gantt introduced the bonus system for completing daily tasks and developed the Gantt Chart to plan and control work.

2. General Administration includes writers who developed theories of what managers do and what constitutes good management practice. This group is often called classical theorists.

Henri Fayol wrote of his personal experiences as Director of a French mining company. He developed a group of management functions: planning, organizing, commanding, coordinating, controlling. In addition, he stated fourteen principles of management:

- division of work
- authority
- discipline
- unity of command
- unity of direction
- subordination of individual interests to the general interest
- remuneration
- centralization
- scalar chain
- order
- equity
- stability of tenure of personnel
- initiative
- esprit de corps

These fourteen principles represent universal truths that Fayol believed could be taught in schools and universities. Max Weber was a German sociologist who developed a theory of authority structures and he described work based on authority relationships. This "ideal bureaucracy" included: division of labor, authority, hierarchy, formal selection, formal rules and regulations, impersonality, and career orientation.

3. The Human Resources Approach focuses on human behavior in management situations. Robert Owen proposed that employees be treated more humanely and that laws should be set to regulate child labor. Hugo Munsterberg suggested the use of psychological tests to improve employee selection decisions and to improve employee motivation. Mary Parker Follett argued that the organization should be based on the group ethic instead of individualism. Chester Barnard saw organizations as social systems that require human cooperation. Barnard also believed that authority comes from workers--not managers--because workers must decide to follow managerial orders (acceptance theory).

    The Hawthorne Studies were undertaken by a group of researchers. The Hawthorne Studies were conducted at the Western Electric Company's Hawthorne Plant and lasted from 1924 until 1932. Elton Mayo and several other researchers studied several aspects of work: redesign of jobs, changes in the length of the work day and work week, introduction of rest periods, and individual versus group wage plans. These studies centered on the importance of the way workers are treated on the job. The conclusions reached from these studies had a major impact on the direction of management theory.

    The Human Relations Movement (a subgroup of the human resources approach) includes contributors such as: Dale Carnegie, Abraham Maslow, and Douglas McGregor. Dale Carnegie believed that the way to success was through winning the cooperation of others. Abraham Maslow proposed a hierarchy of needs with each need acting as a motivator beginning with physiological needs. As a person moves through the hierarchy, needs that are already achieved are no longer motivators. Douglas McGregor proposed that some workers have little ambition and dislike work (Theory X) while other workers enjoy work and seek responsibility (Theory Y).

    Behavioral Science theorists relied on scientific methods for the study of organizational behavior. Researchers such as Fred Fiedler, Victor Vroom and Frederick Herzberg have made important contributions to the understanding of leadership, employee motivation, and the design of jobs.

4. The Quantitative Approach is the use of mathematical statistics to improve decision making. This approach evolved after World War II. This research involved the application of statistics, optimization models, information models, and computer simulations. Techniques such as linear programming, work scheduling, and inventory models were used to improve managerial decision making.

5. In recent years, there has been a concern for developing a unifying framework for management. Three approaches have been developed that attempt to integrate information learned in the first four stages of management history.

    The Process Approach is a circular approach to management using the four functions: planning, organizing, leading, and controlling. According to this approach, managers continuously follow a circular pattern from planning through controlling and return to planning. The Systems Approach defines an organization as a set of interrelated and interdependent parts that are arranged in a manner that produces a unified whole. The Contingency Approach concentrates on the development of situational variables that moderate decision making. In other words, appropriate actions depend on the situation. Some

21

examples of contingency factors include: organization size, routineness of task technology, environmental uncertainty, and individual differences.

Many trends and issues impact the way managers do their work.

1. Globalization - The world is a global marketplace and managers must be able to adapt to techniques, systems and cultures that are different from those in the United States.

2. Work Force Diversity - There is diversity in the work force in terms of gender, race, ethnicity, and other characteristics. Managers are recognizing that the "melting pot" approach to differences in workers is no longer acceptable. Instead, managers are learning to recognize and celebrate diversity.

3. Ethics - There is a perception that ethical standards of business are too low. In response to this concern, many companies are developing ethics codes and ethics training programs.

4. Stimulating Innovation and Change - The external environment of business continues to change rapidly. In the 1990's and beyond, organizations will have to be flexible to prosper.

5. Total Quality Management (TQM) - Concern for quality products and services continues to be a goal of business. TQM is a philosophy that is driven by customer expectations and needs. Some TQM components include quality control groups, process improvement, team work, improved supplier relationships, and listening to customer needs.

6. Empowerment - Managers are recognizing that workers often have better skills and more knowledge than managers about the best way to perform their jobs. These workers should be given the authority to make job-related decisions.

7. The Bi-Modal Work Force - The variety of jobs available is not as great as it was in the past. Many high-paying blue collar jobs have been lost to technology improvements such as robots. Most jobs today fall into two categories: low-paying service jobs and high-skilled jobs that provide monetary rewards for middle and upper class lifestyles.

KEY TERMS AND DEFINITIONS

1. division of labor - The breakdown of jobs into narrow, repetitive tasks.

2. Industrial Revolution - The advent of machine power, mass production, and efficient transportation.

3. scientific management - The use of the scientific method to define the "one best way" for a job to be done.

4. therbligs - A classification scheme for labeling seventeen basic hand motions.

5. Gantt chart - A graphic bar chart that shows the relationship between work planned and completed on one axis and time elapsed on the other.

6. general administrative theorists - Writers who developed general theories of what managers do and what constitutes good management practice.

7. classical theorists - The term used to describe the scientific management theorists and general administrative theorists.

8. principles of management - Universal truths of management that can be taught in school.

9. bureaucracy - A form of organization marked by division of labor, hierarchy, rules and regulations, and impersonal relationships.

10. human resources approach - The study of management that focuses on human behavior.

11. traditional view of authority - The view that authority comes from above.

12. acceptance view of authority - The theory that authority comes from the willingness of subordinates to accept it.

13. Hawthorne Studies - A series of studies during the 1920's and 1930's that provided new insights into group norms and behavior.

14. human relations movement - The belief for the most part unsubstantiated by research that a satisfied worker would be productive.

15. behavioral science theorists - Psychologists and sociologists who relied on the scientific method for the study of organizational behavior.

16. quantitative approach - The use of mathematical statistics to improve decision making.

17. process approach - Management performs the functions of planning, organizing, leading, and controlling.

18. systems approach - A theory that sees an organization as a set of interrelated and interdependent parts.

19. closed systems - Systems that neither are influenced by nor interact with their environments.

20. open systems - Dynamic systems that interact with and respond to their environments.

21. contingency approach - Recognizing and responding to situational variables as they arise.

22. work force diversity - Employees in organizations are heterogeneous in terms of gender, race, ethnicity, or other characteristics.

23. total quality management (TQM) - A philosophy of management that is driven by customer needs and expectations.

24. empowerment - Increasing the decision-making discretion of workers.

25. bi-modal work force - Employees tend to perform either low-skilled service jobs for near-minimum wage or high-skilled, well-paying jobs.

TRUE/FALSE QUESTIONS

1.   T   F   Management links together ideas and research findings from many diverse specializations such as psychology, sociology, and mathematics.

2.   T   F   Four distinct approaches that explain the history of management include: scientific management, general administrative theory, the human resources approach, and the behavioral science approach.

3.   T   F   Henri Fayol was a major contributor to the scientific approach to management.

4.   T   F   Frederick Taylor wanted to create a mental revolution among both workers and managers by developing a science for work.

5.   T   F   Frank Gilbreth developed ideas about improving work time and motion by studying pig iron being loaded onto rail cars.

6.   T   F   Frederick Taylor believed that he could increase productivity by improving job methods and offering workers a bonus if they completed their assigned task for the day.

7.   T   F   Bureaucracy is not unlike scientific management in its ideology because both emphasize rationality, predictability, impersonality, technical competence, and authoritarianism.

8.   T   F   Both scientific management and general administrative theorists viewed organizations as machines.

9.   T   F   The functional view of the manager's job owes its origin to Henri Fayol.

10. T   F   Robert Owen suggested the use of psychological tests to improve employee selection.

11. T   F   The acceptance view of authority was developed by Max Weber.

12. T   F   The Hawthorne Studies consisted of several different experiments and lasted over a period of twelve years.

13. T   F   Members of the Human Relations Movement include Abraham Maslow and Douglas McGregor.

14. T F Behavioral science theorists tried to build a science of organization behavior by conducting objective research, not by writing about their personal opinions.

15. T F The quantitative approach to management had little impact on management.

16. T F Approaches designed to integrate management theories include process, systems, and contingency approaches.

17. T F Organizations are open systems.

18. T F Some interdependent factors in an organization system include individuals, groups, attitudes, motives, formal structure, interactions, status, and authority.

19. T F The work force is less heterogeneous than it was twenty years ago.

20. T F Managers today are often more effective when they coach and cheer their workers on than when they tell workers what to do.

MULTIPLE CHOICE QUESTIONS

21. The first major step toward developing a formal theory of management:

    a. began with the Egyptian Pyramids and the Great Wall of China
    b. began in the early 1900's
    c. began after World War II
    d. began during the industrial revolution

22. The person who developed the idea of teaching management principles in schools and universities:

    a. Frederick Taylor
    b. Max Weber
    c. Henri Fayol
    d. Henry Gantt

23. The person who developed a science for work by studying pig iron movements and shovel sizes:

    a. Frederick Taylor
    b. Max Weber
    c. Henri Fayol
    d. Henry Gantt

24. The person who developed the idea for giving a bonus if a person finished his assigned task for the day:

    a. Frederick Taylor
    b. Max Weber
    c. Henri Fayol
    d. Henry Gantt

25. The person who described the "ideal bureaucracy":

a. Frederick Taylor
b. Max Weber
c. Henri Fayol
d. Henry Gantt

26. The person who described management functions and fourteen principles of management:

a. Frederick Taylor
b. Max Weber
c. Henri Fayol
d. Henry Gantt

27. Henri Fayol was a contributor to this approach to the study of management:

a. scientific management
b. general administrative approach
c. human resources approach
d. quantitative approach

28. Another name for the classical approach to management:

a. scientific management
b. general administrative approach
c. human resources approach
d. quantitative approach

29. This approach to the study of management was developed after World War II:

a. scientific management
b. general administrative approach
c. human resources approach
d. quantitative approach

30. Robert Owen was a contributor to this historical era in management:

a. scientific management
b. general administrative approach
c. human resources approach
d. quantitative approach

31. The development of a hierarchy of needs is part of this historical approach to management:

a. scientific management
b. general administrative approach
c. human resources approach
d. quantitative approach

32. The bar chart that was developed to help managers plan and control work was part of this management approach:

    a. scientific management
    b. general administrative approach
    c. human resources approach
    d. quantitative approach

33. The Hawthorne Studies were a part of this approach to management:

    a. scientific management
    b. general administrative approach
    c. human resources approach
    d. quantitative approach

34. The acceptance view of authority was an idea developed during this approach to management:

    a. scientific management
    b. general administrative approach
    c. human resources approach
    d. quantitative approach

35. Managers began to use techniques such as linear programming for decision making during this historical era of management:

    a. scientific management
    b. general administrative approach
    c. human resources approach
    d. quantitative approach

36. The Gantt Chart was developed during this historical management phase:

    a. scientific management
    b. general administrative approach
    c. human resources approach
    d. quantitative approach

37. Industrial psychology was developed as a discipline of study during this era:

    a. scientific management
    b. general administrative approach
    c. human resources approach
    d. quantitative approach

38. Therbligs were used in a bricklaying study during this era:

    a. scientific management
    b. general administrative approach
    c. human resources approach
    d. quantitative approach

39. This approach is characterized by a search for "one best way":

    a. scientific management
    b. general administrative approach
    c. human resources approach
    d. quantitative approach

40. Which is not an idea developed by Mary Parker Follett?

    a. Managers should rely on formal authority to lead workers.
    b. An organization should be based on a group ethic and not on individualism.
    c. Managers and workers are partners.
    d. The manager's job is to coordinate group efforts.

41. A common thread that united human relations supporters like Carnegie, Maslow, and McGregor was an unshakable optimist about:

    a. the formal organization
    b. authority
    c. peoples' capabilities
    d. group dynamics

42. The quantitative approach to management is also called:

    a. classical approach
    b. systems approach
    c. process approach
    d. management science

43. The process approach was originally introduced by:

    a. Frederick Taylor
    b. Henri Fayol
    c. Robert Owen
    d. Henry Gantt

44. Which is true for an organization system?

    a. The organization has interrelated parts.
    b. The organization has parts that are interdependent.
    c. The organization has inputs and outputs.
    d. All of the above are true for organization systems.

45. An integrative approach to management where decisions are dependent on situational factors:

    a. systems approach
    b. process approach
    c. contingency approach
    d. quantitative approach

46. An integrative approach to management that was originally developed by Henri Fayol:

   a. systems approach
   b. process approach
   c. contingency approach
   d. quantitative approach

47. An integrative approach to management where the organization is characterized as a group of parts that work together to form a whole:

   a. systems approach
   b. process approach
   c. contingency approach
   d. quantitative approach

48. Harold Koontz wrote about a management theory "jungle" and advocated this approach:

   a. systems approach
   b. process approach
   c. contingency approach
   d. quantitative approach

49. Which of the following is not an integrative approach to management?

   a. systems approach
   b. process approach
   c. contingency approach
   d. quantitative approach

50. An integrative approach where the external environment is an important consideration:

   a. systems approach
   b. process approach
   c. contingency approach
   d. all of the above

51. Development of a unifying framework for management began in earnest:

   a. after World War II
   b. in the early 1980's
   c. during the time of the Hawthorne Studies
   d. in the early 1960's

52. This current trend requires that managers rethink their reliance on Frederick Taylor's idea of telling workers "one best way" to do a job:

   a. bi-modal work force
   b. work force diversity
   c. total quality management
   d. empowerment

29

53. This current trend requires that managers rethink the concept of treating all workers alike:

    a. bi-modal work force
    b. work force diversity
    c. total quality management
    d. empowerment

54. This current trend challenges many managers to determine how to motivate low-paid employees who have little chance for increased wages:

    a. bi-modal work force
    b. work force diversity
    c. total quality management
    d. empowerment

2 - 1 APPLICATION CASE

TODAY'S MANAGERS' VIEWS OF THE HISTORY OF MANAGEMENT

What developments from each historical phase of management theory do you think are concepts that managers use today?

Use an example of a company you know about and list specific information from the history of management that the manager probably uses in managing the business today.

Company: _____

1.   Scientific Management

2.   General Administrative Theory

3.   Human Resources Approach

4.   Quantitative Approach

32

2 - 2 APPLICATION CASE

YOU ARE THE MANAGEMENT THEORIST

As a production manager of a wood products company you recognize your
responsibility to produce the product efficiently. Recently, a salesperson introduced
you to a new machine that would allow your company to significantly improve
efficiency and still maintain high levels of quality in the production of book cases. The
new machine melds a protective, plastic surface to the particle board used in making
the book cases. You are unsure if your employees would be willing to accept the new
equipment since it will require significant amounts of training time.

Since your company does have the funds to invest in this equipment, you have asked
your assistant to study relevant facts for the decision. The new equipment would
impact the job of 40 of the 100 company employees. Training for these workers will
last for one month. During this time, the plant will continue to operate, but the 40
employees who work with the machine will be producing at a low volume of output.
In addition to the slow production rate, it is likely that the workers will scrap about
25% of their production. It is estimated that in about six months the 40 employees who
are working on the new machine will have gradually increased to productivity rates that
were standard before the new equipment was installed and in nine months productivity
will be 20% better than it was before the new machines were installed.

Pretend you are each of the management scholars listed below. What would you
consider as you make your decision and what is your decision in regard to purchasing
the new machine?

1.   Frederick Taylor

2.   Henri Fayol

3.   Elton Mayo

4.   Robert McNamara (one of the "Whiz Kid" military officers who used quantitative methods in World War II.)

2 - 3 APPLICATION CASE

THE CONTINGENCY APPROACH TO MANAGEMENT

Give examples to illustrate how contingency factors might impact operations for some specific organizations listed below.

1. SIZE (How would a small clothing store operate differently from a large chain operated department store?)

2. ROUTINENESS OF TASK TECHNOLOGY (How would a mechanized furniture production process operate differently than a nonroutine custom manufacturing furniture production company?)

3. ENVIRONMENT UNCERTAINTY (How would a restaurant with little environmental uncertainty operate differently than a restaurant that operates in a resort area and must cater to different types of customers demanding a wide variety of menu items?)

4. INDIVIDUAL DIFFERENCES (How would a worker who has a college degree and several kinds of technical skills be treated differently from a worker who has very little formal schooling and no technical skills?)

2 - 4 APPLICATION CASE

CURRENT TRENDS AND ISSUES

How might the current trends and issues listed below impact the production company in Application Case 2 - 2?

1. globalization

2. work force diversity

3. empowerment

4. total quality management

5. bi-modal work force

Chapter 3

Organizational Culture and Environment: The Constraints

CHAPTER OUTLINE	CORRESPONDING LEARNING OBJECTIVES
I. The Manager: Omnipotent or Symbolic?	1. Differentiate the symbolic view from the omnipotent view of management.
A. The Omnipotent View	
B. The Symbolic View	
C. Reality Suggests a Synthesis	
II. The Organization's Culture	
A. What is Organizational Culture?	
	2. Define organizational culture.
	3. Identify the ten characteristics that make up an organization's culture.
B. The Source of Culture	4. Explain how culture constrains managers.
C. Strong Versus Weak Cultures	
D. Influence on Management Practice	
III. The Environment	
A. Defining the Environment	
1. General Versus Specific Environment	
	5. Distinguish between general and specific environments.

CHAPTER OUTLINE	CORRESPONDING LEARNING OBJECTIVES

    2. Assessing Environmental Uncertainty

                                        6.   Contrast certain and uncertain environments.

    3. The Organization and Its Environment

B. The Specific Environment

    1. Suppliers

    2. Customers

    3. Competitors

    4. Government

    5. Pressure Groups

C. The General Environment

    1. Economic Conditions

    2. Political Conditions

    3. Social Conditions

    4. Technological Conditions

D. Influence on Management Practice

                                          7.   Explain how the environment constrains managers.

CHAPTER OVERVIEW

    Two views of managers are the symbolic view and the omnipotent view. The dominate view of managers in management theory and in today's society is the omnipotent view. This view holds that managers are directly responsible for the success or failure of an organization. The symbolic view holds that the manager has only a limited effect on organizational outcomes. Probably it is not realistic to view managers in either perspective, but as a combination of both views. This is true because the manager is not all powerful or all knowing, but he/she does have some latitude for control and influence in the organization.

The manager is constrained in his/her actions partly because of the organization's culture. The organization culture is the personality of the company. The culture governs how managers and workers should behave. This behavior is governed by unwritten rules and shared values. The culture of the organization remains relatively static over time. Cultures can be analyzed by assessing how an organization rates on ten characteristics. These characteristics include: individual initiative, risk tolerance, direction, integration, management support, control, identity, reward system, conflict tolerance, and communication patterns.

Organization cultures operate differently in different companies. Some companies have very strong cultures. This means that the key values are intensely held and widely shared by organization members. Most organizations have moderate to strong cultures. Generally, the culture is derived from the founder of the organization and it is internalized by workers who perpetuate it over time. As the culture becomes stronger, the manager becomes more constrained in his/her activities.

The external environment also constrains the manager's actions. The external environment is defined as forces outside the organization that affect an organization's performance. The general environment includes everything outside the organization such as economic factors, political conditions, social factors, and technological factors. These conditions may affect the environment, but the impact may/may not be important. The specific environment is the part of the external environment that is directly relevant to company operations. Some examples of the specific environment are suppliers, customers, competitors, government agencies, and public pressure groups.

There is a certain amount of uncertainty in the environment. This uncertainty can be explained by considering the amount of complexity and the degree of change in the environment. Complexity refers to the number of external components and the amount of knowledge that the organization has about these components. The degree of change or stability refers to the amount of change that is occurring in the external factors.

It is important that managers study both external environmental factors and the organization culture. This is true because managers are influenced by their environment and must also interact with it.

KEY TERMS AND DEFINITIONS

1. omnipotent view - The view that managers are directly responsible for the success or failure of an organization.

2. symbolic view - The view that management has only a limited effect on substantive organizational outcomes owing to the large number of factors outside of management's control; however, management greatly influences symbolic outcomes.

3. organizational culture - A system of shared meaning within an organization that determines, in large degree, how employees act.

4. strong cultures - Organizations in which the key values are intensely held and widely shared.

5.	whistle blowing - Reporting unethical practices by your employer to outsiders such as the press, government agencies, or public interest groups.

6.	environment - Outside institutions or forces that affect an organization.

7.	general environment - Everything outside the organization.

8.	specific environment - The part of the environment that is directly relevant to the achievement of an organization's goals.

9.	environmental uncertainty - The degree of change and complexity in an organization's environment.

10.	environmental complexity - The number of components in an organization's environment and the extent of an organization's knowledge about its environmental components.

TRUE/FALSE QUESTIONS

1.	T	F	The dominant view in management theory and in society is that much of an organization's success is due to forces outside the manager's control.

2.	T	F	The quality of an organization's managers determines the quality of the organization itself.

3.	T	F	The symbolic view of the manager is that an organization's outcomes are influenced by a number of factors outside the control of management.

4.	T	F	Internal constraints exist within every organization that restrict a manager's decision options.

5.	T	F	External constraints come from the organization culture.

6.	T	F	Because of all of the constraints (both internal and external), managers are not very powerful.

7.	T	F	The personality of the organization is the organization culture.

8.	T	F	Organization culture is used to evaluate whether or not organization members like the company values.

9.	T	F	An organization culture is relatively enduring over time and relatively static in its propensity to change.

10.	T	F	Organization cultures are of about the same importance for each organization.

11.	T	F	Organization culture is usually a reflection of the vision of company founders.

12.   T   F An organization culture is particularly relevant to managers because it establishes constraints upon what they can and cannot do.

13.   T   F The organization culture is usually written down in the formal policies of the organization.

14.   T   F The general environment includes suppliers, customers, and competitors.

15.   T   F The specific environment is unique to each organization and changes as the organization changes.

16.   T   F Environmental uncertainty refers to the amount of change and complexity in the organization environment.

17.   T   F An organization that deals with fewer customers, suppliers, competitors, and government agencies has more uncertainty in its external environment than a company that deals with more customers, suppliers, competitors, and government agencies.

18.   T   F Managers want to minimize the amount of uncertainty in the environment because it threatens organization effectiveness.

19.   T   F Government regulation limits the choices available to managers.

20.   T   F A manager does not need to adapt his/her practices to social conditions in the environment.

MULTIPLE CHOICE QUESTIONS

21.   Which is true for the omnipotent view of a manager?

    a. A manager only has a limited effect on organization outcomes.
    b. Managers are directly responsible for the success or failure of an organization.
    c. Results of organization actions are influenced by many factors outside the control of management.
    d. The manager's role is to create the illusion of control for the benefit of stockholders, customers, employees, and the public.

22.   Which is the most realistic view of a manager?

    a. omnipotent view
    b. symbolic view
    c. combination of omnipotent and symbolic views
    d. none of the above

23.   Which is not true for organization culture?

    a. Culture cannot be analyzed.
    b. Culture is the personality of the company.
    c. Culture governs how managers behave.
    d. Culture is based on perceptions.

24. In organizations whose culture conveys a basic mistrust of employees, managers are more likely to use:

    a. a democratic leader style
    b. an authoritative leader style
    c. either style is appropriate
    d. neither style is appropriate

25. Which is not a characteristic used to analyze organization culture?

    a. management support
    b. reward system
    c. company size
    d. communication patterns

26. An organization culture:

    a. changes routinely
    b. is relatively enduring over time
    c. changes when new workers come into the organization
    d. never changes

27. Which is true for a strong corporate culture?

    a. Key values are intensely held and widely shared.
    b. Key values have little influence on employees.
    c. It is unclear what is important and what is not important to workers.
    d. Culture is not likely to constrain managers.

28. The term that best describes the part of the environment that is directly relevant to achievement of organization goals:

    a. environment
    b. general environment
    c. specific environment
    d. environmental uncertainty

29. Which is true for the specific environment?

    a. It includes economic factors, political factors, social factors, and technological factors.
    b. It includes factors that may affect the organization, but their relevance is not clear.
    c. It is made up of suppliers, customers, the economy, and technological factors.
    d. It is unique to each organization and changes as conditions change.

30.   If components in the environment change frequently, the environment is said to be:

a. stable
b. dynamic
c. simple
d. complex

31.   If there are few components in the environment and the manager understands these components, the environment is said to be:

a. stable
b. dynamic
c. simple
d. complex

32.   This type of environment occurs when there are few new competitors, few new technological breakthroughs, and little activity by pressure groups:

a. stable
b. dynamic
c. simple
d. complex

33.   If an organization signs an agreement to produce items for a large department store and this lessens the number of buyers, there is:

a. a decrease in complexity
b. an increase in complexity
c. a decrease in stability
d. an increase in uncertainty

34.   If an organization has to begin dealing with more external factors and more change in these factors, there is:

a. a decrease in complexity
b. an increase in complexity
c. a decrease in stability
d. an increase in uncertainty

35.   Suppliers include:

a. materials and equipment needed to produce the product
b. government, customers, and competitors
c. materials, equipment, financial resources suppliers, and labor resources suppliers
d. none of the above

36. The specific environment includes:

a. suppliers, customers, competitors, government, and pressure groups
b. suppliers, competitors, and technology
c. customers, suppliers, society, and pressure groups
d. government, pressure groups, the economy, and suppliers

37. The general environment includes:

a. economic factors, government, social factors, and technology
b. economic factors, political factors, social factors, and technological factors
c. suppliers, customers, competitors, government, and pressure groups
d. customers, suppliers, society, and pressure groups

38. Which is true for the general environment?

a. The general environment does not have as large an impact on company actions as the specific environment.
b. The general environment has more impact on company actions than the specific environment.
c. The general environment has about the same impact on company actions as the specific environment.
d. The general environment does not affect the company's actions.

39. Political conditions include:

a. general stability of the country
b. specific attitudes that elected government officials hold toward the role of business in society
c. general stability of the country and specific attitudes that elected government officials hold toward the role of business in society
d. none of the above

40. From the mid 1930's to the late 1970's, the political environment in the United States:

a. changed very little
b. moved toward the government playing a smaller role in society
c. did not change at all, because the same political factors were important during those years
d. moved toward the government playing a larger role in society

41. Social conditions include:

a. consumer customs
b. consumer tastes
c. consumer values
d. all of the above

42. What is the relationship of the organization and the environment?

    a. The organization interacts with and is influenced by its environment.
    b. The organization is influenced by its environment.
    c. The environment influences the organization.
    d. All of the above statements explain the organization and environment relationship.

43. What is the influencing environmental factor when interest rates increase and firms find it difficult to borrow funds?

    a. economic factor
    b. technological factor
    c. social factor
    d. competitive factor

44. What is the influencing environmental factor when new substitutes are developed by other companies?

    a. economic factor
    b. technological factor
    c. social factor
    d. competitive factor

45. What is the influencing environmental factor when ideas are developed for improving production machinery?

    a. economic factor
    b. technological factor
    c. social factor
    d. competitive factor

46. What is the influencing environmental factor when the aging population requires that a company change its product?

    a. economic factor
    b. technological factor
    c. social factor
    d. competitive factor

3 - 1 APPLICATION CASE

CHARACTERISTICS OF CULTURE

Research the organization culture of a large organization such as Apple Computer, IBM, Ford Motor Company, or Proctor & Gamble.

For the company you selected, identify specifics for each of the ten characteristics used to assess the culture.

1. MEMBER IDENTITY

2. GROUP EMPHASIS

3. PEOPLE FOCUS

4. UNIT INTEGRATION

5. CONTROL

6. RISK TOLERANCE

7. REWARD CRITERIA

8. CONFLICT TOLERANCE

9. MEANS-ENDS ORIENTATION

10. OPEN SYSTEMS FOCUS

After learning about the organization culture for the company, do you think you could work for the company?

Explain why or why not? (Be sure to discuss specific characteristics that you can/cannot deal with in the work setting.)

3 - 2 APPLICATION CASE

THE IMPACT OF CULTURE ON THE MANAGEMENT FUNCTIONS

Think about the impact that the organization culture has on each of the management functions. List differences for the two diverse cultures explained in Table 3 - 1 of your textbook. (Table 3 - 2 in your textbook will help you identify the factors for each management function.)

	ORGANIZATION A	ORGANIZATION B
Planning		
Organizing		

	ORGANIZATION A	ORGANIZATION B
Leading		
Controlling		

3 - 3 APPLICATION CASE

ENVIRONMENTAL UNCERTAINTY

Choose an organization you know about or a company such as Apple Computer or Proctor & Gamble and illustrate the amount of uncertainty in the external environment.

1.   How much complexity is there in the environment? (Use the two extremes simple/complex to describe complexity.)

2.   How much change is there in the environment? (Use the two extremes stable/dynamic to describe the degree of change.)

3. Determine how the company must operate considering both the degree of change and the amount of complexity in the environment. (Use Table 3 - 3 in your textbook for this exercise.)

3 - 4 APPLICATION CASE

EXTERNAL ENVIRONMENTAL FACTORS

Think of the impact the external environment has on company operations. Choose a company you know about and give specific examples to illustrate which external factors are particularly important to the company.

1. Specific Environment (suppliers, customers, competitors, government, and pressure groups)

2. General Environment (economic conditions, political conditions, social conditions, technological conditions)

Chapter 4

International Management:
Responding to a Global Environment

CHAPTER OUTLINE	CORRESPONDING LEARNING OBJECTIVES
I. Who Owns What?	1. Explain the importance of viewing management from a global perspective.
II. Attacking Parochialism	2. Describe problems created by national parochialism.
III. The Changing Global Environment	
A. From Multinationals to Transnationals	3. Contrast multinational and transnational corporations.
B. Regional Trading Alliances	4. Explain why many countries have become part of regional trading alliances.
1. U.S.-Canadian Alliance	
2. The European Community	
3. U.S. Mexico Border Zones	
4. U.S.-Mexico Free Trade	
5. What's Next? A Pacific Rim Block?	
C. So Long Communism, Hello Capitalism!	
IV. How Organizations Go International	5. Describe the typical stages by which organizations go international.

CHAPTER OUTLINE	CORRESPONDING LEARNING OBJECTIVES
V. Managing in a Foreign Environment	
A. The Legal-Political Environment	
B. The Economic Environment	
C. The Cultural Environment	6. List four dimensions of national culture.
1. Individualism Versus Collectivism	7. Describe the U.S. culture according to the four dimensions.
2. Power Distance	
3. Uncertainty Avoidance	
4. Quantity Versus Quality of Life	
5. A Guide for U.S. Managers	

CHAPTER OVERVIEW

Americans tend to be parochial in their attitude toward other people in the world. This means that Americans tend to assume that other people act and feel the same way they do. This causes interesting problems for managers who try to apply U.S. values and customs to foreign cultures. Successful global management requires that managers be sensitive to differences in customs and practices in different countries.

Several forces are reshaping the global environment. These include:

1. The growing impact of multinationals - Multinational corporations are companies that maintain significant operations in two or more countries simultaneously. Many multinational corporations decentralize decision making in each local country. These corporations are called transnational corporations (TNC).

2. Regional trading alliances - Some examples include: the European Community, the U.S. Canadian alliance, the U.S. Mexico border zones, and U.S. Mexico-free trade. The European Community is twelve nations that became one market in 1992. As a single European market, there are no longer national barriers to employment, investment, and trade. Canada and the United States signed a Free Trade Agreement in 1989 that seeks to create a unified North America. The U.S. Mexico border zones allow companies to set up plants along the Mexican side of the U.S. border to help develop both sides of the impoverished

region. Discussion is now underway to create a U.S.-Mexico free trade agreement.

3.   Communism to capitalism - Capitalism is spreading throughout the world. This change provides even more markets for corporations.

Organizations typically move through several stages before becoming global organizations:

1.   Passive Response - Products are exported to foreign countries.

2.   Initial Overt Entry - The corporation contracts with foreign representatives to sell the product in another country and/or contracts with foreign manufacturers to produce its products.

3.   Established International Operations - Corporations may pursue a variety of activities: setting up foreign subsidiaries, entering into joint ventures, and licensing/franchising operations.

A manager who operates in global environments must carefully consider the external environment. The legal-political environment includes the stability of foreign governments and the specific laws that govern business practices in the country. The economic environment includes two major factors: fluctuating exchange rates and diverse tax policies. The cultural environment is the national culture of the country. The national culture is attitudes and perspectives shared by individuals from a specific country that shape their behavior and the way they see the world.

The cultural environment is more complex than either the legal or economic environment. Geert Hofstede developed a framework to improve understanding of differences in national cultures. This framework includes four dimensions:

1.   Individualism versus collectivism - Individualism is a loosely knit social framework where people look after their own interests. Collectivism refers to societies where people expect others in their family or work group to look after them and protect them when they are in trouble.

2.   Power Distance refers to the extent to which a society accepts the unequal distribution of power in organizations. If there is low power distance, society plays down the inequalities of supervisors and employees. The opposite is true in high power distance societies.

3.   Uncertainty Avoidance refers to the degree to which people tolerate risk and unconventional behavior. In low uncertainty avoidance societies people are relatively tolerant of behavior and opinions that differ from their own. However, in high uncertainty avoidance societies, people feel threatened by those who have different opinions and beliefs.

4.   Quantity versus Quality of Life - Some cultures value assertiveness and the acquisition of money and material goods (quantity of life) while other cultures value concern for others and the importance of relationships (quality of life).

Hofstede's research results can be used by managers who operate in international environments. A manager can review how the United States ranked on each criteria and use this information in decision making. If a country ranks similarly to the U.S. on the four dimensions, the manager knows the country's culture is similar to the U.S. culture and managers should be able to adjust easily to the culture in that country. If a country ranks very differently from the U.S. on the four dimensions, the manager knows that much adjustment will need to be made so that managers can fit in the country's culture.

KEY TERMS AND DEFINITIONS

1. parochialism - A selfish, narrow view of the world; an inability to recognize differences between people.

2. multinational corporations - Companies that maintain significant operations in more than one countries simultaneously but manage them all from one base in a home country.

3. transnational corporation - Companies that maintain significant operations in more than one country simultaneously and decentralize decision making in each operation to the local country.

4. European Community- Currently the 330 million people living in the following twelve countries: Belgium, Denmark, France, Greece, Ireland, Italy, Luxembourg, Netherlands, Portugal, Spain, the United Kingdom, and Germany.

5. Maquiladoras - Domestic Mexican firms that manufacture or assemble products for a foreign company. The products are then sent back to the foreign company for sale and distribution.

6. national culture - The attitudes and perspectives shared by individuals from a specific country that shape their behavior and the way they see the world.

7. individualism - A cultural dimension in which people are supposed to look after their own interests and those of their immediate family.

8. collectivism - A cultural dimension in which people expect others in their group to look after them and protect them when they are in trouble.

9. power distance - A cultural measure of the extent to which a society accepts the unequal distribution of power in institutions and organizations.

10. uncertainty avoidance - A cultural measure of the degree to which people tolerate risk and unconventional behavior.

11. quantity of life - A national culture attribute describing the extent to which societal values are characterized by assertiveness and materialism.

12. quality of life - A national culture attribute that reflects the emphasis on relationships and concern for others.

TRUE/FALSE QUESTIONS

1. T   F   People with a parochial perspective recognize that people in other countries have different ways of living and working.

2. T   F   Successful global management requires enhanced sensitivity to differences in national customs and practices.

3. T   F   Since international businesses have been around for centuries, multinational corporations are not a recent phenomenon.

4. T   F   Diverse political systems, laws, and customs faced by managers of multinational corporations provide both problems and opportunities.

5. T   F   There are currently 330 million people and twelve nations making up the European Community.

6. T   F   In 1992, the European Community countries became a single market by eliminating border controls, border taxes, and border subsidies.

7. T   F   TNC's maintain operations in more than one country, but manage them from one base in a home country.

8. T   F   Maquiladoras are Mexican companies operating assembly plants along the U.S. side of the U.S.- Mexican border.

9. T   F   The primary reason the legal-political environment is a concern to managers who operate internationally is because foreign governments are unstable.

10. T   F   Research indicates that the national culture has a greater effect on employees than does their organization culture.

11. T   F   A framework to help managers better understand differences in national cultures was developed by Geert Hofstede.

12. T   F   Collectivism is a concern of power distance in evaluating national cultures.

13. T   F   Individualism refers to a tight social framework in which people expect others in groups of which they are a part to look after them and protect them when they are in trouble.

14. T   F   Power distance is a measure of the degree to which people tolerate risk and unconventional behavior.

15. T   F   A high power distance society accepts wide differences in power in organizations.

16. T   F   In societies that have low uncertainty avoidance, people feel relatively secure.

17. T F In terms of quality and quantity of life, Hofstede found that the U.S. has the highest quantity of life rating.

18. T F The U.S. is strongly individualistic, but low on power distance.

MULTIPLE CHOICE QUESTIONS

19. Which is not true for people who have a parochial view of the world?

    a. They view the world solely through their own eyes.
    b. They do not recognize people have different ways of living and working.
    c. Most Americans do not have this view of the world.
    d. This view is detrimental to managers who operate internationally.

20. Which is true for multinational corporations?

    a. A MNC has significant operations in more than one country.
    b. The concept of MNC has been around for centuries.
    c. A MNC focuses on developing specific, different strategies and products for each country.
    d. A MNC is a large corporation.

21. An example of regional cooperation in global competition is:

    a. European Community
    b. U.S.-Canadian Alliance
    c. U.S.-Mexico Border Zones
    d. all of the above

22. The nations united in 1992 to become a single market are called:

    a. European Community
    b. U.S.-Canadian Alliance
    c. U.S.-Mexico Border Zones
    d. U.S.-Mexico Free Trade

23. Cooperation of nations to allow assembly plants to be set up across the border to improve impoverished conditions of the area:

    a. European Community
    b. U.S.-Canadian Alliance
    c. U.S.-Mexico Border Zones
    d. U.S.-Mexico Free Trade

24. This plan has the objective of allowing countries to become more competitive with the U.S. and Japan:

    a. European Community
    b. U.S.-Canadian Alliance
    c. U.S.-Mexico Border Zones
    d. U.S.-Mexico Free Trade

25. The desire is to create a unified North America by phasing out tariffs on most goods traded between two countries:

    a. European Community
    b. U.S.-Canadian Alliance
    c. U.S.-Mexico Border Zones
    d. Pacific Rim

26. The legal-political environment is an important consideration in foreign environments because:

    a. all foreign environments are unstable
    b. laws are similar in foreign nations, but different from the U.S.
    c. differences in U.S. and foreign operations require that managers understand constraints under which they operate in foreign nations
    d. none of the above

27. Economic concerns are important for corporations that operate in the international environment because of:

    a. fluctuating exchange rates
    b. fluctuating value of the foreign investment
    c. diverse tax policies
    d. all of the above

28. Which is not true for the cultural environment?

    a. The cultural environment is fairly straightforward.
    b. Often "natives" are not capable of explaining unique characteristics of their culture to outsiders.
    c. The national culture has a greater effect on employees than does their organizational culture.
    d. Obtaining information about a country's culture is more difficult than obtaining economic and legal information.

29. People in America have the following cultural characteristics:

    a. informal, competitive, individualistic, high power distance
    b. value for punctuality, value for cleanliness, individualistic, and competitive
    c. informal, noncompetitive, and direct
    d. none of the above

30. The country that has both high uncertainty and quantity of life as cultural dimensions:

    a. United States
    b. Canada
    c. Denmark
    d. Japan

31. The country that has power distance as a cultural dimension:

    a. Israel
    b. Mexico
    c. New Zealand
    d. Austria

32. The measure of degree to which people tolerate risk and unconventional behavior:

    a. individualism
    b. collectivism
    c. power distance
    d. uncertainty avoidance

33. People expect others in their group to look out after them:

    a. individualism
    b. collectivism
    c. power distance
    d. uncertainty avoidance

34. The extent to which a society accepts the unequal distribution of power in an organization:

    a. individualism
    b. collectivism
    c. power distance
    d. uncertainty avoidance

35. Which in not one of the dimensions from Hofstede's study of national culture?

    a. power distance
    b. culture avoidance
    c. quantity versus quality of life
    d. individualism versus collectivism

36. An employee who shows a great deal of respect for those in authority is:

    a. low in power distance
    b. low in uncertainty avoidance
    c. high in power distance
    d. high in uncertainty avoidance

37. Stress and aggressiveness of workers because of ambiguity in the society illustrates:

    a. low power distance
    b. low uncertainty avoidance
    c. high power distance
    d. high uncertainty avoidance

38. Low job mobility and lifetime employment policies, formal rules, little tolerance for unconventional behavior and ideas illustrates:

    a. low power distance
    b. low uncertainty avoidance
    c. high power distance
    d. high uncertainty avoidance

39. The inequities of managers and workers is played down; workers are not in awe of the boss illustrates:

    a. low power distance
    b. low uncertainty avoidance
    c. high power distance
    d. high uncertainty avoidance

40. An American manager transferring to which country would need little adjustment to culture?

    a. Venezuela
    b. Peru
    c. England
    d. Singapore

41. If this trade agreement is negotiated, there will be a free-trading zone from the Yukon to the Yucatan that consolidates 360 million consumers into a $6 trillion market:

    a. European Community
    b. U.S.-Canadian Alliance
    c. U.S.-Mexico Border Zone
    d. U.S.-Mexico Free Trade

42. In this stage of evolution into a global organization, a company might contract with a foreign manufacturer to product products for sale in that country:

    a. established international operations
    b. passive response
    c. transnational operations
    d. initial overt entry

43. Which of the following is not an action related to Stage III of evolution into a global organization (established international operations):

    a. foreign subsidiary
    b. joint venture
    c. export
    d. licensing/franchising

4 - 1 APPLICATION CASE

PAROCHIALISM

1. Think of four or five examples that indicate that Americans tend to be parochial. (Hint: An example in your text is monolingualism.)

2. What specific things can you do to make sure you do not have a parochial attitude?

4 - 2 APPLICATION CASE

INTERNATIONAL EXTERNAL ENVIRONMENT

Choose a product or service that you think would sell well internationally. Choose a specific country such as Japan, China, Russia, France, Germany, Sweden.

List specific considerations that are important in your analysis of the external environment of that country.

PRODUCT/SERVICE AND COUNTRY _____

1. Considerations for the LEGAL-POLITICAL international environment:

2. Considerations for the CULTURAL international environment:

3. Considerations for the ECONOMIC international environment:

4 - 3 APPLICATION CASE

SELLING BARBIE TO JAPAN

One of Mattel's best-selling products is the Barbie doll. It sold so well in the United States that Mattel decided to market the doll in Japan. The doll did not sell well in Japan.

1.   What cultural factors did Mattel not take into account when marketing the doll?

2.   What changes would you make to improve sales in Japan?

4 - 4 APPLICATION CASE

HOFSTEDE'S FOUR CULTURAL DIMENSIONS

Your corporation has decided to market home appliances to an Eastern European nation. Researchers have used Hofstede's four cultural dimensions to try to determine how to set up business operations in the country. Initially, the company plans to market refrigerators and stoves that are produced in the United States. If the venture is successful, the company will build a production plant in the country.

Research indicates that the culture of the country is: low in power distance, high in uncertainty avoidance, high in quantity of life, and high in collectivism.

Based on these research results, what is your plan for beginning operations in the country. (Concentrate on plans for personnel policies, authority relationships, and motivation techniques.)

Chapter 5

Social Responsibility and Managerial Ethics

CHAPTER OUTLINE	CORRESPONDING LEARNING OBJECTIVES
I. What is Social Responsibility?	
A. Two Opposing Views	1. Explain the classical and socioeconomic views of social responsibility.
1. The Classical View	
2. The Socioeconomic View	
B. Arguments for and Against Social Responsibility	2. List the arguments for and against business being socially responsible.
1. Arguments For	
2. Arguments Against	
C. From Obligations to Responsiveness	3. Differentiate social responsibility from social responsiveness.
II. Social Responsibility and Economic Performance	4. Describe the relationship between corporate social responsibility and economic performance.
III. Is Social Responsibility Just Profit-Maximizing Behavior?	
IV. A Guide Through the Maze	5. Define stakeholders and describe their role in social responsibility.
V. Managerial Ethics	6. Define ethics.
A. Three Different Views On Ethics	7. Differentiate three views on ethics.
B. Factors Affecting Managerial Ethics	8. Identify the factors that affect ethical behavior.

CHAPTER OUTLINE	CORRESPONDING LEARNING OBJECTIVES
1. Stages of Moral Development	
	9. Describe the stages of moral development.
2. Individual Characteristics	
3. Structural Variables	
4. Organization's Culture	
5. Issue Intensity	
C. Toward Improving Ethical Behavior	10. Discuss various ways in which organizations can improve the ethical behavior of their employees.
1. Selection	
2. Codes of Ethics and Decision Rules	
3. Top Management's Leadership	
4. Job Goals	
5. Ethics Training	
6. Comprehensive Performance Appraisal	
7. Independent Social Audits	
8. Formal Protective Mechanisms	
VI. A Final Thought	

CHAPTER OVERVIEW

Two opposing views of social responsibility are the classical view and the socioeconomic view. According to the classical view, management's only social responsibility is to maximize profits. One of the most outspoken advocates of the classical view is Milton Friedman. Friedman believes that when managers try to work for the "social good", they undermine the market mechanism. Advocates of the socioeconomic view suggest that profits are important, but are not the first priority of business. The primary responsibility of business is to ensure its survival. The best way to ensure the survival of business is to protect and improve society's welfare.

Several points have been discussed both "for" and "against" social responsibility. The major arguments that support the assumption of business social responsibility include the following:

1. Public expectations
2. Long-run profits
3. Ethical obligation
4. Public image
5. Better environment
6. Discouragement of further government regulation
7. Balance of responsibility and power
8. Stockholder interests
9. Possession of resources
10. Superiority of prevention over cures

The major arguments against social responsibility include the following:

1. Violation of profit maximization
2. Dilution of purpose
3. Costs
4. Too much power
5. Lack of skills
6. Lack of accountability
7. Lack of broad public support

The three definitions below help specify just what is meant by social responsibility. Social responsibility is defined as a social obligation, beyond that required by law and economics, for a firm to pursue long-term goals that are good for society. This definition assumes that the business obeys the law, pursues economic interests, and in its effort to do good for society, differentiates between right and wrong. Definitions of two concepts that are similar to social responsibility help to explain social responsibility.

1. Social obligation is the obligation of business to meet its economic and legal responsibilities.

2. Social responsiveness is the capacity of a firm to adapt to changing societal conditions.

Results of several research studies indicate that socially responsible activities result in higher economic performance. There is little evidence that suggests that a company's socially responsible actions significantly reduce its long-term economic performance. Some people suggest that the notion of social responsibility is nothing more than a public relations concept. It might be true that socially responsible actions are nothing more than profit-maximizing actions in disguise. Cause-related marketing is a term that is used to describe social actions taken by companies that are motivated directly by profits. Firms such as American Express and Coca-Cola make no apologies for capitalizing on the public's social conscience. Does this evidence mean that socially responsible actions are really just profit maximizing behavior? Certainly not all socially responsible actions are just cause-related marketing, but the motivation for some of these actions is profits.

An important consideration in social responsibility is to whom companies are socially responsible. Depending on a manager's view of social responsibility, different groups are considered stakeholders of the organization. History indicates that the domain of social responsibility is continually expanding. The stakeholders for the four stages of domain are as follow:

Stage 1 - owners and managers
Stage 2 - owners, managers, and employees
Stage 3 - owners, managers, employees, constituencies in the organization's specific environment
Stage 4 - all of society

Ethics commonly refers to the rules and principles that define right and wrong conduct. A manager makes decisions differently depending on which of the three different views of ethics he/she believes.

1. Using the utilitarian view, a manager makes decisions solely on the basis of their outcomes or consequences.

2. Using the rights view of ethics, a manager makes decisions that respect and protect basic rights of individuals.

3. Using the theory of justice view, a manager makes decisions by trying to impose and enforce rules fairly and impartially.

The manager's actions related to ethics are a combination of several issues: the manager's stage of moral development, individual characteristics, the company structure, the organization culture, and the issue intensity. The three stages of moral development are as follow:

1. Preconventional Level - Individuals make moral decisions based on their own personal consequences.

2. Conventional Level - Individuals make moral decisions based on expectations of others and on maintaining order in society (follow the law).

3. Principled Level - Individuals make moral decisions based on moral principles.

Moral development can end at any stage. Managers at higher stages are more likely to behave ethically than mangers at lower stages of moral development.

Every manager has certain values (convictions about what is right and wrong), but these values are influenced by ego strength and locus of control. Ego strength is the strength of one's convictions and locus of control measures the degree to which people believe they are the master of their own fate. Organization structure guides ethical behavior through formal rules, job descriptions, actions of top managers, reward mechanisms, etc. The content and strength of the organization culture also will influence ethical behavior. A culture that is likely to shape high ethical standards is one that is high in risk tolerance, direction, and conflict tolerance. Also, a strong culture will exert more influence on managers than a weak one. When the moral intensity is high, managers recognize the importance of the ethical choice.

If top managers are seriously interested in reducing unethical behavior several things can be done:

1. Selection - Managers can hire individuals who have personal values that are consistent with the organization's needs.
2. Code of Ethics - Managers can develop a code of ethics to govern behavior. A code of ethics is a formal statement of an organization's primary values and the ethical rules it expects its employees to follow.
3. Top Management Leadership - A code of ethics requires commitment from top managers. Top managers set the cultural tone by their reward and punishment practices related to ethical behavior.
4. Job Goals - Employees should have explicit and realistic goals.
5. Ethics Training - Seminars and workshops can provide guidance for employees on ethical behavior. These training sessions will reinforce the company standards of conduct, clarify which practices are/are not permissible, and allow employees to see that others in the organization must deal with similar ethical dilemmas.
6. Comprehensive Performance Appraisal - The annual performance review should include a measure of the employee's ethical conduct.
7. Independent Social Audits - Routine evaluations of management practice in regard to the code of ethics will deter some unethical behavior because managers will fear being caught.
8. Formal Protective Mechanisms - Ethical advisors could be hired and an ethical appeals process could be instituted to make sure that those who raise ethical questions will not risk being fired.

KEY TERMS AND DEFINITIONS

1. classical view - The view that management's only social responsibility is to maximize profits.

2. socioeconomic view - The view that management's social responsibility goes well beyond making of profits to include protecting and improving society's welfare.

3. social responsibility - An obligation, beyond that required by the law and economics, for a firm to pursue long-term goals that are good for society.

4. social obligation - The obligation of a business to meet its economic and legal responsibilities.

5. social responsiveness - The capacity of a firm to adapt to changing societal conditions.

6. cause-related marketing - Performing social actions that are motivated directly by profits.

7. stakeholders - Any constituency in the environment that is affected by an organization's decisions and policies.

8. ethics - Rules and principles that define right and wrong conduct.

9. utilitarian view of ethics - Decisions are made solely on the basis of their outcomes or consequences.

10. rights view of ethics - Decisions are concerned with respecting and protecting basic rights of individuals.

11. theory of justice view of ethics - Decision makers seek to impose and enforce rules fairly and impartially.

12. preconventional level - Individuals make moral decisions based on their own personal consequences.

13. conventional level - Individuals make moral decisions based on expectations of others and on maintaining order in society.

14. principled level - Individuals make moral decisions based on moral principles.

15. values - Basic convictions about what is right and wrong.

16. ego strength - A personality characteristic that measures the strength of a person's convictions.

17. locus of control - A personality attribute that measures the degree to which people believe they are masters of their own fate.

18. code of ethics - A formal statement of an organization's primary values and the ethical rules it expects its employees to follow.

TRUE/FALSE QUESTIONS

1. T F The classical view of social responsibility states that a manager's social responsibility goes beyond making a profit.

2. T F The most outspoken advocate of the classical view of social responsibility is Milton Friedman.

3. T F Supporters of the socioeconomic view contend that managers must accept social obligations and the costs that go with them so that profits can be maximized in the long-term.

4. T F Social obligation is the capacity of a firm to respond to social pressures.

5. T F Social responsibility does not require business to determine what is right or wrong, but business is guided only by social norms.

6. T F When a company follows pollution control standards because they have been established by the federal government, the company is being socially responsible.

7.   T F At the conventional level of moral development, individuals make decisions based on moral principles.

8.   T F At the preconventional level of moral development, individuals make decisions based on their own personal consequences.

9.   T F The focus of the recent efforts by colleges to raise students' ethical awareness and standards is an attempt to move students to the principled level of moral decision making.

10.   T F The characteristics of the ethical issue itself affects a manager's ethical behavior.

11.   T F When both concentration of effect and immediacy of consequences are high, ethical intensity is reduced.

12.   T F Social responsiveness is social actions that are motivated directly by profits.

13.   T F Ethics is commonly defined as social responsibility.

14.   T F A manager is following the theory of justice view of ethics if he pays employees more than minimum wage because he believes minimum wage is an inadequate rate to pay for basic financial commitments.

15.   T F According to the rights view of ethics, decisions are made on the basis of outcomes or consequences.

16.   T F The theory of justice view sacrifices the welfare of minorities in the interest of the majority.

17.   T F Personality variables that influence individuals' actions according to what is right or wrong include strength of conviction and belief in control of their own fate.

18.   T F Values are basic convictions about right and wrong that are developed in the early years of life.

19.   T F A culture that is likely to shape high ethical standards is one that is low in risk tolerance and low in conflict tolerance.

20.   T F Codes of ethics should be clearly written so that ethical options are specifically identified.

21. Corporations have a social responsibility to the larger society that creates and sustains them.

    a. classical view
    b. socioeconomic view
    c. cause-related marketing
    d. issue intensity

22. An example is hiring lobbyists and providing financial support for Political Action Committees in order to minimize surprises and enforce social policies that benefit the firm:

    a. classical view
    b. social obligation
    c. cause-related marketing
    d. issue intensity

23. A social responsibility belief that managers do not have the expertise to decide how society "should" be:

    a. classical view
    b. socioeconomic view
    c. cause-related marketing
    d. issue intensity

24. A primary interest of managers should be protecting the interests of their stockholders by maximizing profits:

    a. classical view
    b. socioeconomic view
    c. cause-related marketing
    d. issue intensity

25. Which is not an argument for social responsibility?

    a. public expectations
    b. better environment
    c. costs
    d. profits

26. An argument for social responsibility related to improving quality of life in a community:

    a. public expectations
    b. better environment
    c. costs
    d. profits

27. An argument for social responsibility related to financial security in the long-term:

   a. public expectations
   b. better environment
   c. costs
   d. profits

28. Those who argue against social responsibility because of violation of profit maximization would suggest that:

   a. profits are lower with social responsibility
   b. society does not want social responsibility because product selling prices increase
   c. business is most socially responsible when it concentrates on economic interests
   d. costs are lower with social responsibility

29. Those who argue against social responsibility because of costs would suggest that:

   a. social responsibility costs are passed on to the consumer
   b. costs are lower with social responsibility
   c. profits are higher with social responsibility
   d. all of the above

30. An example is a company improving air pollution standards to the minimum levels required by law.

   a. social responsibility
   b. social obligation
   c. social responsiveness
   d. issue intensity

31. An example is a company that voluntarily recalls a toy when it is discovered that it is unsafe:

   a. social responsibility
   b. social obligation
   c. social responsiveness
   d. issue intensity

32. An example is a car company that improves their engines so that their cars get higher than the legally required minimum standard for miles per gallon:

   a. social responsibility
   b. social obligation
   c. social responsiveness
   d. issue intensity

33. Closing a plant that puts 500 people out of work versus closing a plant that puts 50 people out of work is an example of this characteristic of issue intensity:

   a. immediacy of consequences
   b. proximity to the victim
   c. probability of harm
   d. greatness of harm

34. Reducing retirement benefits of current retirees versus reducing retirement benefits of current employees between the ages of 40 and 50 is an example of this characteristic of issue intensity:

   a. immediacy of consequences
   b. proximity to the victim
   c. probability of harm
   d. greatness of harm

35. Layoffs in your own plant versus layoffs you hear about in a far away state is an example of this characteristic of issue intensity:

   a. immediacy of consequences
   b. proximity to the victim
   c. probability of harm
   d. greatness of harm

36. Which of the following variables is not a factor that affects managerial ethics?

   a. issue intensity
   b. stage of moral development
   c. organization culture
   d. All are factors that affect managerial ethics.

37. Strategy of choosing social actions because they will increase profits:

   a. preconventional level
   b. organization culture
   c. principles level
   d. cause-related marketing

38. A manager who makes decisions to promote workers based on merit because she believes this is fair to everyone has this view on ethics:

   a. utilitarian view
   b. rights view
   c. theory of justice view
   d. code of ethics

39. A manager who sets a policy that allows a worker to challenge the fairness of promotion policies because he wants to make sure that individuals' rights are protected has this view on ethics:

    a. utilitarian view
    b. rights view
    c. theory of justice view
    d. code of ethics

40. An example of this view of ethics is a manager who sets a policy that requires that employees wear safety glasses even though employees do not like these glasses. The manager believes the glasses will make the workplace safer for everyone and the company will be less likely to be involved in a law suit:

    a. utilitarian view
    b. rights view
    c. theory of justice view
    d. code of ethics

41. Which is not true for values?

    a. Values are developed from parents, teachers, friends, and others who influence a person.
    b. Values of different managers in the organization are basically the same.
    c. Values are basic convictions about what is right and wrong.
    d. Values are developed in a person's early years.

42. If a company were selling unsafe, high tar cigarettes to third world countries, a manager with high ego strength would be likely to:

    a. say he believes that since the cigarettes are unsafe, the company should not sell them, and then he actively campaigns to persuade the company to stop selling the cigarettes
    b. say he believes that the cigarettes are unsafe and the company should not sell them, but does nothing to encourage the company to stop the practice
    c. not say what he thinks, but informally suggest that the company stop selling the cigarettes
    d. not act to change even if he believes the cigarettes are unsafe

43. If a company were selling unsafe, high tar cigarettes to third world countries a manager with an external locus of control would be likely to:

    a. say he believes that since the cigarettes are unsafe, the company should not sell them, and then he actively campaigns to persuade the company to stop selling the cigarettes
    b. say he believes that the cigarettes are unsafe and the company should not sell them, but does nothing to encourage the company to stop the practice
    c. not say what he thinks, but informally suggest that the company stop selling the cigarettes
    d. not act to change even if be believes the cigarettes are unsafe

44. An organization is more likely to shape high standards for ethical behavior if:

   a. managers performance is based on "outcomes"
   b. there is much pressure in an organization
   c. objectives and performance goals are unclear
   d. the culture is high in risk tolerance and high in conflict tolerance

45. Which of the following is not a way to improve ethical behavior in a company?

   a. Select employees who have value systems consistent with the company ideals.
   b. Write a company code of ethics.
   c. Make sure job goals and job descriptions are informal.
   d. Provide ethics training programs for employees.

46. Top managers are role models in both word and action because they:

   a. imply that their behavior is acceptable for others
   b. can punish behavior
   c. can reward behavior with promotions
   d. all of the above

47. Which of the following is a benefit of ethics training?

   a. Workers are reminded that top managers want workers to consider ethical issues in their decisions.
   b. Managers become more confident that they are doing the right thing when they have to take unpopular stands.
   c. The organization's standards of conduct are reinforced.
   d. all of the above

5 - 1 APPLICATION CASE

STAGES OF MORAL DEVELOPMENT

Dumac, Inc. markets pesticides to farmers in countries such as Costa Rica, Mexico, and Brazil. These pesticides have been banned for use in the United States for several years, but are legal products in the countries where the company sells the pesticides. Since fruits and vegetables are imported from these countries into the U.S., it is possible that U.S. citizens could be harmed by the pesticide residue of the imported produce.

Discuss the thought process (for the three levels of moral development) and the decision a marketing manager would make in regard to selling the pesticide that is illegal in the U.S. to other countries.

1.   PRECONVENTIONAL LEVEL

2.   CONVENTIONAL LEVEL

3.   PRINCIPLED LEVEL

5 - 2 APPLICATION CASE

THREE VIEWS ON ETHICAL BEHAVIOR

A sales representative for a large industrial manufacturer sells component parts for furniture. He has a rather large sales territory, but somehow manages to visit his customers regularly. The customers are manufacturing plants that need the components to produce sofas, recliners, and dining room sets. Several issues have arisen in the last six months that have required ethical judgment from the sales representative.

1. One customer offered John a free sofa if he would ship more material than was invoiced. John declined.
2. John purchased several meals for his wife and child when they accompanied him on a trip and charged these to his company expense account.
3. John often uses his company car when doing personal errands.
4. Since John works very hard for the company on nights and weekends, he sometimes tells his boss he is working out of town Friday afternoon. John really takes the day off.
5. One of John's best customers regularly purchases large quantities of a particular material. John told the customer that the price would increase 10% next month. The customer ordered a large quantity of the material.
6. John refused to "swap" orders with another sales representative. The other sales representative wanted to meet his sales quota and needed a $1000 sale to meet the quota. John had already passed his quota so he would not have lost anything if he had exchanged an order with the other sales representative.

Which ethical view does John take when making decisions related to his sales job? (You may believe he uses some combination of the three views.) Explain your opinion.

5 - 3 APPLICATION CASE

CODE OF ETHICS

Write a code of ethics for student behavior at your college or university. (Hint: Include ways of handling issues that you must deal with at your university. Some examples might include: cheating, studying, library privileges, computer use/misuse, dorm policies, and general courtesy.)

Chapter 6

Decision Making: The Essence of the Manager's Job

CHAPTER OUTLINE	CORRESPONDING LEARNING OBJECTIVES
I. The Decision-Making Process	1. Outline the steps in the decision-making process.
A. Identifying a Problem	
B. Identifying Decision Criteria	
C. Allocating Weights to the Criteria	
D. Developing Alternatives	
E. Analyzing Alternatives	
F. Selecting an Alternative	
G. Implementing the Alternative	
H. Evaluating Decision Effectiveness	
II. The Pervasiveness of Decision Making	
III. The Rational Decision Maker	2. Define the rational decision maker.
A. Assumptions of Rationality	3. Explain the limits to rationality.
B. Limits to Rationality	4. Describe the perfectly rational decision maker.
C. Bounded Rationality	5. Describe the boundedly rational decision maker.
IV. Problems and Decisions: A Contingency Approach	6. Identify the two types of decision problems and the two types of decisions that are used to solve them.
A. Types of Problems	

CHAPTER OUTLINE	CORRESPONDING LEARNING OBJECTIVES

B. Types of Decisions

    1. Programmed Decisions
    2. Nonprogrammed Decisions

C. Integration

V. Analyzing Decision Alternatives   7. Differentiate certainty, risk, and uncertainty decision conditions.

A. Certainty

B. Risk

C. Uncertainty

VI. Group Decision Making   8. Identify the advantages and disadvantages of group decisions.

A. Advantages and Disadvantages

B. Effectiveness and Efficiency

C. Techniques for Improving Group Decision Making   9. Describe four techniques for improving group decision making.

    1. Brainstorming
    2. Nominal Group Technique
    3. Delphi Technique
    4. Electronic Mail

CHAPTER OVERVIEW

Decision making is a process or sequence of steps leading to selection of a decision from several alternatives. The eight steps in the decision-making process are described below:

1. Identifying a Problem - The decision maker recognizes a difference between "what is" and "what should be." The problem is recognized by comparing actual affairs with company standards. In addition, before a situation can be characterized as a problem, the decision maker must be under some pressure to take action and have the resources that are necessary to take action. Managers must be careful at this stage to make sure that problems are identified and not just symptoms of problems.

2. Identifying Decision Criteria - The decision criteria includes what is relevant in a decision. The decision maker will have several criteria that are important in the decision. Any criteria not identified as important in the decision situation is not considered in the decision.

3. Allocating Weights to the Criteria - The decision maker will assign weights to the criteria according to the priority or importance of the criteria to the decision maker.

4. Developing Alternatives - The decision maker lists the possible alternatives, but does not try to evaluate the alternatives.

5. Analyzing Alternatives - The decision maker should analyze each alternative using the criteria for the decision and the weights that have been allocated to the criteria. Some criteria can be evaluated on an objective basis, but often the decision maker must use his/her judgment in determining the value of some criteria.

6. Selecting the Best Alternative - The decision maker chooses the alternative that received the highest score in Step 5.

7. Implementing the Alternative - This step includes communicating the decision to those who are affected and getting their commitment to the decision.

8. Evaluating Decision Effectiveness - The decision maker will evaluate the decision effectiveness by determining if the decision has corrected the problem. If the problem has not been solved, the decision maker will have to return to an earlier step in the process and proceed. Sometimes the decision maker may even have to go back to Step 1 of the decision process.

Almost everything a manager does involves decision making. Some decisions are complex and others are routine. A rational decision maker is fully objective, logical, and chooses the alternative that maximizes some specific goal. The assumptions of rationality for business decisions include:

1. problem clarity
2. goal orientation
3. known options
4. clear preferences
5. constant preferences
6. no time or cost constraints
7. maximum payoff

Some decisions do include all of these assumptions of rationality. However, most decisions that managers face do not meet all of these tests. Often managerial decision making is not exactly logical, consistent, or systematic.

This is true because:

1. There are limits to an individual's information-processing capacity.
2. Decision makers tend to intermix solutions with problems.
3. Perceptual biases can distort problem identification.
4. Often decision makers select information for its accessibility instead of its quality.

5. Decision makers may commit to a specific alternative early in the decision process.
6. When decisions are not working, often managers become even more committed to making them work.
7. Prior decisions constrain current choices.
8. There is a continual "bargaining" among managers who have different interests in the organization.
9. Time and costs constrain decision makers.
10. There is a strong conservative bias in most organization cultures.

Even though managers are not perfectly rational, this does not mean that they do not follow a rational approach to decision making. Managers operate under the assumptions of bounded rationality. This means that the key to decision making is to find a solution that is "good enough". Managers satisfice in their decision making by: setting up simplified models that capture the essential features of a problem.

Sometimes management problems are well-structured and sometimes they are ill-structured. The well-structured problem is straightforward and easily defined, while the ill-structured problem is ambiguous or incomplete. Programmed decisions are used to deal with well-structured problems. Usually the manager has policies, procedures, and rules that specify how routine problems will be handled. However, ill-structured problems require a nonprogrammed approach. This means that a unique decision must be developed for the problem. Most decisions are a combination of programmed and nonprogrammed decision making. Even the most programmed decision contains an element of judgment on the part of management and nonprogrammed decisions usually contain some element of policy that specifies the process for solving the problem.

Three different conditions for making decisions include:

1. Certainty - The manager knows the best decision because all alternatives and their outcomes are known.
2. Risk - The decision maker can identify alternatives and knows enough about each alternative to set probabilities for the alternatives.
3. Uncertainty - The decision maker does not know enough about a decision to assign probabilities to alternatives and may not even be able to list alternatives.

Most managerial decision makers must solve problems under conditions of risk and under conditions of uncertainty. Very few managerial decisions are certainty decisions.

Group decisions are often made in organizations. Some advantages of group decision making include:

1. Provides more complete information.
2. Generates more alternatives.
3. Increases acceptance of a solution.
4. Increases legitimacy.

Some disadvantages of group decision making include:

1. Time consuming.
2. Minority domination.
3. Pressures to conform.
4. Ambiguous responsibility.

Groups may interact in several ways to make decisions. Brainstorming is an informal method used to generate as many alternatives as possible without criticism from the group. The nominal group technique requires that the group meet together, but members operate independently by writing ideas down before the meeting and by choosing a final decision after the group has discussed the alternatives. The Delphi Technique is a group approach where group members never meet face-to-face. Instead, group members give opinions by answering questionnaires. These questionnaires are complied with all group members' ideas and redistributed to the group for further suggestions. Electronic meetings link groups through computer technology.

KEY TERMS AND DEFINITIONS

1. decision-making process - A set of eight steps that include formulating a problem, selecting an alternative, and evaluating the decision's effectiveness.

2. problem - A discrepancy between an existing and a desired state of affairs.

3. decision criteria - Criteria that define what is relevant in a decision.

4. implementation - Conveying a decision to those affected and getting their commitment to it.

5. rational - Describes choices that are consistent and value-maximizing within specified constraints.

6. escalation of commitment - An increased commitment to a previous decision despite evidence that it may have been wrong.

7. bounded rationality - Behavior that is rational within the parameters of a simplified model that captures the essential features of a problem.

8. satisficing - Acceptance of solutions that are "good enough".

9. well-structured problems - Straight-forward, familiar, easily defined problems.

10. ill-structured problems - New problems in which information is ambiguous or incomplete.

11. programmed decision - A repetitive decision that can be handled by a routine approach.

12. procedure - A series of interrelated sequential steps that can be used to respond to a structured problem.

13. rule - An explicit statement that tells managers what they ought or ought not to do.

14. policy - A guide that establishes parameters for making decisions.

15. nonprogrammed decisions - Unique decisions that require a custom-made solution.

16.   certainty - A situation in which a manager can make accurate decisions because the outcome from every alternative is known.

17.   risk - Those conditions in which the decision maker has to estimate the likelihood of certain outcomes.

18.   uncertainty - A situation in which a decision maker has neither certainty nor reasonable probability estimates available.

19.   groupthink - The withholding by group members of different views in order to appear in agreement.

20.   brainstorming - An idea-generating process that encourages alternatives while withholding criticism.

21.   nominal group technique - A decision-making technique in which group members are physically present, but they operate independently.

22.   Delphi technique - A group decision-making technique in which members never meet face-to-face.

23.   electronic meetings - Decision-making groups that interact by way of linked computers.

TRUE/FALSE QUESTIONS

1.   T   F   The decision-making process is designed for individual decision making rather than group decision making.

2.   T   F   A problem is a discrepancy between an existing and desired state of affairs.

3.   T   F   Some discrepancies may not be considered problems because there is no pressure to take action to correct the situation.

4.   T   F   In Step 4 of the decision-making process, (Developing Alternatives) the manager appraises the alternatives.

5.   T   F   In the analyzing alternatives phase of decision making, the manager makes some assessments subjectively.

6.   T   F   Implementation is merely conveying the decision to those affected.

7.   T   F   Evaluating decision effectiveness is a mechanism for control.

8.   T   F   Evaluating the decision may cause managers to return to an earlier step in the decision process.

9.   T   F   Decision making is important for only two management functions: planning and leading.

10.   T   F   Decision making is synonymous with managing.

11.   T   F   Managers make dozens of routine decisions every day.

12.   T   F   Most decisions that managers face do not meet all of the tests of rationality.

13.   T   F   Sometimes rationality in decision making is limited because of prior decisions that have been made by managers.

14.   T   F   Well-structured problems are usually solved with nonprogrammed decisions.

15.   T   F   Lower-level managers usually deal with repetitive problems and rely on programmed decisions.

16.   T   F   Most decisions made by managers are made under conditions of certainty.

17.   T   F   When the decision maker knows the probability of occurrences of alternatives, the decision is made under conditions of uncertainty.

18.   T   F   For effective decision making, larger groups are preferred over smaller groups.

19.   T   F   The nominal group technique is a group decision-making method in which members meet face-to-face, but operate independently.

20.   T   F   Groupthink means that group members will feel free to have different views from other group members.

MULTIPLE CHOICE QUESTIONS

21. The control mechanism in the decision-making process is:

    a. allocating weights to the criteria
    b. developing alternatives
    c. evaluating decision effectiveness
    d. analyzing alternatives

22. A manager who determines that cost, speed, and enlarging capability are relevant to his decision to purchase a new photocopy machine is an example of this phase of the decision-making process:

    a. allocating weights to the criteria
    b. identifying decision criteria
    c. developing alternatives
    d. formulating a problem

23. Decision making is an important activity for the following management functions:

   a. planning and controlling
   b. planning, organizing, and controlling
   c. planning
   d. planning, organizing, leading, and controlling

24. A perfectly rational decision maker would:

   a. be fully objective and logical
   b. select the alternative that maximizes a specific goal
   c. define a problem carefully
   d. follow all of the above

25. Which is not an assumption of a rational decision maker?

   a. time and cost constraints
   b. clear preferences
   c. maximum payoff
   d. goal orientation

26. Escalation of commitment is:

   a. usually effective
   b. a contingency approach in decision making
   c. a limit to rationality in decision making
   d. profit maximizing

27. Decision makers tend to:

   a. intermix solutions with problems
   b. make perfectly rational decisions
   c. select information for its quality rather than its accessibility
   d. wait until the end of the decision process to commit to a decision

28. Bounded rationality is:

   a. conveying a decision to those affected and getting their commitment to it
   b. the withholding by group members of different views in order to appear in agreement
   c. behavior that is rational within the parameters of a simplified model that captures the essential features of a problem
   d. an explicit statement that tells managers what they ought or ought not to do

29. Decisions that are routine are called:

   a. nonprogrammed decisions
   b. programmed decisions
   c. ill-structured problems
   d. well-structured problems

30. The manager of a retail clothing store just found out that some "name brand" merchandise was actually brought into the U.S. illegally. This is an example of:

    a. a well-structured problem
    b. satisficing
    c. an ill-structured problem
    d. a programmed decision

31. Policies, procedures, and rules are developed to help managers deal with:

    a. well-structured problems
    b. groupthink
    c. bounded rationality
    d. nonprogrammed decisions

32. Which of the following is the procedure for snack breaks in a production company?

    a. Each production worker is entitled to a snack break in the morning and in the afternoon each work day.
    b. No food is to be taken into the work area. All snacks must be eaten in the break room.
    c. Employees will be given a morning break beginning at 10 a.m. for production line one and continuing at fifteen minute intervals until all four production lines have taken a break. Workers should report to the production line after a fifteen minute break.
    d. All statements above are procedures.

33. Which of the following is a rule for snack breaks in a production company?

    a. Each production worker is entitled to a snack break in the morning and in the afternoon each work day.
    b. No food is to be taken into the work area. All snacks must be eaten in the break room.
    c. Employees will be given a morning break beginning at 10 a.m. for production line one and continuing at fifteen minute intervals until all four production lines have taken a break. Workers should report to the production line after a fifteen minute break.
    d. All statements above are rules.

34. Which of the following is a policy for snack breaks in a production company?

    a. Each production worker is entitled to a snack break in the morning and in the afternoon.
    b. No food is to be taken into the production area. All snacks must be eaten in the break room.
    c. Employees will be given breaks beginning at 10 a.m. for production line one and continuing at fifteen minute intervals until all four production lines have taken a break. Workers should report to the production line after a fifteen minute break.
    d. All statements above are policies.

35. Lower level managers usually deal with:

    a. ill-structured problems
    b. programmed decisions
    c. nonprogrammed decisions
    d. nonroutine decisions

36. As a worker moves to higher levels in the organization, he/she is more likely to encounter:

    a. ill-structured problems
    b. nonprogrammed decisions
    c. nonroutine decisions
    d. all of the above types of decisions

37. Most decisions made in organizations are:

    a. fully nonprogrammed
    b. fully programmed
    c. some combination of programmed and nonprogrammed
    d. nonroutine

38. Organizational effectiveness is facilitated by the use of:

    a. programmed decisions
    b. nonprogrammed decisions
    c. ill-structured problems
    d. nonroutine decisions

39. John can repair a saw at Quality Production, Inc. in two hours while it takes Mike five hours to make repairs. Assuming that both workers are present, the manager will always choose John to make repairs to the saws. This is a decision under:

    a. conditions of certainty
    b. conditions of risk
    c. conditions of uncertainty
    d. none of the above

40. A manager has no idea what alternatives are available for new computer support systems and does not know how she can determine this information. This is a decision under:

    a. conditions of certainty
    b. conditions of risk
    c. conditions of uncertainty
    d. none of the above

41. A manager chooses among three alternatives for advertising (billboards, radio, and newspapers) based on research indicating success in sales for the three alternatives. This is a decision under:

    a. conditions of certainty
    b. conditions of risk
    c. conditions of uncertainty
    d. none of the above

42. Advantages for group decision making include:

    a. increases acceptance of the solution
    b. time consuming
    c. pressure to conform
    d. all of the above

43. Disadvantages for group decision making include:

    a. increases acceptance of the solution
    b. provides more complete information
    c. pressure to conform
    d. all of the above

44. Related to the effectiveness of a decision:

    a. If effectiveness is defined as speed, groups are more effective.
    b. If effectiveness is defined as accuracy, groups tend to be more effective.
    c. If effectiveness is defined as creativity, individuals tend to be more effective.
    d. If effectiveness is defined as acceptance, individuals tend to be more effective.

45. Groupthink:

    a. increases effectiveness in decision making
    b. generates more alternatives
    c. means programmed decision making
    d. is the withholding by group members of different views in order to appear in agreement

46. Four ways to make group decisions more creative include:

    a. nominal group technique, brainstorming, Delphi technique, electronic meetings
    b. satisficing, groupthink, nominal group technique, brainstorming
    c. nominal group technique, programmed decision, satisficing, electronic meetings
    d. Delphi technique, brainstorming, satisficing, groupthink

47. A group decision-making method in which group members meet face-to-face, but operate independently:

   a. brainstorming
   b. nominal group technique
   c. Delphi technique
   d. electronic meetings

48. A group decision-making method in which group members never meet face-to-face:

   a. brainstorming
   b. nominal group technique
   c. Delphi technique
   d. groupthink

49. An advantage of the Delphi technique is:

   a. It insulates group members from the undue influence of others.
   b. It is very efficient since it can be done very quickly.
   c. It is useful in developing a wide range of alternatives.
   d. All of the above are advantages.

50. Which is not a characteristic of the nominal group technique?

   a. Members meet as a group and write down ideas independently.
   b. Members present their ideas and these are discussed by the group.
   c. Members independently rank the ideas after discussion by the group.
   d. Members work together to rank the ideas after group discussion.

6 - 1 APPLICATION CASE

DECISION MAKING FOR THE GAP, INC.

The Gap, Inc. is a retail clothing store chain consisting of The Gap, Banana Republic, and GapKids. These stores provide fashion clothing for men, women, and children. The merchandise mix in the stores is well-made "classic" clothing that sells for moderate prices. Mickey Drexler has been President of The Gap, Inc. for approximately eight years. He has made several major changes in the stores during this time. Some of these changes include:

1. Clothing lines that appeal to adult shoppers were added. (The store had been known as a "jeans store" for teenagers.)

2. The look of the store was changed from "crowded" aisles and an unrelated mix of merchandise to modular shelves and neatly folded merchandise.

For one of these decisions made by Drexler, formulate a problem and work through the decision-making process. (You will have to make some assumptions and use your imagination!)

1. Identify the Problem.

2. Identify Decision Criteria.

3. Allocate Weights to the Criteria.

4. Develop Alternatives.

5. Analyze the Alternatives.

6. Select an Alternative.

7. Implement the Alternative.

8. Evaluate Decision Effectiveness.

6 - 2 APPLICATION CASE

CONDITIONS FOR MAKING DECISIONS AT MCDONALD'S

Customers of fast food restaurants have changed in recent years. These customers often decide to stay home and use their microwave, not to eat red meat at all, or to shop for burgers wherever the price is lower. McDonald's is still very successful, but managers realize that decisions must be made now to ensure that success continues. For example, the average McDonald's serves salads and chicken and eating areas are more spacious now. Pizza is also being served in some McDonald's outlets.

Consider conditions for decision making at McDonald's. List several possible decisions that might be made under conditions of certainty, risk, and uncertainty. (Hint: Some possible decisions might be related to store hours, product mix, promotion plans, inventory/ordering decisions, etc.)

1. Certainty Decisions

2. Risk Decisions

3. Uncertainty Decisions

6 - 3 APPLICATION CASE

PROBLEMS ENCOUNTERED IN DECISION MAKING

Each of the managers discussed below has specific problems making decisions.

1. The Bored Manager - John has been employed in an organization for several years. He is content to follow the same routines year after year, but he has reached a level in the corporation where it is difficult to just follow routine policies.

2. The Indecisive Boss - Jean is so scared of making a wrong decision that she often decides not to make decisions. When she feels she must decide, her decisions are usually related to minor occurrences in the organization.

3. The Obsolete Manager - Donna has not kept up with changes in the organization in regard to new technology, new products, new managerial methods. She has twenty years experience in a managerial position.

4. The Impatient Manager - Tom has only worked in a managerial capacity for eighteen months. His co-workers believe he expects to solve major company problems over the weekend.

Which manager(s) would prefer to make only programmed decisions? Why?

Which manager(s) would prefer to make many nonprogrammed decisions? Why?

Which conditions for making decisions would each manager be most comfortable with for his/her organization: certainty, risk, or uncertainty? Why?

Are any of these managers likely to use group decision making? If so, which types of group decision making?

Chapter 7

Foundations of Planning

CHAPTER OUTLINE	CORRESPONDING LEARNING OBJECTIVES

I. The Definition of Planning

1. Define planning.

II. The Purpose of Planning

2. Explain the benefits of planning.

III. Planning and Performance

IV. Myths about Planning

V. Types of Plans

    A. Strategic Versus Operational Plans

3. Distinguish between strategic and operational plans.

    B. Short-Term Versus Long-Term Plans

    C. Specific Versus Directional Plans

4. State when directional plans are preferred over specific plans.

VI. Contingency Factors in Planning

5. Identify four contingency factors in planning.

    A. Level in the Organization

    B. Life Cycle of the Organization

    C. Degree of Environmental Uncertainty

    D. Length of Future Commitments

6. Explain commitment concepts.

VII. Objectives: The Foundation of Planning

    A. Multiplicity of Objectives

CHAPTER OUTLINE	CORRESPONDING LEARNING OBJECTIVES
B. Real versus Stated Objectives	7. Explain why an organization's stated objectives might not be its real objectives.
C. Traditional Objective Setting	
D. Management by Objectives	
1. What is MBO? 2. MBO's Common Elements	8. Describe a typical MBO program.
3. Does MBO Work?	
	9. Explain how MBO establishes goals as motivators.
	10. Describe the conditions under which MBO is most likely to succeed.

CHAPTER OVERVIEW

All managers engage in planning, but it might be only the informal variety. In this chapter, planning is discussed from the perspective of formal planning. Specific objectives are formulated covering a period of years at the beginning of the planning phase. Planning gives managers direction, reduces the impact of change, minimizes waste and redundancy, and sets the standards to facilitate control. Reviews of research studies indicate that generally speaking, formal planning is associated with higher profits, higher return on assets, and other positive financial results. However, it cannot be said that organizations that formally plan always outperform those that do not plan formally.

Some myths and misconceptions about planning include the following:

1. Planning that proves inaccurate is a waste of management's time.

2. Planning can eliminate change.

3. Planning reduces flexibility.

Plans can be divided into three different types, described as follow: breadth (strategic versus operational), time frame (short-term versus long-term), and specificity (specific versus directional).

BREADTH - Strategic plans establish the organization's overall objectives and operational plans specify the details for how the overall objectives are to be achieved. Operational plans tend to cover shorter time periods. Strategic plans usually cover longer time periods, cover a broader area, and deal with fewer specifics than operational plans.

116

TIME FRAME - Short-term plans are for less than one year and long-term plans cover a period in excess of five years. Strategic plans include both long-term and short-term plans, but operational plans tend to be mostly short-term plans.

SPECIFICITY - Specific plans are clearly defined and directional plans set out general guidelines. When uncertainty is high, it is preferable to use directional plans.

Several contingency factors affect planning:

1. Level in the Organization - As managers progress in the organization hierarchy, their planning role becomes more strategy oriented.

2. Life Cycle of the Organization - Planning is not the same throughout the life cycle of the organization. Managers must rely more on directional plans in the organization's infancy. During the growth stage, plans become more specific. From maturity to decline, plans need to be more directional. Also, short-term plans are more prevalent during the formative and decline stages and long-term plans are more prevalent during maturity.

3. Degree of Environmental Uncertainty - The greater the environmental uncertainty, the more plans should be directional and based on the short-term.

4. Length of Future Commitments - Plans should extend far enough into the future to see through current commitments. The more that current plans affect future commitments, the longer the time frame for which managers should plan.

Objectives are goals and desired outcomes for individuals, groups, or the entire organization. Organizations have more than one goal. Often, it is assumed that for-profit organizations have only one goal: profits. Emphasis on only one goal ignores other goals that must also be reached if long-term profits are to be achieved. Some examples of objectives are: profitability, growth, market share, social responsibility, employee welfare, product quality, and efficiency.

Stated objectives are official statements of what an organization says are its objectives. However, often these stated objectives are not the same as the organization's real objectives. Real objectives are objectives that an organization actually pursues, as defined by the actions of its members.

Objectives have traditionally been used by top managers to control workers. Management by Objectives (MBO) is an alternative to the traditional approach to planning. MBO is a system in which subordinates and managers jointly determine specific performance objectives, periodically meet to assess the subordinate's progress, and rewards given are based on progress in achieving the jointly set goals. Four ingredients common to MBO programs are goal specificity, participative decision making, an explicit time period, and performance feedback. Several research studies confirm that hard or difficult goals result in a higher level of individual performance than do easy goals, that specific hard goals result in higher levels of performance than do no goals at all or the generalized goal of "do your best", and that feedback on one's performance leads to higher performance. These conclusions indicate that MBO can be a valuable tool for organizations. This does not mean that MBO programs are always successful. Some problems that could cause MBO to fail include an unsupportive culture, lack of top management commitment, and organizational constraints that undermine MBO ideology.

117

KEY TERMS AND DEFINITIONS

1. strategic plans - Plans that are organizationwide, establish overall objectives, and position an organization in terms of its environment.

2. operational plans - Plans that specify details on how overall objectives are to be achieved.

3. short-term plans - Plans that cover less than one year.

4. long-term plans - Plans that extend beyond five years.

5. specific plans - Plans that are clearly defined and leave no room for interpretation.

6. directional plans - Flexible plans that set out general guidelines.

7. life cycle of the organization - Four stages which organizations go through: formation, growth, maturity, and decline.

8. commitment concept - Plans should extend far enough to see through current commitments.

9. objectives - Desired outcomes for individuals, groups, or entire organizations.

10. stated objectives - Official statements of what an organization says - and what it wants various publics to believe - are its objectives.

11. real objectives - Objectives that an organization actually pursues, as defined by the actions of its members.

12. traditional objective setting - Objectives are set at the top and then broken down into subgoals for each level in an organization. The top imposes its standards on everyone below.

13. Management by Objectives (MBO) - A system in which specific performance objectives are jointly determined by subordinates and their superiors, progress toward objectives is periodically reviewed, and rewards are allocated on the basis of this progress.

TRUE/FALSE QUESTIONS

1. T F Planning is concerned with desired "ends", but not "means".

2. T F All managers engage in planning, even though for some managers all of their planning is informal.

3.   T   F   Planning gives direction, reduces the impact of change, minimizes waste, and sets standards to facilitate control.

4.   T   F   Organizations that formally plan always outperform those that do not formally plan.

5.   T   F   In those research studies where formal planning has not led to higher performance, the environment is typically the culprit.

6.   T   F   Planning that proves inaccurate is a waste of management's time.

7.   T   F   Planning reduces flexibility.

8.   T   F   Strategic plans specify details on how overall objectives are to be achieved.

9.   T   F   Short-term plans cover less than a year.

10. T   F   When uncertainty is high, it is preferable to use directional plans instead of specific plans.

11. T   F   As managers rise in the hierarchy, their planning becomes more operational.

12. T   F   Managers should rely more heavily on directional plans in an organization's infancy.

13. T   F   Short-term planning is more prevalent than long- term planning in the maturity stage of the organization life cycle.

14. T   F   Objectives are goals or desired outcomes.

15. T   F   All organizations have multiple objectives.

16. T   F   Real objectives are official statements of what an organization says are its objectives.

17. T   F   In MBO, objectives are unilaterally set by the boss and assigned to workers.

18. T   F   A lack of top management commitment and involvement will quickly undermine any MBO program.

MULTIPLE CHOICE QUESTIONS

19.   The purpose of planning is to:

   a.   give direction
   b.   reduce the impact of change
   c.   set standards to facilitate control and minimize redundancy
   d.   all of the above

20. Which is not true for planning?

    a. Planning forces managers to look ahead and anticipate change.
    b. Planning makes coordination of activities more difficult.
    c. Planning includes developing objectives.
    d. Without planning, there is no control.

21. Which of the following is not one of the three broad categories of plans that managers develop:

    a. time frame
    b. direction
    c. specificity
    d. breadth

22. Plans that specify details on how overall objectives are to be achieved:

    a. operational
    b. strategic
    c. specific
    d. directional

23. Flexible plans that set out general guidelines:

    a. operational
    b. strategic
    c. specific
    d. directional

24. Plans that are organization wide, establish overall objectives, and position an organization in terms of its environment:

    a. operational
    b. strategic
    c. specific
    d. directional

25. Plans that are clearly defined and leave no room for interpretation:

    a. operational
    b. strategic
    c. specific
    d. directional

26. Plans that extend beyond five years:

    a. short-term
    b. specific
    c. operational
    d. long-term

27. An example is a complete, exact plan for training employees:

    a. short-term
    b. specific
    c. operational
    d. long-term

28. An example is a plan developed that illustrates how a company can increase its market share:

    a. short-term
    b. specific
    c. operational
    d. long-term

29. Plans that cover less than one year:

    a. short-term
    b. specific
    c. operational
    d. long-term

30. Operational plans tend to:

    a. cover shorter time periods than strategic plans
    b. include a broader area than strategic plans
    c. be much less specific than strategic plans
    d. tend to be long-term plans

31. A plan that is described by its level of SPECIFICITY:

    a. operational
    b. directional
    c. short-term
    d. none of the above

32. A plan that is described by its BREADTH:

    a. operational
    b. directional
    c. short-term
    d. none of the above

33. A contingency factor in planning related to organization stages such as growth and maturity:

    a. level in the organization
    b. life cycle in the organization
    c. degree of environmental uncertainty
    d. length of future commitments

34. An example of this contingency factor in planning is that as managers progress in the hierarchy, their planning role becomes more strategy oriented:

    a. level in the organization
    b. life cycle in the organization
    c. degree of environmental uncertainty
    d. length of future commitments

35. An example of this contingency factor in planning is that the more current plans affect future commitments, the longer the time frame for planning should be:

    a. level in the organization
    b. life cycle in the organization
    c. degree of environmental uncertainty
    d. length of future commitments

36. An example of this contingency factor in planning is that if rapid technological, social, or economic changes occur, well-defined plans will likely hinder an organization's performance:

    a. level in the organization
    b. life cycle in the organization
    c. degree of environmental uncertainty
    d. length of future commitments

37. Objectives:

    a. provide direction for management decisions
    b. are goals of the organization
    c. are desired outcomes for individuals, groups, or entire organizations
    d. all of the above

38. Routinely a university has at least fifty students per class even though the university policy is to hold classes at thirty students. This illustrates:

    a. real objective
    b. traditional objective setting
    c. stated objective
    d. MBO

39. An approach to setting objectives from top managers downward through the organization:

    a. real objective
    b. traditional objective setting
    c. stated objective
    d. MBO

40. An example is a boss and worker who together decide that the worker will increase his productivity by 8 percent over the next year. Throughout the year the boss and worker meet to assess progress and at the end of the year the worker is rewarded because he achieved his goal:

   a. real objective
   b. traditional objective setting
   c. stated objective
   d. MBO

41. An example is an official statement that the university class size will be kept at thirty students:

   a. real objective
   b. traditional objective setting
   c. stated objective
   d. MBO

42. Which is not true for MBO?

   a. MBO includes participative decision making.
   b. A specific time period is set for the planning and achievement of goals.
   c. The worker receives performance feedback.
   d. There is no need for specific goals.

43. According to research studies, which contingency variable may explain the instances when MBO fails?

   a. organization constraints that undermine MBO ideology
   b. unsupportive culture
   c. lack of top management commitment
   d. all of the above

44. Which is not a conclusion related to MBO from research on the topic?

   a. Feedback on one's performance leads to higher performance.
   b. Hard goals result in a higher level of individual performance than do easy goals.
   c. Participation seems to induce individuals to establish more difficult goals.
   d. Participation decreases one's goal aspiration level.

7 - 1 APPLICATION CASE

TYPES OF PLANS

Consider your career plans for the next five to ten years. Give specific examples of your plans to illustrate your understanding of BREADTH, TIME FRAME, and SPECIFICITY in planning.

1.   BREADTH - strategic plan

2.   BREADTH - operational plan

3.   TIME FRAME - short-term plan

4. TIME FRAME - Long-term plan

5. SPECIFICITY - specific plan

6. SPECIFICITY - directional plan

7 - 2 APPLICATION CASE

CONTINGENCY FACTORS IN PLANNING

You work for an organization that produces shirts for sale to Wal-Mart stores. The organization employs approximately 400 production workers and 50 managers. Explain how the contingencies listed below would affect the organization's plans. (Hint: Relate to specificity, breadth, and time frame of planning for each situation.)

1. Environmental uncertainty is low because Wal-Mart purchases all of the company's product and has a contract with the production company for ten years.

2. Production supervisors (low organizational level) must coordinate and devise plans for meeting the Wal-Mart orders.

3.   Top managers (high organizational level) work on developing future plans for the organization.

4.   The organization is in the maturity phase of the organization life cycle.

7 - 3 APPLICATION CASE

PLANNING FOR WINTER SURVIVAL

You have just crash-landed somewhere in the woods of northern Minnesota or southern Manitoba. It is 11:32 a.m. in mid-January. The small plane in which you were traveling was destroyed except for the frame. The pilot and copilot have been killed, but no one else is seriously injured.

The crash came suddenly before the pilot had time to radio for help or inform anyone of your position. Since your pilot was trying to avoid a storm, you know the plane was considerably off course. The pilot announced shortly before the crash that you were eighty miles northwest of a small town that is the nearest known habitation.

You are in a wilderness area made up of thick woods broken by many lakes and rivers. The last weather report indicated that the temperature would reach minus 25 degrees in the daytime and minus 40 degrees at night. The men and women in your party are wearing business attire (including pants and jackets), street shoes, and overcoats.

While escaping from the plane your group salvaged the fifteen items listed below. Assume that you are the group leader and in charge of planning and the group of people will stick together in their search for help.

Rank the items below according to their importance to the group. (Number 1 is the most important item and number 15 is the least important.) REMEMBER YOUR PLANS COULD SAVE OR CAUSE HARM TO THE FIVE PEOPLE IN THE GROUP!!

ITEM	RANKING
Compress kit with 28 feet of gauze	_____
Ball of steel wool	_____
Cigarette lighter	_____
Loaded .45 caliber pistol	_____
Newspaper (one per person)	_____
Compass	_____
Two ski poles	_____
Knife	_____
Sectional air map made of plastic	_____
30 feet of rope	_____
Family size chocolate bar (one per person)	_____

ITEM	RANKING
Flashlight with batteries	_____
Quart of 85 proof whiskey	_____
Extra shirt and pants for each person	_____
Can of shortening	_____

Explain your reasoning for your rankings:

(Source: Ritchie, J.B. and Thompson, Paul, Organization and People, West Publishing Company, 3rd edition, 1984, pp. 264- 265.)

Chapter 8

Strategic Planning and Management

CHAPTER OUTLINE	CORRESPONDING LEARNING OBJECTIVES
I. The Increasing Importance of Strategic Planning	1. Explain the importance of strategic planning.
II. Levels of Strategy	2. Differentiate corporate, business-, and functional-level strategies.
A. Corporate-Level Strategy	
B. Business-Level Strategy	
C. Functional-Level Strategy	
III. The Strategic Management Process	
A. Step 1: Identifying the Organization's Current Mission, Objectives, and Strategies	3. Outline the steps in the strategic management process.
B. Step 2: Analyzing the Environment	
C. Step 3: Identifying Opportunities and Threats	
D. Step 4: Analyzing the Organization's Resources	
E. Step 5: Identifying Strengths and Weaknesses	
F. Step 6: Reassessing the Organization's Mission and Objectives	
	4. Explain SWOT analysis.
G. Step 7: Formulating Strategies	
H. Step 8: Implementing Strategies	
I. Step 9: Evaluating Results	

CHAPTER OUTLINE	CORRESPONDING LEARNING OBJECTIVES

IV. Corporate-Level Strategic Frameworks

    A. Grand Strategies

        1. Stability

        2. Growth

        3. Retrenchment

        4. Combination

    B. Corporate Portfolio Matrix

        5. Describe the four business groups in the BCG matrix.

V. Business-Level Strategic Frameworks

    A. Adaptive Strategies

        6. Identify and contrast the four business-level strategies.

        1. Defenders

        2. Prospectors

        3. Analyzers

        4. Reactors

    B. Competitive Strategies

        1. Industry Analysis

        2. Selecting a Competitive Advantage

        3. Sustaining a Competitive Advantage

        7. Describe how to assess an organization's competitive advantage.

VI. TQM as a Strategic Weapon

VII. Entrepreneurship: A Special Case of Strategic Planning

CHAPTER OUTLINE	CORRESPONDING LEARNING OBJECTIVES
A. What is Entrepreneurship?	8. Explain what entrepreneurship is.
B. Characteristics of Entrepreneurs	9. Compare how entrepreneurs and bureaucratic managers approach strategy.
C. Impetus for Entrepreneurship	
D. Comparing Entrepreneurs and Traditional Managers	
E. Strategy and the Entrepreneur	

CHAPTER OVERVIEW

The fact that strategic planning plays a critical role in an organization's success has been widely recognized for only about twenty years. Before the 1970's, managers' future plans were merely extensions of past actions. Changing external environmental conditions of the 1970's forced managers to develop a systematic means of analyzing the environment, assessing the organization's strengths and weaknesses, and identifying opportunities where the organization could gain a competitive advantage. Today strategic planning is important for corporations as well as government agencies, hospitals, and educational institutions.

It is necessary for organizations to have different strategies for organization activities at different levels in the organization. These different levels of strategies include: corporate-level strategy, business-level strategy, and functional-level strategy.

1. Corporate-level strategy is the overall strategy set by top managers to determine the different businesses in which the organization should be involved.

2. Business-level strategy is the strategy for each different business of the organization. Typical strategic plans include the products/services the organization will offer and the customers it wants to reach. When an organization is involved in several different businesses, planning can be facilitated by creating strategic business units (SBU's). These SBU's are single businesses or related businesses that have their own distinct mission and competitors.

3. Functional-level strategy is the strategy that is set for each functional area to support the business-level strategy.

The strategic management process is a nine step process encompassing strategic planning, implementation, and evaluation.

Step 1: Identifying the Organization's Current Mission, Objectives, and Strategies -- In this stage, managers determine the mission or purpose of the organization so that the scope of products/services can be identified.

Step 2: Analyzing the Environment -- Managers must analyze factors in the external environment that have an impact on the company. Some of the external factors that companies must consider include competition, pending legislation, and supply of labor. Knowledge of these factors will help managers understand trends that may affect company operations.

Step 3: Identifying Opportunities and Threats -- After the environment has been analyzed, managers should be able to recognize the external factors that provide important opportunities and/or pose threats to the organization.

Step 4: Analyzing the Organization's Resources -- Managers study the internal environment of the organization to determine important internal factors for company success.

Step 5: Identifying Strengths and Weaknesses -- In this step, managers seek to identify important internal strengths and weaknesses. The knowledge of strengths and weaknesses will allow managers to identify unique skills and resources the organization can use to gain competitive advantage.

Step 6: Reassessing the Organization's Mission and Objectives -- After assessment of opportunities, threats, strengths, and weaknesses (SWOT analysis), managers need to reevaluate the company mission and objectives. Some modification of the mission and objectives may be necessary if they are not realistic. If the mission and objectives are realistic, managers are ready to begin formulating strategic alternatives.

Step 7: Formulating Strategies -- Specific strategies must be set for all three levels of the organization: corporate- level, business-level, and functional-level. Managers should use the decision making process to develop strategic alternatives. This step is completed when managers have developed a set of strategies that will give the organization a competitive advantage.

Step 8: Implementing Strategies -- Good leadership and motivated middle- and lower-level managers are important if the selected strategies are to be applied successfully.

Step 9: Evaluating Results -- Finally, managers must control the situation by making adjustments to the strategy and implementation as needed.

Corporate-level strategy can be determined by using the grand strategy framework and the corporate portfolio matrix. Four possible grand strategies that might be pursued by managers include: stability, growth, retrenchment, and combination.

1. Stability is characterized by an absence of significant change. Examples of this strategy include continuing to serve the same clients by offering the same product or service and by maintaining market share. Stability is a good strategy choice when managers believe that organization performance is satisfactory and the environment is stable and unchanging.

134

2. Growth is characterized by plans to increase the level of the organization's operations. Growth can be achieved by direct expansion, merging with other organizations, and by diversification. Example indicators of growth include increasing revenues, increasing numbers of employees, and increasing market share.

3. Retrenchment is characterized by reductions in organization size or diversity of operations. Often organizations choose retrenchment in response to aggressive foreign competition, deregulation, mergers and acquisitions, and major technological breakthroughs.

4. Combination is a strategy of pursuing two or more strategies simultaneously. For example, one division in the organization might be pursuing growth while another division is in retrenchment.

The Boston Consulting Group (BCG) Matrix is a corporate portfolio matrix that is used to guide resource allocation decisions based on market share and growth of SBU's. This matrix was developed in the early 1970's. Four business groups are identified in the matrix:

1. Cash cows are products that demonstrate low growth, but have a high market share. This means that these products generate large amounts of cash, but potential for future growth is limited. The strategy for the cash cow products is to "milk" them by using the cash that is generated for investment for other promising opportunities.

2. Stars are products that demonstrate high growth and high market share. This means that these products are fast- growing and hold a dominate share of the market. However, these products might or might not produce a positive cash flow because of the need to invest in new plant and equipment or product development. The strategy for star products is to invest heavily so that the product can eventually be developed into a cash cow.

3. Question marks are products that demonstrate high growth and low market share. This means that these products are speculative, risky products because even though profits are high, the low market share limits potential. The strategy for question marks is two-fold: some question marks should be sold off and others should be turned into stars.

4. Dogs are products that demonstrate low growth and low market share. This means that these products do not generate much cash or require much cash. These products hold no promise for improved performance. The best strategy for dogs is to divest or liquidate.

It is important to remember that the BCG matrix assumes the existence of a cumulative learning curve. This means that it is assumed that when a business increases the amount of product manufactured, the per-unit cost of the product will decrease. For the BCG matrix, this assumption means that the businesses that hold the largest market share will have the lowest costs.

In recent years, the corporate portfolio matrix concept (especially the BCG matrix) has become a less popular approach for developing strategy. Four reasons explain the loss of popularity:

135

1. Cost reduction due to greater cumulative experience has not been automatic.

2. The portfolio concept assumes that an organization's businesses can be divided into a reasonable number of independent units.

3. Many dogs have shown consistently higher levels of profitability than their growing competitors with dominant market shares.

4. Considering the rate of growth in the economy and the fact that there can be only one industry leader for a particular product, by definition most products would be considered dogs using the BCG matrix.

Despite these negative aspects of the corporate portfolio matrix, it is still a useful tool in strategy development. This is true because it provides a framework for understanding different businesses and establishing priorities for making strategic resource allocation decisions.

Two approaches for developing **business-level strategy** include the adaptive strategy approach and the competitive strategy approach. The adaptive strategy approach includes four strategic types: defenders, prospectors, analyzers, and reactors. Research indicates that success can be achieved with any of the first three strategies if there is a good fit between the strategy and the business unit's environment, internal structure, and managerial processes.

1. Defenders seek stability by producing only a limited set of products directed at a narrow segment of the total potential market.

2. Prospectors seek innovation by finding and exploiting new product and market opportunities.

3. Analyzers seek to minimize risk by following competitors' innovations, but only after they have proven successful.

4. Reactors respond inappropriately, perform poorly, and are reluctant to commit themselves aggressively to a specific strategy. The reactor strategy often leads to failure.

An example of the competitive strategy approach for developing business-level strategy is Michael Porter's five forces model for achieving competitive advantage. The five forces that dictate the rules of competition in any industry include the following:

1. Barriers to entry -- Economies of scale, brand identity, and capital requirements determine how easy or hard it is for new competitors to enter an industry.

2. Threats of substitutes -- Switching costs and buyer loyalty determine the degree to which customers are likely to switch their business to a competitor.

3. Bargaining power of buyers -- Buyer's volume, buyer information, and the availability of substitute products determine the amount of influence that buyers will have in an industry.

4. Bargaining power of suppliers -- Degree of supplier concentration and the availability of substitute inputs determine the power that suppliers will have over firms in the industry.

5.   Rivalry among existing competitors -- Industry growth and product differences determine how intense rivalry will be among firms in the industry.

Managers can assess the industry attractiveness by evaluating it in terms of these five factors. The five factors directly influence the prices that a firm can charge, its cost structure, and its investment requirements. Porter suggests three possible strategies for gaining competitive advantage:

1.   cost-leadership strategy (low cost producer in an industry) -- An organization can be the low cost leader in an industry by improving efficiency of operations, developing economies of scale, technological innovation, low-cost labor, or preferential access to raw materials.

2.   differentiation strategy (unique in its industry) -- An organization can differentiate by emphasizing high quality, excellent service, innovative design, technological capability, or an unusually positive brand image.

3.   focus strategy (cost or differentiation in a narrow market segment) -- An organization can obtain an advantage either by providing the product at low cost or by providing a unique product for a specific market to the exclusion of other segments of the market.

Sometimes organizations are "stuck in the middle" or unable to gain advantage through cost leadership, differentiation, or focus. Often organizations are stuck in the middle because they reach beyond their competitive advantage. In addition, organizations must be able to sustain their competitive advantage over the long-term if the company is to be successful.

A number of organizations are using Total Quality Management as a way to develop a competitive advantage in their industries. The incremental improvements in quality and process associated with TQM can develop into sustained differentiation from competitors. TQM can be used as a strategic tool by manufacturing or service organizations and by profit/not-for-profit organizations.

Strategic planning is also necessary for entrepreneurs. Entrepreneurship refers to undertaking ventures, pursuing opportunities, innovating, and starting businesses. Generally, small business owners are considered entrepreneurs. However, not all small business owners are entrepreneurs because they do not innovate or take risks. Entrepreneurs can also be found in large corporations, and are called intrapreneurs. These intrapreneurs create the entrepreneurial spirit in large organizations.

Entrepreneurs approach strategy differently from typical bureaucratic managers. They approach strategy by looking for opportunities and figuring out how to capitalize on these opportunities while typical bureaucratic managers focus on the resources that they control. Entrepreneurs tend to be independent types who prefer to be responsible for solving problems, for setting goals, and for reaching these goals by their own efforts. They value independence and take calculated risks when they feel they can control the outcome.

KEY TERMS AND DEFINITIONS

1.   corporate-level strategy - Seeks to determine what businesses a corporation should be in.

2. business-level strategy - Seeks to determine how a corporation should compete in each of its businesses.

3. strategic business unit (SBU) - A single business or collection of businesses that is independent and formulates its own strategy.

4. functional-level strategy - Seeks to determine how to support the business-level strategy.

5. strategic management process - A nine step process encompassing strategic planning, implementation, and evaluation.

6. mission - The purpose of the organization.

7. distinctive competence - The unique skills and resources that determine the organization's competitive weapons.

8. SWOT analysis - Analysis of an organization's strengths and weaknesses, and its environmental opportunities and strengths.

9. stability strategy - A corporate-level strategy characterized by an absence of significant change.

10. growth strategy - A corporate-level strategy that seeks to increase the level of the organization's operations. This typically includes increasing revenues, employees, and/or market share.

11. retrenchment strategy - A corporate-level strategy that seeks to reduce the size or diversity of an organization's operations.

12. combination strategy - A corporate-level strategy that pursues two or more of the following strategies-- stability, growth, or retrenchment--simultaneously.

13. BCG matrix - Strategy tool to guide resource allocation decisions based on market share and growth of SBU's.

14. cash cows - Products that demonstrate low growth, but have a high market share.

15. stars - Products that demonstrate high growth and high market share.

16. question marks - Products that demonstrate high growth, but low market share.

17. dogs - Products that demonstrate low growth and low market share.

18. cumulative learning curve - Assumes that when a business increases the amount of product manufactured, the per- unit cost of the product will decrease.

19. defenders - A business-level strategy that seeks stability by producing only a limited set of products directed at a narrow segment of the total potential market.

20. prospectors - A business-level strategy that seeks innovation by finding and exploiting new product and market opportunities.

21. analyzers - A business-level strategy that seeks to minimize risk by following competitors' innovations, but only after they have proven successful.

22. reactors - A business-level strategy that characterizes inconsistent and unstable decision patterns.

23. cost-leadership strategy - The strategy an organization follows when it wants to be the lowest-cost producer in its industry.

24. differentiation strategy - The strategy a firm follows when it wants to be unique in its industry along dimensions widely valued by buyers.

25. focus strategy - The strategy a company follows when it pursues a cost or differentiation advantage in a narrow segment of the market.

26. stuck in the middle - Descriptive of organizations that cannot compete through cost-leadership, differentiation, or focus strategies.

27. entrepreneurship - A process by which individuals pursue opportunities, fulfilling needs and wants through innovation, without regard to the resources they currently control.

28. intrapreneurship - Creating the entrepreneurial spirit in a large organization.

TRUE/FALSE QUESTIONS

1. T   F   Strategic planning is a concept that applies only to business organizations.

2. T   F   Organizations that are in multiple businesses need to develop different strategies for different organization levels.

3. T   F   Corporate-level strategy seeks to answer the question: How should we compete in each of our businesses?

4. T   F   Corporate-level strategy integrates business-level strategy for different SBU's.

5. T   F   Functional-level strategy answers the question: How do we support the business-level strategy?

6. T   F   The strategic management process and strategic planning are synonymous terms.

7. T   F   After analyzing organization resources, the manager needs to develop a list of opportunities and threats.

8. T F Managers identify strengths and weaknesses to determine where the company can develop distinctive competencies.

9. T F Organization culture has little impact on strategic planning.

10. T F The final step in the strategic management process is implementation of the strategy.

11. T F An approach to corporate-level strategy is called the adaptive strategy framework.

12. T F A corporate-level strategy that seeks to reduce size or diversity of the organization operations is called retrenchment.

13. T F The location of a product on the BCG matrix is determined by company market share and anticipated market growth.

14. T F According to the BCG matrix, cash cows have low market share, but high anticipated market growth.

15. T F Of the four strategies in the adaptive strategy framework, the prospector strategy often leads to failure.

16. T F According to Michael Porter, understanding industry competitive factors is not essential in developing strategic alternatives.

17. T F A focus strategy is a cost-leadership or differentiation strategy that has been developed for a specific market.

18. T F Entrepreneurs can be defined as small business owners.

MULTIPLE CHOICE QUESTIONS

19. Which was true for strategic plans before the 1970's, but is no longer true today?

    a. Strategic plans are specific, desired actions the company chooses to gain competitive advantage.
    b. Strategic plans are primarily based on what the organization has done in the past.
    c. Strategic planning is considered essential for success.
    d. Strategic planning is an important activity for hospitals, government agencies, and educational institutions.

20. Business-level strategy seeks to answer the question:

    a. How do we support the selected strategy?
    b. In what set of businesses should we be involved?
    c. How should we compete in each of our businesses?
    d. none of the above

21. Which of the following is an example of a functional-level strategy?

    a. plans to integrate operations of three product areas
    b. plans that pinpoint consumers between the ages of 25 and 35 as the target customer group
    c. plans that involve the selection of two primary product areas for focus of operations
    d. plans determining how marketing and production can work together to produce a consumer product

22. Which step in the strategic management process includes developing distinct competencies?

    a. Analyzing the Environment
    b. Identifying Opportunities and Threats
    c. Analyzing Organization Resources
    d. Identifying Strengths and Weaknesses

23. Which step in the strategic management process is complete when management has grasped what is taking place in its environment and is aware of trends that might affect operations?

    a. Analyzing the Environment
    b. Identifying Opportunities and Threats
    c. Analyzing Organization Resources
    d. Identifying Strengths and Weaknesses

24. For which step in the strategic management process are pending legislation and competitors' activities important considerations?

    a. Analyzing the Environment
    b. Identifying Opportunities and Threats
    c. Analyzing Organization Resources
    d. Identifying Strengths and Weaknesses

25. For which step in the strategic management process are determining employee skills and determining the organization's cash position important considerations?

    a. Analyzing the Environment
    b. Identifying Opportunities and Threats
    c. Analyzing Organization Resources
    d. Identifying Strengths and Weaknesses

26. Which step in the strategic management process includes developing a list of factors in the external environment that impact the company positively and factors that impact the company negatively?

    a. Analyzing the Environment
    b. Identifying Opportunities and Threats
    c. Analyzing Organization Resources
    d. Identifying Strengths and Weaknesses

27. Which is true for formulating strategies in the strategic management process?

    a. Strategies should be selected for the corporate-, business-, and functional-levels that will give the company a competitive advantage.
    b. Formulation of strategy should follow the decision-making process.
    c. Managers should develop and evaluate alternatives and determine which ones will allow the organization to best capitalize on its resources and opportunities in the environment.
    d. all of the above

28. A merger is an example of this corporate-level strategy:

    a. growth
    b. stability
    c. retrenchment
    d. combination

29. Selling off parts of the business is an example of this corporate-level strategy:

    a. growth
    b. stability
    c. retrenchment
    d. combination

30. Organizations that sell off an unprofitable product line and expand another product line are following this corporate-level strategy:

    a. growth
    b. stability
    c. retrenchment
    d. combination

31. Which product category in the BCG matrix has low growth and low market share?

    a. cash cow
    b. question mark
    c. star
    d. dog

32. The strategy for products that fit this category of the BCG matrix is to generate funds so that investments can be made in other products:

    a. cash cow
    b. question mark
    c. star
    d. dog

33. If managers can improve market share for this product category, the product can be turned into a star:

   a. cash cow
   b. question mark
   c. star
   d. dog

34. Which product category in the BCG matrix has high growth and high market share?

   a. cash cow
   b. question mark
   c. star
   d. dog

35. Which product category in the BCG matrix has a twofold strategy: one of risk taking investment and another of divesting the product?

   a. cash cow
   b. question mark
   c. star
   d. dog

36. A strategy in the adaptive strategy framework that is characterized by a loose organization structure:

   a. defender
   b. reactor
   c. prospector
   d. analyzer

37. A strategy in the adaptive strategy framework that often leads to failure:

   a. defender
   b. reactor
   c. prospector
   d. analyzer

38. A strategy in the adaptive strategy framework that involves seeking stability, providing a narrow set of products, and focusing on a narrow segment of the population:

   a. defender
   b. reactor
   c. prospector
   d. analyzer

39. This adaptive strategy involves imitating competitors:

    a. defender
    b. reactor
    c. prospector
    d. analyzer

40. This adaptive strategy involves seeking innovation:

    a. defender
    b. reactor
    c. prospector
    d. analyzer

41. Which of Michael Porter's competitive forces is related to switching costs?

    a. barriers to entry
    b. threats of substitute products
    c. bargaining power of buyers
    d. bargaining power of suppliers

42. Which of Michael Porter's competitive forces is related to availability of substitute inputs?

    a. barriers to entry
    b. threats of substitute products
    c. bargaining power of buyers
    d. bargaining power of suppliers

43. Which of Michael Porter's competitive forces is related to developing economies of scale?

    a. barriers to entry
    b. threats of substitute products
    c. bargaining power of buyers
    d. bargaining power of suppliers

44. Which of Michael Porter's competitive forces is related to buyer loyalty?

    a. barriers to entry
    b. threats of substitute products
    c. bargaining power of buyers
    d. bargaining power of suppliers

45. Which of Michael Porter's competitive forces is related to capital requirements?

    a. barriers to entry
    b. threats of substitute products
    c. bargaining power of buyers
    d. bargaining power of suppliers

46. Which of Porter's strategies is set when companies take advantage of economies of scale?

    a. cost-leadership
    b. focus
    c. differentiation
    d. combination

47. An example of this strategy is producing a product for weight conscious people in sufficient numbers to gain economies of scale:

    a. cost-leadership
    b. focus
    c. differentiation
    d. combination

48. Users of this strategy would emphasize brand image to compare themselves to rivals:

    a. cost-leadership
    b. focus
    c. differentiation
    d. combination

49. How can organizations sustain a competitive advantage?

    a. reducing price to gain volume (if there are strong economies of scale)
    b. creating barriers that make imitation difficult
    c. contracting with suppliers
    d. all of the above

50. An entrepreneur is:

    a. an individual who undertakes ventures, pursues opportunities, and starts businesses
    b. a small business owner
    c. a person in a large company with an entrepreneurial spirit
    d. all of the above

51. Which of the following illustrate characteristics of entrepreneurs?

    a. independent, not afraid of taking chances, desire rules and order
    b. independent, delegate to others, not afraid of taking chances
    c. prefer to take calculated risks, independent
    d. independent, wild risk taker

52. The entrepreneur's strategy emphasis is driven by:

    a. resources available
    b. search for opportunities
    c. constraints of structure
    d. none of the above

8 - 1 APPLICATION CASE

THE STRATEGIC MANAGEMENT PROCESS

Your university operations are based on strategic plans that have been developed. Use the strategic management process to analyze the university and develop strategies you think the university should pursue for the **next five years.** (You may want to choose one department of the organization such as Student Affairs, School of Business, or an athletic team.)

1.   Identify the current mission, objectives, and strategies.

2/3.   Analyze the external environment. What are the opportunities and threats?

4/5.   Analyze the organization resources. What are the strengths and weaknesses?

6.   Reassess the mission and objectives.

7. Formulate strategies.

8. Implement strategies. (Explain how strategies **should** be implemented.)

9. Evaluate results. (Explain how results **should** be evaluated.)

8 - 2 APPLICATION CASE

CORPORATE-LEVEL STRATEGIES

Which of the strategies listed below are stability strategies, growth strategies, retrenchment strategies, combination strategies?

1. Phillip Morris company purchased Kraft to help increase revenues from falling cigarette sales.

2. Hershey's purchased Peter Paul Almond Joy and Mounds and York Peppermint Patties.

3. Some airline companies have cut fares to try to keep revenues strong.

4. Campbell's Soups continues to keep condensed soups as their main product.

5.   Federal Express has begun a strategy of expanding into overseas markets.

6.   Polaroid is beginning to focus on conventional film in addition to "instant" film.

7.   Guess (jeans) founders sold part of the company assets to Jordache.

8.   Service Merchandise Company, Inc. intends to continue selling sporting goods, housewares, electronics, toys, gift items, and jewelry in a "catalog showroom" store format.

THE BOSTON CONSULTING GROUP MATRIX

What are the stars, cash cows, question marks, and dogs for Walt Disney? Explain why you categorize each business segment the way you do.

Some business divisions for Walt Disney are:

Walt Disney Attractions (Disney World, Disneyland, Tokyo Disneyland, Disney-MGM
        Studio Theme Park)
Walt Disney Studios (Touchstone Pictures, Buena Vista Pictures, Buena Vista Home
        Video, Buena Vista Television, Disney Channel, Walt Disney Records)
Disney Consumer Products

1.   STARS

2.   QUESTION MARKS

3.   CASH COWS

4.   DOGS

Chapter 9

Planning Tools and Techniques

CHAPTER OUTLINE	CORRESPONDING LEARNING OBJECTIVES
I. Techniques for Assessing the Environment	1. Describe techniques for assessing the environment.
A. Environmental Scanning	
B. Forecasting	
1. Types of Forecasts	
2. Forecasting Techniques	2. Contrast qualitative and quantitative forecasting.
3. Forecasting Effectiveness	
C. Benchmarking for TQM	
II. Budgets	3. Describe why budgets are popular.
A. Types of Budgets	
1. Revenue Budgets	
2. Expense Budgets	
3. Profit Budgets	
4. Cash Budgets	
5. Capital Expenditure Budgets	
6. Variable Budgets	
B. Approaches to Budgeting	4. List two approaches to budgeting.
1. Incremental Budgets	
2. Zero-Base Budgets	

CHAPTER OUTLINE	CORRESPONDING LEARNING OBJECTIVES
III. Operational Planning Tools	
A. Scheduling	
1. The Gantt Chart	5. Differentiate Gantt and load charts.
2. The Load Chart	
3. PERT Network Analysis	6. Identify the steps in a PERT network.
B. Break-even Analysis	7. State the factors that determine a product's break-even point.
C. Linear Programming	8. Describe the requirements for using linear programming.
D. Queueing Theory	
E. Probability Theory	
F. Marginal Analysis	
G. Simulation	9. Discuss how simulation can be a planning tool.
IV. Time Management: A Guide for Personal Planning	
A. Time as a Scarce Resource	
B. Focusing on Discretionary Time	
C. How Do You Use Your Time?	
D. Five Steps to Better Time Management	10. List five steps toward better time management.

CHAPTER OUTLINE	CORRESPONDING LEARNING OBJECTIVES

E. Some Additional Points to Ponder

   1. Follow the 10-90 Principle

   2. Know Your Productivity Cycle

   3. Remember Parkinson's Law

   4. Group Less Important Activities Together

   5. Minimize Disruptions

   6. Beware of Wasting Time in Poorly Run Meetings

CHAPTER OVERVIEW

Managers in both small and large organizations are using environmental scanning to anticipate and interpret changes in their environments. Environmental scanning is the screening of much information to detect emerging trends and create scenarios. The importance of environmental scanning was first recognized (outside the national security establishment) by firms in the life insurance industry in the late 1970's. One of the fastest growing areas of environmental scanning -- competitor intelligence -- seeks to identify who competitors are, what they are doing, and how their actions will affect the focus organization. Examples of competitor intelligence include collecting information about competitors from news reports and annual reports and buying the competitor's product and analyzing it. Managers usually focus their research on three or four environmental issues that are especially important for the company and develop scenarios for these issues. Environmental scanning creates the foundation for forecasting.

Forecasting is predicting future outcomes. Forecasting can be qualitative and/or quantitative. Qualitative forecasts require the manager to use judgment and opinions, while quantitative forecasts involve math models and use of past data to forecast the future. Managers develop several different kinds of forecasts. Probably the two most popular forecasts are revenue forecasts and technological forecasts. Forecasting is not always completely accurate because managers do not usually deal with static environments. Forecasting effectiveness can be improved if managers use simple forecasting methods, use a variety of forecasting methods, compare every forecast with "no change", and shorten the length of forecasts.

157

Benchmarking is also an effective tool for strategic planning. Benchmarking allows managers to improve quality by analyzing and copying the methods of leaders in various fields. The benchmarking process typically involves 4 steps:

1. Form a benchmark planning team.

2. Collect data on company operations and for competitors.

3. Analyze the data to identify performance gaps and determine the cause of differences.

4. Prepare and implement an action plan that will allow your company to meet or exceed the standards of others.

Budgets are also important planning tools for managers. A budget is a numerical plan. Managers typically prepare budgets for revenues, expenses, and capital expenditures. Revenue budgets project future sales and expense budgets list the primary activities undertaken by a unit and allocate a dollar amount to each. Capital expenditure budgets are used to forecast investment in property, buildings, and major equipment. Other budgets used by managers include: cash budgets, fixed budgets, and variable budgets.

Managers can choose from among two approaches to budgeting. Incremental budgets require that funds be allocated to departments according to the previous time period. This traditional approach is not as popular as it was in recent years because inefficiencies tend to be hidden and it is difficult for management to "cut out funds" once they have been allocated. Zero-base budgeting (ZBB) is a system in which budget requests start from scratch, regardless of previous appropriations. This means that managers must justify their budget requests in detail from scratch for each budget period. The ZBB process is used to evaluate every organizational activity, assign it a priority, and determine if the activity should continue, be modified, or be terminated. This process does have some disadvantages: increased paperwork, time for preparation, and a manager's favorite project often has its benefits inflated.

In addition to budgets and forecasting, managers often use operational planning tools. These are defined as follow:

1. The Gantt Chart is a bar graph with time on the horizontal axis and the activities to be scheduled on the vertical axis. The bars show output, both planned and actual, over a period of time. This chart is used by a manager for scheduling and controlling work achievement.

2. A Load Chart is a modified Gantt Chart that allows managers to plan and control capacity utilization for work stations.

3. PERT Network Analysis is a technique for scheduling complicated projects comprising many activities, some of which are interdependent. PERT allows managers to monitor a project's progress, identify possible bottlenecks and shift resources as necessary to keep the project on schedule.

4. Break-even Analysis is a technique for identifying the point at which total revenue is just sufficient to cover total costs. In order to calculate break-even, a manager must know the unit price of the product being sold, the variable cost per unit, and total fixed costs. (Variable costs are costs that change in

proportion to output and fixed costs are costs that do not change regardless of volume.) Break-even can be useful for several decisions: sales objectives can be established, volume increases needed to break even if a company has a loss can be determined, and volume that a company can afford to lose and still break even can be determined.

5. Linear Programming is a mathematical technique that solves resource allocation problems. In order to use linear programming, a manager needs to develop an objective function and constraints for the situation. The objective function is either to maximize profit or minimize costs. The constraints represent limits on the situation. Some examples of limits might be available amounts of raw materials and available levels of worker time. The results of these problems will allow managers to get "the best use" of limited resources.

6. Queueing Theory is a technique that balances the cost of having a waiting line against the cost of service to maintain the line.

7. Probability Theory is the use of statistics to analyze past predictable patterns and to reduce risk in future plans.

8. Marginal Analysis is a planning technique that assesses the incremental costs or revenues in a decision.

9. Simulation is a model of a real-world phenomenon that contains one or more variables that can be manipulated in order to assess their impact.

It is important that managers learn to schedule their own time effectively. Managers who are effective time managers know what activities they want to accomplish, the best order for completion of the activities, and deadlines for completion of the activities. It is impossible for managers to control all of their time. The majority of a manager's time is spent responding to requests, demands, and problems initiated by others. This response time is uncontrollable. However, a manager does have some discretionary time that he/she controls. There are several ways that managers can get better use of their discretionary time:

1. Make a list of objectives.
2. Rank the objectives according to their importance.
3. List the activities necessary to achieve the objectives.
4. For each objective, assign priorities to the various activities required to reach the objective.
5. Schedule activities according to the priorities that have been set.

Some additional hints that should help managers use their time more effectively include the following:

1. Follow the 10-90 Principle - Ten percent of most manager's time produces 90 percent of their results.
2. Know your productivity cycle.
3. Remember Parkinson's Law - Work expands to fill the time available.
4. Group less important activities together.
5. Minimize disruptions.
6. Beware of wasting time in poorly run meetings.

KEY TERMS AND DEFINITIONS

1. environmental scanning - The screening of much information to detect emerging trends and create scenarios.

2. competitor intelligence - Environmental scanning activity that seeks to identify who competitors are, what they're doing, and how their actions will affect the focus organization.

3. scenario - An consistent view of what the future is likely to be.

4. forecasts - Predictions of future outcomes.

5. revenue forecasting - Predicting future revenues.

6. technological forecasting - Predicting changes in technology and when new technologies are likely to be economically feasible.

7. quantitative forecasting - Applies a set of mathematical rules to a series of past data to predict future outcomes.

8. qualitative forecasting - Uses the judgment and opinions of knowledgeable individuals to predict future outcomes.

9. benchmarking - The search for the best practice among competitors or noncompetitors that leads to their superior performance.

10. budget - A numerical plan for allocating resources to specific activities.

11. revenue budget - A budget that projects future sales.

12. expense budget - A budget that lists the primary activities undertaken by a unit and allocates a dollar amount to each.

13. profit budget - A budget used by separate units of an organization that combines revenue and expense budgets to determine the unit's profit contribution.

14. cash budget - A budget that forecasts how much cash an organization will have on hand and how much it will need to meet expenses.

15. capital expenditure budget - A budget that forecasts investments in property, buildings, and major equipment.

16. fixed budget - A budget that assumes a fixed level of sales or production.

17. variable budget - A budget that takes into account those costs that vary with volume.

18. incremental budget - A budget that allocates funds to departments according to allocations in the previous period.

19. zero-base budgeting (ZBB) - A system in which budget requests start from scratch, regardless of previous appropriations.

20. scheduling - A listing of necessary activities, their order of accomplishment, who is to do each, and time of completion.

21. Gantt Chart - A bar graph with time on the horizontal axis and the activities to be scheduled on the vertical axis. The bars show output, both planned and actual, over a period of time.

22. load chart - A modified Gantt Chart that schedules capacity by work stations.

23. Program Evaluation and Review Technique (PERT) - A technique for scheduling complicated projects comprising many activities, some of which are interdependent.

24. events - End points that represent the completion of major activities in a PERT network.

25. activities - The time or resources needed to progress from one event to another in a PERT network.

26. critical path - The longest sequence of activities in a PERT network.

27. PERT network - A flowchart like diagram showing the sequence of activities needed to complete a project and the time or cost associated with each.

28. break-even analysis - A technique for identifying the point at which total revenue is just sufficient to cover total costs.

29. linear programming - A mathematical technique that solves resource allocation problems.

30. queueing theory - A technique that balances the cost of having a waiting line against the cost of service to maintain that line.

31. probability theory - The use of statistics to analyze past predictable patterns and to reduce risk in future plans.

32. marginal analysis - A planning technique that assesses the incremental costs or revenues in a decision.

33. simulation - A model of a real-world phenomenon that contains one or more variables that can be manipulated in order to assess their impact.

34. time management - A personal form of scheduling time effectively.

35. response time - Uncontrollable time spent responding to requests, demands, and problems initiated by others.

36. discretionary time - The part of a manager's time that is controllable.

TRUE/FALSE QUESTIONS

1. T F Environmental scanning refers to screening large amounts of information to detect emerging trends and create a set of scenarios.

2. T F Managers in both small and large organizations are increasingly turning to environmental scanning to anticipate and interpret changes in their environment.

3. T F Environmental scanning makes forecasting unnecessary.

4. T F The basis for revenue forecasts is historical revenue figures, revenue trends, and changes in the environment.

5. T F Quantitative forecasting uses judgment and opinions of knowledgeable individuals to predict future outcomes.

6. T F Budgets are one planning device that most managers, regardless of their level in the organization, help to formulate.

7. T F In time of severe competition or recession, managers typically look first at the revenue budget to achieve economic efficiency.

8. T F The most popular approach to budgeting is the zero-base budget.

9. T F An incremental budget allocates funds to activities that are needed to achieve a specific objective.

10. T F In a zero-base budget system, budget requests start from scratch, regardless of previous appropriations.

11. T F A modified Gantt Chart that schedules capacity by work stations is called PERT.

12. T F PERT allows managers to monitor a project's resources as necessary to keep the project on schedule.

13. T F Break-even analysis is a technique for identifying the point at which total revenue is just sufficient to cover fixed costs.

14. T F Selecting transportation routes that minimize shipping costs and allocating a limited advertising budget among various product brands are two uses for linear programming technology.

15. T F Marginal analysis is a planning technique that balances the cost of having to wait in line against the cost of service to maintain that line.

16. T F The part of a manager's time that he/she can control is called response time.

17. T F The 10-90 Principle states that 10 percent of most managers time produces 90 percent of their results.

162

MULTIPLE CHOICE QUESTIONS

18. Which is not true for environmental scanning?

    a. The importance of environmental scanning was first recognized (outside the national security establishment) by firms in the life insurance industry in the late 1970's.
    b. Environmental scanning is a technique used by large businesses, but not often used by small businesses.
    c. Competition intelligence is one of the fastest growing areas of environmental scanning.
    d. Environmental scanning is used to anticipate and interpret changes in an organization's environment.

19. The basis for revenue forecasts is:

    a. changes in the environment
    b. historical revenue amounts
    c. trends for revenue figures
    d. all of the above

20. A qualitative forecasting technique is:

    a. regression model
    b. substitution effect
    c. customer evaluation
    d. time series analysis

21. A forecasting method that applies a set of math rules to past data to predict future outcomes:

    a. sales-force competition
    b. quantitative forecast
    c. jury of opinion
    d. qualitative forecast

22. Budgets can be set for which of the following?

    a. improving time and space
    b. revenue and expenses and capital expenditures
    c. the use of material resources
    d. all of the above

23. This budget would help reveal potential shortages or surpluses of cash:

    a. expense budget
    b. cash budget
    c. profit budget
    d. revenue budget

24. This budget is essentially a planning device for marketing and sales activities:

    a. expense budget
    b. cash budget
    c. profit budget
    d. revenue budget

25. This budget lists the primary activities undertaken by a division to achieve its goal and allocates a dollar amount needed for each division to operate:

    a. expense budget
    b. cash budget
    c. profit budget
    d. revenue budget

26. This budget allows managers to forecast future needs for property, buildings, and major equipment:

    a. capital expenditure budget
    b. fixed budget
    c. variable budget
    d. cash budget

27. This budget helps managers to better plan costs by specifying cost schedules for varying levels of income:

    a. capital expenditure budget
    b. fixed budget
    c. variable budget
    d. cash budget

28. A method that allows managers to improve quality by analyzing and then copying the methods of major competitors:

    a. environmental scanning
    b. forecast
    c. benchmarking
    d. budget

29. One problem with this budget is that activities have a way of becoming immortal:

    a. incremental budget
    b. zero-base budget
    c. revenue budget
    d. none of the above

30. This budget shifts the burden of proof to the manager to justify why his/her actions should get any budget at all:

    a. incremental budget
    b. zero-base budget
    c. revenue budget
    d. none of the above

31. Inefficiencies in operation tend to grow when this budget is used because they tend to get hidden:

    a. incremental budget
    b. zero-base budget
    c. revenue budget
    d. none of the above

32. Which is not true for zero-based budgeting?

    a. Zero-base budgeting requires much time to prepare and increases paperwork in the budgeting process.
    b. Zero-base budgeting is appropriate for most organizations.
    c. Important activities that managers want funded tend to have their benefits inflated.
    d. Zero-Base budgeting is compatible with managing declining resources.

33. This scheduling technique uses a bar graph to illustrate planned activities and their completion over a period of time:

    a. load chart
    b. Gantt chart
    c. PERT
    d. Critical Path

34. The longest time through the network for a PERT project:

    a. activity
    b. critical path
    c. event
    d. PERT network

35. A flowchart diagram that illustrates the flow of activities from start to finish:

    a. activity
    b. critical path
    c. event
    d. PERT network

36. In building an office building, pouring concrete for the foundation in two weeks is an example:

   a. activity
   b. critical path
   c. event
   d. PERT network

37. In building an office building, the point where builders have completed the foundation and the frame:

   a. activity
   b. critical path
   c. event
   d. PERT network

38. In PERT, the amount of time an activity would take under ideal conditions:

   a. optimistic time
   b. most likely time
   c. pessimistic time
   d. none of the above

39. This time is weighted four times the other times in PERT:

   a. optimistic time
   b. most likely time
   c. pessimistic time
   d. none of the above

40. Which is true for break-even analysis?

   a. Break-even is so simple it is not very valuable to managers.
   b. To calculate break-even, a manager needs to know two things: unit price of the product being sold and the variable costs per unit.
   c. An organization breaks even when total revenue is just enough to equal the organization's fixed costs.
   d. Break-even is a tool used for planning that can help managers set their sales objectives.

41. This linear programming formula is used to set up one of two possible desired outcomes: maximize profit or minimize cost:

   a. constraints
   b. feasibility region
   c. objective function
   d. none of the above

42. A candy company produces two kinds of candy using the same ingredients and has the following available this week: 500 pounds of chocolate, 300 pounds of sugar, and 100 pounds of nuts. Managers must know these values to write the _____ for the linear programming problem:

a. constraints
b. feasibility region
c. objective function
d. none of the above

43. Using this technique, a dry cleaner who wonders whether she should take on a new customer would not consider total revenue and total costs, but rather additional revenue and costs generated by this particular order:

a. probability theory
b. marginal analysis
c. simulation
d. queueing theory

44. A model of some real world situation that is manipulated to assess the impact on a company if the situation is really introduced into the company:

a. probability theory
b. marginal analysis
c. simulation
d. queueing theory

45. Which is not a step to better time management?

a. List activities necessary to achieve objectives.
b. Try to schedule work in the mornings.
c. Schedule your activities according to priorities you set.
d. Make a list of objectives and rank them according to their importance.

9 - 1 APPLICATION CASE

BUDGETS

Consider budgets from your perspective as a student. Set up budgets for your time and expenses for one typical school week. (Be sure to include specific amounts of time and dollars spent for activities.)

TIME BUDGET

EXPENSE BUDGET

Monitor your time and expenses for a week. Were you successful in following the budgets?

Based on this experience, what are the advantages and disadvantages of budgets?

9 - 2 APPLICATION CASE

BREAK-EVEN ANALYSIS

Find the break-even point for the following: A company produces and sells dolls. The best-selling doll is a replica of the original Shirley Temple doll which sells for $20. Variable costs are $12 per doll and total fixed costs are $45,000.

1. How many units does the company need to sell to break-even?

2. What is the break-even point in dollars?

3. What is the break-even point if the company sells the dolls for $24?

4. What is the break-even point in dollars if the company sells the dolls for $24?

PLANNING TOOLS

Think of specific examples when managers would need to use the following planning tools. (Select specific examples for supermarkets, movie theaters, and the assembly line production of automobiles.) You should include one example for each type of company for each planning tool.

1.   PERT

2.   Linear Programming

3.   Queueing Theory

4.   Simulation

Chapter 10

Foundations of Organizing

CHAPTER OUTLINE	CORRESPONDING LEARNING OBJECTIVES

I. Defining Organization Structure and Design

    1. Define organization structure.

II. Basic Organization Design Concepts

  A. Division of Labor

    2. Identify the advantages and disadvantages of division of labor.

    1. The Classical View

    2. The Contemporary View

  B. Unity of Command

    1. The Classical View

    2. The Contemporary View

  C. Authority and Responsibility

    1. The Classical View

    3. Contrast power with authority.

    2. The Contemporary View

  D. Span of Control

    4. Explain why wider spans of control are related to increased efficiency.

    1. The Classical View

    2. The Contemporary View

  E. Departmentalization

    5. Identify the five different ways by which management can departmentalize.

CHAPTER OVERVIEW

Organization structure describes the organization's framework. The structure can be divided into three parts as follow:

1. Complexity considers how much differentiation there is in an organization.

2. Formalization is the degree to which an organization relies on rules and procedures to direct the behavior of employees.

3. Centralization considers where the decision-making authority lies (centralized at top levels or decentralized throughout the organization).

When managers construct or change an organization's structure, they are engaged in organization design.

Most of the classical concepts of organization design were developed more than sixty years ago. For the most part, they still provide valuable insights into how to design effective and efficient organizations. The five basic principles that have guided organization design over the years include the following:

1. Division of Labor - A job is broken down into several steps with each step being completed by a separate person. Division of labor makes efficient use of the diversity of employees' skills. Classical writers viewed division of labor as an unending source of increased productivity. However, by the 1960's managers began to understand that jobs can become too specialized. Jobs that are over-specialized cause several problems: stress, boredom, low productivity, poor quality, fatigue, high turnover, and increased absenteeism.

2. Unity of Command - A worker should have only one superior to whom he/she is directly responsible. For the most part, managers still believe this is important, but there are some instances where managers appropriately choose to violate the unity of command principle.

3. Authority and Responsibility - Authority is the right inherent in a manager's position to give orders and expect that they be carried out. Responsibility is the obligation to perform. Authority and responsibility must exist simultaneously. When a manager delegates responsibility, he/she must also provide adequate authority so the worker can carry out the assigned task. However, even though a manager assigns responsibility to others, the manager is still ultimately responsible. The classical writers also distinguished between two forms of authority relationships: line and staff. Line authority is the chain of command authority that allows a manager to give orders. Staff authority is authority that supports, assists, and advises holders of line authority. The classical writers were naive in their assumption that managers were all powerful because of their authority. More recently managers have learned that several kinds of power exist in an organization and this power can be in the hands of managers and/or workers. Power (the capacity to influence decisions) is made up of one's vertical position in the organization and one's distance from the power core. The five sources of power include the following: coercive power (punishment), reward power, legitimate power (formal authority), expert power (based on expertise or knowledge), and referent power (based on identification with a person who has desirable resources or personal traits).

4. Span of Control - A manager can effectively manage a specific number of people. Classical writers believed that this number was relatively small (about six people). They also suggested that higher level managers could manage fewer people than lower level managers because of the diverse set of problems at upper levels in the organization. More recently managers have begun to increase their span of control. Contingency factors such as skill level of workers, the similarity of worker tasks, complexity of tasks, the physical proximity of workers, and the preferred style of the manager will help a manager determine the appropriate span of control for his/her work group.

5. Departmentalization - Classical writers believed that workers should be grouped into departments. They did not advocate a single departmentalization method as being most appropriate. However, they did explore several alternatives for departmentalization. Organizations can be departmentalized according to product, function, geography, customer, or process. Today managers still choose from among these five kinds of departmentalization. However, organizations more frequently choose to use customer departmentalization. Many managers have improved flexibility in their rigid departments through the addition of teams and taskforces.

Most of the classical writers believed that bureaucratic structures were the ideal organization design. However, contemporary managers realize that no one organization structure is "best". Two extreme organizational forms are mechanistic structures and organic structures. Mechanistic organizations are high on complexity, formalization, and centralization. Organic organizations are low on complexity, formalization, and centralization. Several contingency variables are used by today's managers to decide if an organization should be more mechanistic or more organic. These contingencies include: strategy, organization size, technology, and environment.

The first important study of the strategy-structure relationship was conducted by Alfred Chandler. Chandler discovered that at the beginning of operations, an organization tends to have a simple, one product strategy. Over time, the company strategy becomes more complex because more products are added and the company becomes more diversified. Chandler proposed that as strategies move from single product to vertical integration to product diversification, management will move from an organic to a more mechanistic organization.

Organization size is an important consideration in developing an organization structure. Research indicates that large organizations tend to use more specialization, more horizontal and vertical differentiation, and more rules than smaller companies.

In the 1960's, Joan Woodward suggested that technology is an important consideration in the determination of organization structure. She studied about 100 manufacturing firms in England. Woodward found that distinct relationships exist between technology and organization structure and the effectiveness of the organizations is related to the "fit" between technology and structure. She found that there is no one best way to organize a company. However, she did suggest that unit and continuous process organizations are most effective with an organic structure and mass production companies are more effective with a mechanistic structure.

Charles Perrow studied knowledge technology as a contingency factor. He suggested that technology be viewed in terms of two dimensions:

1. the number of exceptions individuals encounter in their work (task variability)
2. the type of search procedures followed to find successful methods for responding adequately to these exceptions (problem analyzability)

Perrow suggested that a specific structure is appropriate for an organization depending on its task variability and problem analyzability. He called these technologies: routine, engineering, craft, and nonroutine.

Research has also demonstrated that the environment is a major influence on structure. Organizations tend to be mechanistic when the environment is stable, but organic when the environment is dynamic. Global competition, rapid product innovation, and demands of better quality from customers are some dynamic environmental forces that have caused organizations to develop leaner, more flexible structures.

KEY TERMS AND DEFINITIONS

1. organization structure - An organization's framework as expressed by its degree of complexity, formalization, and centralization.

2. complexity - The amount of differentiation in an organization.

3. formalization - The degree to which an organization relies on rules and procedures to direct the behavior of employees.

4. centralization - The concentration of decision-making authority in upper management.

5. decentralization - The handing down of decision-making authority to lower levels in an organization.

6. organization design - The construction or changing of an organization's structure.

7. unity of command - The principle that a subordinate should have one and only one superior to whom he or she is directly responsible.

8. authority - The rights inherent in a managerial position to give orders and expect them to be obeyed.

9. responsibility - An obligation to perform assigned tasks.

10. line authority - The authority that entitles a manager to direct the work of a subordinate.

11. chain of command - The flow of authority from the top to the bottom of an organization.

12. staff authority - Authority that supports, assists, and advises holders of line authority.

13. power - The capacity to influence decisions.

14. coercive power - Power dependent on fear.

15. reward power - Power based on the ability to distribute anything that others may value.

16. legitimate power - Power based on one's position in the formal hierarchy.

17. expert power - Power based on one's expertise, special skill, or knowledge.

18. referent power - Power based on identification with a person who has desirable resources or personal traits.

19. span of control - The number of subordinates a manager can direct efficiently and effectively.

20. functional departmentalization - Grouping activities by functions performed.

21. product departmentalization - Grouping activities by product line.

22. customer departmentalization - Grouping activities on the basis of common customers.

23.   geographic departmentalization - Grouping activities on the basis of territory.

24.   process departmentalization - Grouping activities on the basis of product or customer flow.

25.   mechanistic organization (bureaucracy) - A structure that is high in complexity, formalization, and centralization.

26.   organic organization (adhocracy) - A structure that is low in complexity, formalization, and centralization.

27.   unit production - The production of items in units or small batches.

28.   mass production - Large-batch manufacturing.

29.   process production - Continuous-process production.

30.   task variability - The number of exceptions individuals encounter in their work.

31.   problem analyzability - The type of search procedures employees follow in responding to exceptions.

TRUE/FALSE QUESTIONS

1.   T   F   The degree to which an organization relies on rules and procedures to direct the behavior of employees is called complexity.

2.   T   F   When managers construct or change an organization structure, they are involved in organization design.

3.   T   F   The principles related to organizing that were developed about sixty years ago are not very useful in today's complex business environment.

4.   T   F   Assembly line production is an example of division of labor.

5.   T   F   There is a point at which human diseconomies from division of labor such as boredom and fatigue exceed the economic advantages of division of labor.

6.   T   F   When managers delegate authority, they must also allocate responsibility.

7.   T   F   A manager is not responsible for decisions made by subordinates when he/she has delegated authority to them.

8.   T   F   Line authority is the authority that supports, assists, and advises holders of staff authority.

9. T F An example of line authority is a marketing director giving orders to a sales manager.

10. T F To have power in an organization, one must have a position of formal authority.

11. T F Demoting employees is an example of referent power.

12. T F Legitimate power and authority are one and the same.

13. T F Setting up departments by separating engineering, accounting, manufacturing, personnel, and marketing departments is functional departmentalization.

14. T F Organizations that must change rapidly in response to environmental change, need mechanistic structures.

15. T F There is a relationship between structure and strategy.

16. T F There is considerable historical evidence that an organization's size has little effect on structure.

17. T F Joan Woodward found that little relationship exists between structure and technology.

18. T F Organic organizations are most effective in stable environments.

MULTIPLE CHOICE QUESTIONS

19. The formalization of organization structure:

    a. considers where the decision-making authority lies
    b. is the degree to which an organization relies on rules and procedures to direct the behavior of employees
    c. considers how much differentiation there is in an organization
    d. all of the above

20. The complexity of organization structure:

    a. considers where the decision-making authority lies
    b. is the degree to which an organization relies on rules and procedures to direct the behavior of employees
    c. considers how much differentiation there is in an organization
    d. all of the above

21. The decision to increase the authority of managers to make decisions and give employees less discretion in making decisions:

    a. unity of command
    b. division of labor
    c. span of control
    d. centralization

22. Each employee in a production company has been given a specific, routine job:

    a. unity of command
    b. division of labor
    c. span of control
    d. centralization

23. A manager decides that he can manage more people and he creates several new product divisions (in his chain of command):

    a. unity of command
    b. division of labor
    c. span of control
    d. centralization

24. An employee answers to one boss who gives him orders related to his job:

    a. unity of command
    b. division of labor
    c. span of control
    d. centralization

25. The unity of command principle was logical when organizations were comparatively simple:

    a. but managers now believe the principle no longer holds true
    b. because it provided for flexibility of operations
    c. and most organizations adhere to this principle today
    d. none of the above

26. Which is not true for the classical view of authority?

    a. Managers are not the only people in organizations with power.
    b. Responsibility cannot be delegated.
    c. Managers should delegate downward to subordinates, giving them prescribed limits within which they must operate.
    d. Authority and responsibility are related.

27. An obligation to perform:

    a. authority
    b. operating responsibility
    c. ultimate responsibility
    d. responsibility

28. Rights inherent in a management position to give orders and expect them to be obeyed:

    a. authority
    b. operating responsibility
    c. ultimate responsibility
    d. responsibility

29. An aspect of responsibility that must be retained by managers:

  a. authority
  b. operating responsibility
  c. ultimate responsibility
  d. none of the above

30. Managers should delegate _____ equal to the amount of delegated authority:

  a. power
  b. operating responsibility
  c. ultimate responsibility
  d. centralization

31. The chain of command follows:

  a. staff authority
  b. line authority
  c. functional authority
  d. power

32. An example of this kind of authority is a legal department advising personnel about discrimination laws:

  a. staff authority
  b. line authority
  c. functional authority
  d. power

33. An example of this kind of authority is a legal department requiring personnel to follow fair hiring laws (Legal department does not answer directly to personnel):

  a. staff authority
  b. line authority
  c. functional authority
  d. power

34. The closer a manager is to the power core:

  a. the more authority the manager has on decisions
  b. the more influence the manager has on decisions
  c. the more legitimate power the manager has on decisions
  d. the less influence the manager has on decisions

35. Requiring people to work overtime is an example of this kind of power:

  a. coercive
  b. reward
  c. expert
  d. referent

36. A person who has worked in the industry for several years and is respected for her work has this kind of power:

    a. coercive
    b. reward
    c. expert
    d. referent

37. Allowing workers to have a day off from work after completing an especially difficult project is an example of this kind of power:

    a. coercive
    b. reward
    c. expert
    d. referent

38. A manager who has power because of her charisma is an example of this kind of power:

    a. coercive
    b. reward
    c. expert
    d. referent

39. Friendliness, acceptance, and praise illustrate this type of power that is available without legitimate authority:

    a. coercive
    b. reward
    c. expert
    d. referent

40. This power develops out of admiration of another person and a desire to be like that person:

    a. coercive
    b. reward
    c. expert
    d. referent

41. Which is not true for span of control?

    a. Classical writers favored small spans so that close control could be maintained.
    b. The number of workers a manager can effectively manage defines the span of control.
    c. Today more organizations are decreasing their spans of control.
    d. The span of control to a large degree determines the number of levels and managers in an organization.

42. An auto manufacturer that divides the company into departments according to different models of automobiles uses this kind of departmentalization:

   a. product
   b. customer
   c. function
   d. process

43. A book publishing company that has several divisions such as children's books, adult novels, and college textbooks uses this kind of departmentalization:

   a. product
   b. customer
   c. function
   d. process

44. A book case manufacturer that has several departments such as wood cutting, staining, and assembly uses this kind of departmentalization:

   a. product
   b. customer
   c. function
   d. process

45. A fast food organization that maintains a central office for marketing, accounting, and personnel uses this kind of departmentalization:

   a. product
   b. customers
   c. function
   d. process

46. Classicists advocated that organization structures for all organizations should have:

   a. low complexity, high formalization, high centralization
   b. high complexity, low formalization, high centralization
   c. high complexity, high formalization, high centralization
   d. high complexity, high formalization, low centralization

47. The mechanistic organization is also referred to as:

   a. adhocracy
   b. bureaucracy
   c. organic
   d. decentralized

48. The first important research on the strategy-structure relationship was conducted by:

   a. Joan Woodward
   b. John French
   c. Charles Perrow
   d. Alfred Chandler

49. Chandler proposed that as strategies move from single product to vertical integration to product diversification:

   a. management structure will change from an organic to a mechanistic organization
   b. management structure will change from a mechanistic to an organic organization
   c. there is no need for a change in structure
   d. none of the above

50. The mass-production technology category in Joan Woodward's research is defined as follows:

   a. continuous process production
   b. large-batch manufacturing
   c. tailor made products
   d. production of items in units or small batches

51. According to Joan Woodward, the most effective structure for unit and process production is:

   a. bureaucracy
   b. mechanistic structure
   c. organic structure
   d. There is no one "best" structure choice for these technologies.

52. A type of technology in Charles Perrow's study that has a large number of exceptions, but the exceptions can be handled in a rational and systematic manner:

   a. routine
   b. engineering
   c. craft
   d. nonroutine

53. A type of technology in Charles Perrow's study that has many exceptions and it is difficult to analyze problems:

   a. routine
   b. engineering
   c. craft
   d. nonroutine

54. Perrow suggested that if problems can be systematically analyzed, these technology cells are appropriate:

a. routine and engineering
b. craft and nonroutine
c. engineering and nonroutine
d. routine and craft

55. Perrow suggested that if problems are familiar, these technology cells are appropriate:

a. routine and engineering
b. craft and nonroutine
c. engineering and nonroutine
d. routine and craft

56. Perrow suggested that if new or unfamiliar problems appear regularly, these technology cells are appropriate:

a. routine and engineering
b. craft and nonroutine
c. engineering and nonroutine
d. routine and craft

10 - 1 APPLICATION CASE

DEPARTMENTALIZATION

The Rock-A-Bye Baby Company has been growing rapidly since its start in 1978. In the beginning, the company produced baby food only. Now the company produces baby food, baby clothes, baby toys, baby furniture, and baby toiletries such as shampoo, lotion, powder, and disposable diapers. The company has nationwide operations and the founder, Janet Williams, is the company President.

Important functional areas for the company include manufacturing, accounting, marketing, research and development, and personnel. The company sells some items wholesale, some items retail, and some to institutional customers (schools and hospitals).

1. Draw 3 possible organization charts Rock-A-Bye Company could select. (Your organization chart could be set up according to function, product, customer, geography, or some combination of these.)

2. Which type of departmentalization is most appropriate for the company? Why?

10 - 2 APPLICATION CASE

LINE, STAFF, AND FUNCTIONAL AUTHORITY

Joe and Jane Jones operate a local retail store chain of five stores. The stores sell a variety of building materials. Personnel who work at the company's main office include the following:

1. Personnel Department - Five employees handle screening of prospective employees, payroll, benefits, training, and other personnel functions.

2. Legal Department - Two employees deal with legal issues related to employment, product safety, work place safety, etc.

3. Accounting Department - Ten employees develop quarterly and end-of-year financial statements, handle budgeting, purchase inventory, etc.

Explain how each of the departments in the organization has line, staff, and functional authority by giving specific examples.

10 - 3 APPLICATION CASE

ORGANIZATION CONTINGENCIES

How would you decide if an organization should be more mechanistic or more organic if the following contingencies are true? (You should determine which structure is more appropriate for each contingency and decide which structure is better overall.)

1.   Strategy - several products
2.   Size - large
3.   Manufacturing Technology - mass production
4.   Knowledge Technology - engineering
5.   Environment - stable

10 - 4 APPLICATION CASE

POWER

Illustrate your understanding of the use of informal power by giving examples for ways students can use power in classroom situations. (Hint: You may want to consider group dynamics for in class work, class discussions, outside of class group activities, or informal conversation among students outside the classroom.)

1. REWARD

2. COERCIVE

3. REFERENT

4. EXPERT

Chapter 11

Organization and Job Design Options

CHAPTER OUTLINE	CORRESPONDING LEARNING OBJECTIVES

I. Mechanistic Design Options

    A. The Functional Structure

                    1. Describe and explain the strengths of the functional structure.

    B. The Divisional Structure

                    2. Contrast the divisional and functional structures.

II. Organic Design Options

    A. The Simple Structure

                    3. Define the simple structure.

    B. The Matrix Structure

                    4. Explain the strengths of the matrix structure.

    C. The Network Structure

                    5. Explain the recent popularity of the network structure.

    D. Organic Appendages

                    6. Identify the advantages of using organic appendages.

        1. The Task Force

        2. The Committee Structure

III. A Buyer's Guide to Organization Design Options

                    7. Contrast job specialization, job enlargement, and job enrichment.

IV. Job Design Options

    A. Job Specialization

    B. Job Rotation

    C. Job Enlargement

    D. Job Enrichment

    E. Work Teams

CHAPTER OUTLINE	CORRESPONDING LEARNING OBJECTIVES
F. The Job Characteristics Model	
1. Core Dimensions	8. Identify the core job dimensions in the job characteristics model.
2. Predictions from the Model	
3. Guides for Managers	
G. Scheduling Options	
1. The Compressed Workweek	
2. Flexible Work Hours	
	9. Describe the advantages and disadvantages of flexible work hours.
3. Job Sharing	
4. Contingent Workers	
5. Telecommuting	
H. TQM and Structural Design	

CHAPTER OVERVIEW

Two design options are appropriate for mechanistic systems: functional structures and divisional structures. A functional structure is a design that groups similar or related occupational specialties together. The major strengths of a functional structure are that organizations can take advantage of economies of scale and can minimize duplication of personnel and equipment. The major weakness of a functional structure is that often managers lose sight of the company's best interest in the pursuit of functional goals. A divisional structure is an organization structure made up of autonomous, self-contained units. This means that each unit has a manager who is responsible for performance, strategic planning, and operational decision-making. The strengths of divisional structure include: a focus on results and corporate headquarters personnel are freed from concern with day-to-day operating details. The divisional form is also an excellent way to develop senior managers because division managers gain a broad range of experience in running their autonomous units. The major disadvantage of divisional structure is duplication of activities and resources.

Organic design options include: simple, matrix, network, task force, and committee structures.

1. A simple structure is low in complexity and formalization, but high in centralization. This structure is most widely used in small businesses in which the manager and owner are one and the same. This structure is fast, flexible, and inexpensive to maintain, and accountability is clear. However, this structure becomes ineffective as the organization grows.

2. A matrix structure assigns specialists from functional departments to work on one or more projects that are led by a project manager. This means that a worker will have two bosses: a project/product boss and a functional boss. The matrix structure creates an overall structure that possesses the strengths of both functional and product departmentalization, while avoiding the weaknesses of both. Some strengths of the functional form are: specialists work together so that the number of specialists is minimized and resources can be shared across product lines. The weakness of a functional form is that coordination is difficult. However, the strength of product departmentalization is that coordination is easier. The primary weakness of the product form is that no one is responsible for the long-run development of the specialities (functions) and this results in duplication of costs. A matrix structure is difficult to organize and operate because confusion is often created and there is a tendency for power struggles between project managers and functional managers.

3. A network structure is a small centralized organization that relies on other organizations to perform its basic business functions on a contract basis. Functional personnel such as accountants, human resources managers, and lawyers are hired on contract from outside sources. This gives management in the company flexibility and allows them to do what they do best. One disadvantage of the network structure is that some control is lost by management.

4. Some organic appendages include: task force structure and committee structure. These are two options that can be used in mechanistic structures to allow them to operate more organically. The task force structure is a temporary structure created to accomplish a specific, well-defined, complex task that requires the involvement of personnel from other organizational subunits. The committee structure brings together a range of individuals from across functional lines to deal with problems.

Job design is the way in which tasks are combined to form complete jobs. Managers have several options in designing jobs: job specialization, job rotation, job enlargement, job enrichment, and work teams.

1. Job specialization is when jobs are broken down into simple, specialized tasks.

2. Job rotation is when workers are allowed to diversify their job activities and avoid boredom by routinely moving to different jobs within the organization.

3. Job enlargement is the horizontal expansion of a job. This means that a worker is given several tasks that require about the same skills instead of one specialized task.

4. Job enrichment is vertical expansion of a job. This means that workers are given more control over their own work. Usually workers in enriched jobs have some supervisory responsibilities such as planning and evaluating work.

5. Work teams are groups of individuals who cooperate in completing a set of tasks. An integrated work team is a group that accomplishes many tasks by making specific assignments to members and rotating jobs among members as the tasks require. Self-managed work teams are more vertically integrated and have a wider range of discretion than integrated work teams. A fully self-managed work team selects its own members and has the members evaluate one another's performance.

The Job Characteristics Model offers a framework for analyzing and designing jobs. A job can be described in terms of five core dimensions:

1. Skill Variety - the amount of different activities required in a job

2. Task Identity - the degree to which a task can be seen to contribute to the whole product

3. Task significance - the degree to which the job has impact on the lives or work of others

4. Autonomy - the degree to which a job provides freedom and independence for workers

5. Feedback - the degree to which the results of a person's job performance are made known to the worker

Skill Variety, Task Identity, and Task Significance combine to create meaningful work. Jobs that possess autonomy give workers a feeling of personal responsibility. A job that provides feedback gives a worker knowledge of results. This model suggests that when a worker has knowledge of results, experienced responsibility, and experienced meaningfulness of work, internal rewards are obtained by the worker. Based on the model, several guides for managers have been developed to help them design jobs:

1. Combine tasks.
2. Create natural work units.
3. Establish client relationships.
4. Expand jobs vertically.
5. Open feedback channels.

Another issue related to job design is scheduling of work. Labor-market conditions, the type of work that has to be done, and employee preferences often cause managers to look for new ways to schedule work. Some possible ways to schedule work include: a compressed workweek, flexible work hours, and job sharing. In addition, managers can schedule work by using contingent workers or telecommuting.

1. A compressed workweek means that workers work the required forty hours, but in four days instead of five days.

2. Flexible work hours or flextime is a scheduling system in which employees are required to work a number of hours a week, but are free, within limits to vary the hours of work.

200

3. Job sharing means that two or more people split a forty hour a week job.

4. Contingent workers are temporary and part-time workers who supplement an organization's permanent work force.

5. Telecommuting is the linking by computer and modem of workers at home with co-workers and management at an office.

Several organizing topics are components of Total Quality Management. Increasing the span of control, flattening the organization structure, and decentralized decision making all help to improve quality and customer service

KEY TERMS AND DEFINITIONS

1. functional structure - A design that groups similar or related occupational specialties together.

2. divisional structure - An organization structure made up of autonomous, self-contained units.

3. simple structure - An organization that is low in complexity and formalization but high in centralization.

4. matrix structure - A structural design that assigns specialists from functional departments to work on one or more projects that are led by a project manager.

5. network structure - A small centralized organization that relies on other organizations to perform its basic business functions on a contract basis.

6. task force structure - A temporary structure created to accomplish a specific, well-defined, complex task that requires the involvement of personnel from other organizational subunits.

7. committee structure - A structure that brings together a range of individuals from across functional lines to deal with problems.

8. job design - The way in which tasks are combined to form complete jobs.

9. job rotation - Periodic lateral job transfers of workers among jobs involving different tasks.

10. job enlargement - The horizontal expansion of a job; an increase in job scope.

11. job scope - The number of different tasks required in a job and the frequency with which the job cycle is repeated.

12. job enrichment - Vertical expansion of a job by adding planning and evaluating responsibilities; an increase in job depth.

13. job depth - Allowing employees greater control over their work by expanding it vertically.

14. work teams - Groups of individuals that cooperate in completing a set of tasks.

15. integrated work team - A group that accomplishes many tasks by making specific assignments to members and rotating jobs among members as the tasks require.

16. self-managed work team - A vertically integrated team that is given almost complete autonomy in determining how a task will be done.

17. job characteristics model - A framework for analyzing and designing jobs; identifies five primary job characteristics, their interrelationships, and impact on outcome variables.

18. skill variety - The degree to which a job includes a variety of activities that call for a number of different skills and talents.

19. task identity - The degree to which a job requires completion of a whole and identifiable piece of work.

20. task significance - The degree to which a job has a substantial impact on the lives or work of other people.

21. autonomy - The degree to which a job provides substantial freedom, independence, and discretion to an individual in scheduling and carrying out his or her work.

22. feedback - The degree to which carrying out the work activities required by a job results in an individual's obtaining direct and clear information about the effectiveness of his or her performance.

23. compressed workweek - A workweek comprised of four ten-hour days.

24. flexible work hours (flextime) - A scheduling system in which employees are required to work a number of hours a week, but are free, within limits, to vary the hours of work.

25. job sharing - The practice of having two or more people split a forty-hour-a-week job.

26. contingent workers - Temporary and part-time workers who supplement an organization's permanent work force.

27. telecommuting - The linking by computer and modem of workers at home with co-workers and management at an office.

TRUE/FALSE QUESTIONS

1. T F In the real world, there are few purely mechanistic or purely organic organizations.

2. T F Making organization design decisions is a universal activity for all managers.

3.   T   F   Mechanistic design options include simple, matrix, network, task force, and committee structures.

4.   T   F   An obvious weakness of a functional structure is that the organization frequently loses sight of its best interests in the pursuit of functional goals.

5.   T   F   The divisional framework creates a set of autonomous "little companies".

6.   T   F   An advantage of divisional structure is that activities and resources are not duplicated.

7.   T   F   The simple structure is the most widely practiced in small businesses in which the manager and the owner are one and the same.

8.   T   F   The matrix structure breaks the unity of command principle.

9.   T   F   A matrix structure is a combination of functional and customer departmentalization.

10.   T   F   Matrix structures can be set up temporarily as well as permanently.

11.   T   F   The multinational matrix simultaneously blends functional and geographic departmentalization.

12.   T   F   Network structures have many vertical levels of management and include functional divisions for accounting, manufacturing, and personnel.

13.   T   F   A task force structure is a temporary structure created to accomplish a specific, well-defined, complex task that requires the involvement of personnel from other organization subunits.

14.   T   F   The strength of committee and task force organization designs is flexibility.

15.   T   F   Functional and task force structures are designed to work well in large organizations that are specialized.

16.   T   F   Job enrichment is horizontal expansion of a job by increasing job scope.

17.   T   F   Job specialization is synonymous with division of labor.

18.   T   F   Fully autonomous work teams select their own members and have the members evaluate one another's performance.

19.   T   F   Task significance, one of the core dimensions in the job characteristics model, is the degree to which a job requires completion of a whole and identifiable piece of work.

20.   T   F   Flextime tends to reduce absenteeism, make planning and control easier, and is less expensive for organizations.

21. Which is not true for functional structures?

    a. A strength is the advantage that occurs from specialization.
    b. A weakness is that the organization frequently loses site of its best interest in the pursuit of functional goals.
    c. It provides good training for future chief executives.
    d. It is a mechanistic approach to structure.

22. A disadvantage of divisional structures is:

    a. There is a focus on results.
    b. Activities and resources are duplicated.
    c. Divisional structures require much involvement by top managers.
    d. It is difficult to develop senior level managers in divisional structures.

23. A simple structure is:

    a. low in complexity, low in formalization, and authority is centralized in one person
    b. high in complexity, low in formalization, and authority is centralized in one person
    c. low in complexity, high in formalization, and authority is centralized in one person
    d. none of the above

24. Which is not an organic design option?

    a. matrix
    b. divisional
    c. task force
    d. network

25. A small centralized organization that relies on other organizations to perform manufacturing, distribution, marketing, and other crucial business functions on a contract basis:

    a. matrix
    b. network
    c. task force
    d. committee

26. A dual chain of command:

    a. matrix
    b. network
    c. task force
    d. committee

27. An example of this structure is when Kellogg temporarily brings together people who have expertise in product design, food research, marketing, finance, and manufacturing to plan and design new cereals:

   a. matrix
   b. network
   c. task force
   d. committee

28. This structure is often used in the aerospace industry:

   a. matrix
   b. network
   c. task force
   d. committee

29. This structure is an excellent choice for a manufacturing firm that is just getting started because it minimizes risks and commitments:

   a. matrix
   b. network
   c. task force
   d. committee

30. Which is not a disadvantage of a matrix structure?

   a. A matrix structure often creates confusion.
   b. There is a tendency for power struggles in the organization.
   c. Coordination is difficult.
   d. All of the above are disadvantages of a matrix structure.

31. A large Wall Street law firm that requires new associates to work for many different partners before choosing an area of specialization is an example of:

   a. job specialization
   b. job rotation
   c. job enlargement
   d. job enrichment

32. An increase in job scope occurs with this type of job design:

   a. job specialization
   b. job rotation
   c. job enlargement
   d. job enrichment

33. An increase in job depth occurs with this type of job design:

   a. job specialization
   b. job rotation
   c. job enlargement
   d. job enrichment

34. A production worker, who in the past has done one specific activity, now does three different activities that require the same kinds of skills:

    a. job specialization
    b. job rotation
    c. job enlargement
    d. job enrichment

35. Production suffers routinely because of training needs with this type of job design. A person is often moved to a new job just when he becomes efficient at his present job:

    a. job specialization
    b. job rotation
    c. job enlargement
    d. job enrichment

36. This type of job design prepares people more rapidly to assume greater responsibility, especially at upper levels:

    a. job specialization
    b. job rotation
    c. job enlargement
    d. job enrichment

37. An example of this type of job design is a worker who has one simple, repetitive job on an assembly line:

    a. job specialization
    b. job rotation
    c. job enlargement
    d. job enrichment

38. Jobs are designed around groups instead of individuals (like building maintenance workers), a large number of tasks are assigned to the group, and these tasks are administered by a manager:

    a. autonomous work team
    b. committee
    c. task force
    d. integrated work team

39. An example of this core dimension of the job characteristics model is a maintenance worker at a nuclear power plant who recognizes that his job is important to society at large:

    a. skill variety
    b. task identity
    c. task significance
    d. autonomy

40. A worker does not really identify with this core dimension of the job characteristics model because he does not use different skills and talents in his job:

    a. skill variety
    b. task identity
    c. task significance
    d. autonomy

41. A worker who schedules her own work and decides how to approach her job, has a feeling of:

    a. skill variety
    b. task identity
    c. task significance
    d. autonomy

42. A worker does not really identify with this core dimension of the job characteristics model because he has a specialized job and he cannot see the importance of his job to the completed product:

    a. skill variety
    b. task identity
    c. task significance
    d. autonomy

43. A job where this core dimension is important gives a worker a feeling of personal responsibility for results:

    a. skill variety
    b. task identity
    c. task significance
    d. autonomy

44. Which is true for motivation and the job characteristics model?

    a. High growth need individuals will respond more positively to the psychological states than will low growth need individuals.
    b. Internal rewards are obtained when one learns that one personally has performed well on a task that one cares about.
    c. The links between the job dimensions and the outcomes are moderated or adjusted for by the strength of the individual's growth need (the employee's desire for self-esteem and self-actualization).
    d. All of the above are true for motivation and the job characteristics model.

45. Which is not a guide from the job characteristics model for designing jobs?

    a. Expand jobs vertically.
    b. Create natural work units.
    c. Use job specialization whenever possible.
    d. Open feedback channels.

46. An example is a salesperson who works in the office from 9 - 11 a.m. and sets the rest of her own work hours:

    a. compressed workweek
    b. flextime
    c. job sharing
    d. telecommuting

47. An example is an accountant who receives work information on his home computer and returns work to the office through a modem from his home:

    a. compressed workweek
    b. flextime
    c. job sharing
    d. telecommuting

48. An example is production employees who work from Monday through Thursday for ten hours each day:

    a. compressed workweek
    b. flextime
    c. job sharing
    d. telecommuting

49. An example is two employees working as Lifestyle Editor for a small town paper. One person works mornings and the other person works afternoons:

    a. compressed workweek
    b. flextime
    c. job sharing
    d. telecommuting

50. Interdependence of workers makes this scheduling method difficult to coordinate for an assembly line:

    a. compressed workweek
    b. flextime
    c. job sharing
    d. telecommuting

51. A disadvantage of this scheduling method is tired workers:

    a. compressed workweek
    b. flextime
    c. job sharing
    d. telecommuting

52. Contingent workers:

    a. are permanent employees who work full time
    b. provide managers with less flexibility in operating
    c. usually have the same health and retirement benefits as other workers
    d. are temporary and part-time workers

11 - 1 APPLICATION CASE

MATRIX STRUCTURE

Future Space Technologies, Inc. is an aerospace firm that builds communication satellite projects that will be sent into space: Alpha, Beta, and Gamma projects. The basic functions of the firm are: engineering, accounting, production, materials and purchasing, and personnel.

1. Construct a matrix organization chart using the above information.

2. Who is the boss over an engineer working in the Beta Project? A production worker in the Gamma Project? An accountant in the Alpha Project?

3. What advantages and disadvantages do you see for the structure of Future Space Technologies, Inc.?

11 - 2 APPLICATION CASE

CHOOSING STRUCTURE ALTERNATIVES

Which type of organizational structure is appropriate for the following strategies? (You should choose from these structures: Simple, Functional, Divisional, and Matrix.)

1. A small company has a single product line. There is stable growth and one decision maker.

2. A large company has multiple projects and stable growth.

3. A large company has a single product line, moderate growth, and a stable environment.

4. A large company has several product lines, stable growth, and self-centered organization units.

5. A medium-sized company sells a single product line. The company is growing rapidly and is concentrating on research and development into new product ideas.

6. A medium-sized company has a single product line, moderate growth, and a stable environment.

11 - 3 APPLICATION CASE

JOB DESIGN OPTIONS AND THE JOB CHARACTERISTICS MODEL

For the following job types, which design option seems appropriate? Why? (You should choose from job specialization, job enlargement, job enrichment.)

1. A production worker who needs meaningful work, but does not want autonomy

2. A production worker who needs meaningful work and also desires autonomy

3. A production worker who only wants to earn a paycheck and is not concerned with meaningful work, knowledge of results, or autonomy

4. A salesperson who needs to feel important to the company, but has difficulty meeting deadlines when he is given too much authority

5. A retail manager who needs knowledge of results and desires autonomy in the operation of her operation.

Do you think any of these jobs should be scheduled some other way than the traditional forty hours per week? Which ones and why?

Chapter 12

Human Resource Management

CHAPTER OUTLINE	CORRESPONDING LEARNING OBJECTIVES
I. Managers and Personnel Departments	
II. The Human Resource Management Process	1. Describe the human resource management process.
III. Important Environmental Considerations	2. Discuss the influence of government regulations on human resource decisions.
IV. Human Resource Planning	
A. Current Assessment	3. Differentiate between job descriptions and job specifications.
B. Future Assessment	
C. Developing a Future Program	
V. Recruitment and Decruitment	4. Contrast recruitment and decruitment options.
VI. Selection	
A. Foundations of Selection	5. Explain the importance of validity and reliability in selection.
1. Prediction	
2. Validity	
3. Reliability	
B. Selection Devices	
1. The Application Form	
2. Written Tests	
3. Performance Simulation Tests	
4. Interviews	

5. Background
Investigation

6. Physical Examination

C. What Works Best and
When

    6. Describe the selection devices that
work best with various kinds of
jobs.

VII. Orientation

VIII. Employee Training

A. Skill Categories

1. Technical

2. Interpersonal

3. Problem Solving

B. Training Methods

    7. Identify the various training
methods.

1. On-the-Job Training

2. Off-the-Job Training

IX. Performance Appraisal

A. Performance Appraisal
Methods

    8. Describe six performance
appraisal methods.

1. Written Essays

2. Critical Incidents

3. Graphic Rating Scales

4. Behaviorally
Anchored Rating
Scales

5. Multiperson
Comparisons

6. Objectives

B. Providing Feedback in the
Appraisal Review

CHAPTER OUTLINE	CORRESPONDING LEARNING OBJECTIVES

X. Career Development

  A. Career Stages   9. Outline the five stages in a career.

      1. Exploration

      2. Establishment

      3. Midcareer

      4. Late Career

      5. Decline

      6. Applying the Career Stage Model

  B. Keys to a Successful Management Career

      1. Select Your First Job Judiciously

      2. Do Good Work

      3. Present the Right Image

      4. Learn the Power Structure

      5. Gain Control of Organizational Resources

      6. Stay Visible

      7. Don't Stay Too Long in Your First Job

      8. Find a Mentor

      9. Support Your Boss

     10. Stay Mobile

     11. Think Laterally

CHAPTER OUTLINE	CORRESPONDING LEARNING OBJECTIVES

XI. Labor-Management Relations

    A. Why Good Labor-Management Relations are Important

    B. The Collective Bargaining Process   10. Explain the collective bargaining process.

        1. Organizing and Certification

        2. Preparation for Negotiation

        3. Negotiation

        4. Contract Administration

XII. Current Issues in Human Resource Management

    A. Managing Work Force Diversity

                    11. Describe how HRM practices can facilitate work force diversity.

    B. Dual-Career Couples   12. Explain why sexual harassment is a growing concern of management.

    C. Sexual Harassment

CHAPTER OVERVIEW

The human resource management (HRM) process is nine steps that should allow the organization to hire workers and sustain high employee performance. The first four steps represent human resources planning. After the organization has hired competent workers, management must help these new workers adapt to the organization and ensure that their job skills are kept current. The last steps of the process are designed to identify performance problems, correct them, and help employees sustain a high level of performance. HRM permeates all four of the management functions: planning, organizing, leading, and controlling.

The federal government increased its influence over HRM operations. Some of the regulations from the 1960's and 1970's that affect HRM include: Equal Pay Act, Age Discrimination Act, Privacy Act, Civil Rights Act, and Mandatory Retirement Act. More recent legislation (1986-1990) includes: Immigration Reform and Control Act, Polygraph Protection Act, Worker Adjustment and Retraining Notification Act, and Americans with Disabilities Act. In addition, many organizations have set up affirmative action programs to enhance the organizational status of members of protected groups. These laws limit the authority of HRM managers to hire, promote, and fire workers.

Human Resource Planning is the process by which management ensures that it has personnel who are capable of completing those tasks that help the organization reach its objectives. Human Resource planning can be summarized into three steps:

1. Assessing Current Human Resources - A manager can take a job inventory to determine the make-up of his/her organization. In addition, a job analysis is developed to define jobs and the behaviors necessary to perform the jobs. Based on information collected from the job analysis process, a manager develops a job description and a job specification for each job. A job description is a written statement of what a jobholder does, how it is done, and why it is done. A job specification states the minimum acceptable qualifications that a person must possess to perform a given job successfully.

2. Assessing Future Human Resource Needs - Managers in the organization should assess the kinds of personnel needs the company will have in the future.

3. Developing a Program to Meet Future Human Resource Needs - It is important for an organization to develop a plan for future personnel needs based on retirements, attrition, firings, etc.

Recruiting is a process of locating, identifying, and attracting capable applicants to the company. Some sources for recruiting include: internal search, advertisements, employee referrals, public employment agencies, private employment agencies, school placement, and temporary help services. Decruitment is techniques for reducing the labor supply within an organization. Some methods of decruitment include: firings, layoffs, attrition, transfers, reduced workweeks, and early retirements.

Selection is a process of screening job applicants to ensure that the most appropriate candidates are hired. Managers should try to develop selection devices that are both valid and reliable. This means that the selection devices should measure the criterion that the company is attempting to measure (valid) and should choose selection devices that provide consistent results (reliable). Selection devices include the following: application forms, written tests, performance simulation tests, interviews, background investigations, and physical examinations. It is important that a manager choose an appropriate mix of selection devices. For example, the application form offers limited information. Traditional written tests are reasonably effective devices for routine jobs. In the late 1980's, written tests began increasing in popularity for a variety of job types. Many managers prefer work samples to written tests because work sampling allows the manager to judge the applicant during actual job performance. If the interview has a place in the selection process, it is most likely among less-routine jobs. Interviews are often not helpful to managers because they are not structured to learn complete information about the applicant. Reference checks are usually worthless for all jobs and physical examinations rarely provide any valid selection information.

After a job candidate has been hired, he/she is usually introduced to the job through an orientation program. The major objective of orientation is to reduce anxiety by helping new workers to become familiar with the work unit, organization policies, and the worker's specific duties in the new job. Many large organizations have formal orientation programs, but the process can be informal as well.

Employees are trained in three skill categories:

1. Technical skills are skills related to learning new technology and new job methods.

2. Interpersonal skills include developing methods for interacting with others, for communicating better, and for reducing conflict in the work unit.

3. Problem-solving skills include activities to help an employee sharpen his/her logic and reasoning abilities.

Employees can be trained either on-the-job or off-the-job or some combination of the two methods. Examples of on-the-job training are job rotation and coaching. Examples of off-the-job training include classroom lectures, films, simulation exercises, and vestibule training.

Performance appraisal is a process of evaluating the worker's performance in order to arrive at objective personnel decisions. These appraisals provide information for personnel planning, for determining training needs, for personnel research, and for determining who is promoted, transferred, or fired. Some performance appraisal methods include: written essays, critical incidents, graphical rating scales, behaviorally anchored rating scales, multiperson comparisons, and management by objectives. After the performance appraisal has been completed, the manager should meet with the worker to explain the results of the appraisal. It is important that this information be communicated in a constructive way and that the manager is fair and impartial in his/her assessment.

Throughout a person's career, he/she will progress through several stages:

1. Exploration is the stage when a person develops expectations about his/her career.

2. Establishment begins with a search for work and includes getting a job, being accepted by co-workers, and learning the job.

3. Midcareer is when a person often faces the first serious career dilemmas. Some people continue to succeed at this stage, while other employees' careers begin to stall or deteriorate.

4. Late Career is a pleasant time when a person can relax and share the knowledge they have learned over time with others in the organization.

5. Decline is when a person decides to retire. This stage is probably most difficult on the most successful workers.

Labor-management relations is the formal interaction between unions and an organization's management. The collective bargaining process is the process for negotiating a union contract and for administrating the contract after it has been negotiated. The collective bargaining process flows as follows: organizing and certification, preparation for negotiation, negotiation, and contract administration.

Several current issues related to HRM are facing today's managers. These include:

1. Managing Work Force Diversity - Organizations must widen their recruiting efforts if they are to achieve diversity in their work force. Many companies offer seminars for current employees in diversity issues.

2. Dual-career couples - Because the number of dual-career couples is increasing, several issues must be dealt with by managers: nepotism, transfers, and conflicts of interest.

3. Sexual harassment - This behavior marked by sexually suggestive remarks, unwanted touching and sexual advances, requests for sexual favors, or other verbal or physical conduct of a sexual nature is illegal and a violation of the federal civil rights law.

KEY TERMS AND DEFINITIONS

1. human resource management (HRM) - Activities necessary for staffing the organization and sustaining high employee performance.

2. bona fide occupational qualifications (BFOQ) - A criterion such as sex, age, or national origin may be used as a basis for hiring if it can be clearly demonstrated to be job related.

3. affirmative action programs - Programs that enhance the organizational status of members of protected groups.

4. human resource planning - The process by which management ensures that it has the right personnel, who are capable of completing those tasks that help the organization reach its objectives.

5. job analysis - An assessment that defines jobs and the behaviors necessary to perform them.

6. job description - A written statement of what a jobholder does, how it is done, and why it is done.

7. job specification - A statement of the minimum acceptable qualifications that an incumbent must possess to perform a given job successfully.

8. recruitment - The process of locating, identifying, and attracting capable applicants.

9. decruitment - Techniques for reducing the labor supply within an organization.

10. selection process - the process of screening job applicants to ensure that the most appropriate candidates are hired.

11. validity - The proven relationship that exists between a selection device and some relevant criterion.

12. reliability - The ability of a selection device to measure the same thing consistently.

13. work sampling - A personnel selection device in which job applicants are presented with a miniature replica of a job and allowed to perform tasks central to that job.

14. assessment centers - Places in which job candidates undergo performance simulation tests that evaluate managerial potential.

15. orientation - The introduction of a new employee into his or her job and the organization.

16. vestibule training - Training conducted away from the work floor in which employees learn on the same equipment they will be using.

17. performance appraisal - The evaluation of an individual's work performance in order to arrive at objective personnel decisions.

18. written essay - A performance appraisal technique in which an evaluator writes out a description of an employee's strengths, weaknesses, past performance, and potential and then makes suggestions for improvements.

19. critical incidents - A performance appraisal technique in which an evaluator lists key behaviors that separate effective from ineffective job performance.

20. graphic rating scale - A performance appraisal technique in which an evaluator rates a set of performance factors on an incremental scale.

21. behaviorally anchored rating scale - A performance appraisal technique in which an evaluator rates employees on specific job behaviors derived from performance dimensions.

22. multiperson comparison - A performance appraisal technique in which individuals are compared to one another.

23. group order ranking - A performance appraisal approach that groups employees into ordered classifications.

24. individual ranking - A performance appraisal approach that ranks employees in order from highest to lowest.

25. paired comparison - A performance appraisal approach in which each employee is compared to every other employee and rated as either the superior or weaker member of the pair.

26. career - The sequence of positions occupied by a person during the course of a lifetime.

27. realistic job preview - Exposing job candidates to both negative and positive information about a job and an organization.

28. mentor - A person who sponsors or supports another employee who is lower in the organization.

29. labor union - An organization that represents workers and seeks to protect their interests through collective bargaining.

30. labor-management relations - The formal interactions between unions and an organization's management.

31. collective bargaining - A process for negotiating a union contract and for administering the contract after it has been negotiated.

32. dual-career couples - Couples in which both partners have a professional, managerial, or administrative occupation.

33. sexual harassment - Behavior marked by sexually suggestive remarks, unwanted touching and sexual advances, requests for sexual favors, or other verbal or physical conduct of a sexual nature.

TRUE/FALSE QUESTIONS

1.   T   F Whether or not an organization has a personnel department, every manager is involved with human resource decisions in his/her unit.

2.   T   F The most critical external factor affecting human resources is social factors.

3.   T   F A bona fide occupational qualification allows managers to use criteria such as sex, age, or national origin as a basis for hiring, without proving a need for selection based on this criteria.

4.   T   F Human resource planning can be condensed into two steps: assessing current human resources and assessing future human resource needs.

5.   T   F A human resource inventory allows management to assess what talents and skills are available in the organization.

6.   T   F A job specification is a written statement of what a jobholder does, how it is done, and why it is done.

7.   T   F The greater the skill required or the higher the position in the organization hierarchy, the more the recruitment process will expand to become a regional or national search.

8.   T   F Some options for decruitment include firing, layoffs, and attrition.

9.   T   F Obvious costs to the organization for accept errors include increased selection costs and discrimination charges.

10. T   F Organizations have been using tests more frequently as a selection device since the 1960's.

11.   T   F   Work sampling is a personnel selection device in which job applicants are presented with a miniature replica of a job and are allowed to perform tasks central to that job.

12.   T   F   The major objective of orientation is to begin job training.

13.   T   F   Most training is directed at upgrading and improving an employee's technical skills.

14.   T   F   Vestibule training is a type of on-the-job training.

15.   T   F   A behaviorally anchored rating scale is a performance appraisal technique in which an evaluator lists key behaviors that separate effective from ineffective job performance.

16.   T   F   It is not important for managers to review an employee's performance appraisal with him/her.

17.   T   F   Evidence indicates that acquiring a mentor who is part of the organization power core is essential for mangers who aspire to make it to the top.

18.   T   F   The negotiation, administration, and interpretation of a labor contract are achieved through collective bargaining.

19.   T   F   The courts have ruled that if an employee who is guilty of sexual harassment is a superior or agent for an organization, then the organization is liable for sexual harassment, regardless of whether the act was authorized or forbidden by the organization or whether the organization knew of the act.

MULTIPLE CHOICE QUESTIONS

20.   The activities in human resource planning include:

a.   orientation and training
b.   human resource planning
c.   identifying and correcting performance problems and helping employees sustain a high level of performance
d.   all of the above

21.   Programs that enhance the organizational status of members of protected groups:

a.   affirmative action programs
b.   bona fide occupational qualification
c.   collective bargaining agreement
d.   all of the above

22. Agreements that usually define such things as recruitment sources, criteria for hiring, and disciplinary practices:

    a. affirmative action programs
    b. bona fide occupational qualification
    c. collective bargaining agreement
    d. all of the above

23. Which of the following is an important consideration for personnel administrators?

    a. affirmative action programs
    b. bona fide occupational qualification
    c. collective bargaining agreement
    d. all of the above

24. A criterion such as sex, age, or national origin that may be used as a basis for hiring if it can be clearly demonstrated to be job related:

    a. affirmative action programs
    b. bona fide occupational qualification
    c. collective bargaining agreement
    d. all of the above

25. During the 1960's and 1970's, the number of federal laws related to human resource management:

    a. decreased
    b. increased slightly
    c. increased dramatically
    d. remained about the same

26. Human resource planning includes:

    a. assessing future human resource needs
    b. assessing current human resources
    c. developing a program to meet future human resource needs
    d. all of the above

27. A human resource inventory is:

    a. employee education, training, prior employment, languages spoken, capabilities, and specialized skills of employees
    b. a statement of what a jobholder does and how it is done
    c. an assessment that defines jobs and the behaviors necessary to perform them
    d. a statement of minimum acceptable qualifications for job candidates

28. This personnel statement for a janitor includes: Job Class 4 and the duties are to clean offices and hallways of the building by vacuuming, dusting, and mopping once each week:

   a. job analysis
   b. job specification
   c. human resource inventory
   d. job description

29. In setting up operations for a new production company, the personnel manager and area managers have developed a list of jobs needed and numbers of people needed for each job. This is a:

   a. job analysis
   b. job specification
   c. human resource inventory
   d. job description

30. A study in the company revealed that 40 percent of workers have college degrees, 20 percent have worked at the company for five years or more, and 25 percent have been trained in the use of computers:

   a. job analysis
   b. job specification
   c. human resource inventory
   d. job description

31. The advertised skills needed for a computer programmer include: college degree, two years experience using an IBM main frame computer, and training on CAD computer software:

   a. job analysis
   b. job specification
   c. human resource inventory
   d. job description

32. Which is not a method for analyzing jobs?

   a. structured questionnaires
   b. interviews with employees
   c. a daily diary kept by employees
   d. all are job analysis methods

33. A process of locating, identifying, and attracting capable applicants:

   a. decruitment
   b. orientation
   c. recruitment
   d. selection

34. Layoffs and reduced workweeks are examples of:

   a. decruitment
   b. orientation
   c. recruitment
   d. selection

35. Screening job applicants to ensure that the most appropriate candidates are hired is:

   a. decruitment
   b. orientation
   c. recruitment
   d. selection

36. A source of potential job candidates that is low in cost and helps build employee morale:

   a. employee referrals
   b. internal search
   c. public employment agencies
   d. private employment agencies

37. A source of potential job candidates that has high cost:

   a. employee referrals
   b. internal search
   c. public employment agencies
   d. private employment agencies

38. If this source of potential job candidates is used, the available candidates tend to be unskilled or minimally skilled:

   a. employee referrals
   b. internal search
   c. public employment agencies
   d. private employment agencies

39. In selection, when a job candidate is selected, but performs poorly there is:

   a. validity
   b. accept error
   c. reliability
   d. reject error

40. The proven relationship that exists between a selection device and some relevant criterion:

   a. validity
   b. accept error
   c. reliability
   d. reject error

41. In selection, when a job candidate is not hired who would have performed successfully on the job:

    a. validity
    b. accept error
    c. reliability
    d. reject error

42. An employee has taken a job skills test three times and scored very differently each time. This suggests that there is a problem with:

    a. validity
    b. accept error
    c. reliability
    d. reject error

43. An assessment center is one method often used for this selection device:

    a. application form
    b. interview
    c. background investigation
    d. performance simulation test

44. A reference check is an example of this selection device:

    a. application form
    b. interview
    c. background investigation
    d. performance simulation test

45. Since the 1960's, the frequency of use of written tests in the selection process has:

    a. increased dramatically
    b. decreased
    c. increased slightly
    d. remained the same

46. Which of the following is a type of test sometimes used as a selection device?

    a. perceptual accuracy
    b. intellectual ability
    c. spatial and mechanical ability
    d. all of the above

47. Executives, supervisors, or trained psychologists evaluate job candidates as the candidates go through two to four days of exercises that simulate real problems they would confront on the job:

    a. physical examination
    b. work sampling
    c. assessment centers
    d. none of the above

48. Which is not a way that a manager can make an interview more valid and reliable?

    a. Use a standardized evaluation form.
    b. Avoid short interviews.
    c. Know as much as can be known about the applicants' different backgrounds, experiences, interests, and test scores before any interviews are held.
    d. Structure a fixed set of questions to be used for all of the interviews related to a specific job.

49. Which question is acceptable for a manager to ask in an interview?

    a. Where were your born?
    b. What church do you attend?
    c. Why are you interested in this job?
    d. Are you married?

50. Training employees to operate a computer is an example of this kind of skill:

    a. interpersonal skill
    b. technical skill
    c. problem-solving skill
    d. none of the above

51. Training of managers to help them improve their logic in handling employee conflicts affects this kind of skill:

    a. interpersonal skill
    b. technical skill
    c. problem-solving skill
    d. none of the above

52. Learning a job by understudying a seasoned veteran is:

    a. a mentor relationship
    b. apprenticeship
    c. coaching
    d. all of the above

53. Training conducted away from the work floor in which employees learn on the same equipment they will be using in their job:

    a. vestibule training
    b. work sampling
    c. assessment centers
    d. all of the above

54. Which is not a use for performance appraisals?

    a. personnel research
    b. making orientation decisions
    c. identify training needs
    d. input for human resource planning

55. For this performance appraisal method, each employee is compared to every other employee and rated as either the superior or weaker member of each comparison group:

    a. critical incident
    b. group order ranking
    c. behaviorally anchored rating scale
    d. paired comparison

56. For this performance appraisal method, an evaluator rates employees on specific job behaviors derived from performance dimensions of the job:

    a. critical incident
    b. group order ranking
    c. behaviorally anchored rating scale
    d. paired comparison

57. At this career stage, a person reaches his first severe career dilemma:

    a. establishment
    b. exploration
    c. late career
    d. midcareer

58. This is the time when a person develops career expectations:

    a. establishment
    b. exploration
    c. late career
    d. midcareer

59. Members of this career group make excellent mentors:

    a. establishment
    b. exploration
    c. late career
    d. midcareer

60. This current issue is a growing concern for managers because it intimidates employees, interferes with job performance, and exposes the organization of liability:

    a. career development
    b. work force diversity
    c. dual-career couples
    d. sexual harassment

12 - 1 APPLICATION CASE

JOB DESCRIPTION AND JOB SPECIFICATION

Write a job description and job specification for one of the following:

1. Manager for a small bakery that sells pastries, made-to-order cakes, and also caters parties. The bakery employs 4 cooks, 2 in-store salespeople, and 1 party consultant.
2. Head Loan officer in a branch office of a regional bank who oversees two other loan officers and is responsible for a department that brings in $5 million in loans each year.
3. Production line worker who needs technical skill to operate a computerized sorting machine.

12 - 2 APPLICATION CASE

RECRUITING SOURCES

Which recruiting sources should be used for the following jobs? Why?

1.   Management trainee for a computer software firm

2.   Computer systems analyst

3.   Production line worker needed for low skilled production task

4. Advertising/commercial artist for a large advertising agency

5. Sales manager for a major drug company

6. Sales trainee for a sporting good company

12 - 3 APPLICATION CASE

CURRENT HUMAN RESOURCE MANAGEMENT ISSUES

Find a current article related to one of the important issues discussed in the chapter such as: sexual harassment, affirmative action programs, assessment centers, dual-career couples, and work force diversity.

Summarize the article.

Discuss your view of the current issue.

What do you think will happen with the issue in the next five years?

Chapter 13

Managing Change and Innovation

CHAPTER OUTLINE	CORRESPONDING LEARNING OBJECTIVES
I. What is Change?	
II. Forces for Change	
A. External Forces	
B. Internal Forces	
C. The Manager as a Change Agent	
III. Two Different Views on the Change Process	1. Contrast the "calm waters" and the "white-water rapids" metaphors of change.
A. The "Calm Waters" Metaphor	
B. The "White-Water Rapids" Metaphor	
C. Putting the two Views in Perspective	
IV. Organizational Inertia and Resistance to Change	
A. Resistance to Change	2. Explain why people are likely to resist change.
B. Techniques for Reducing Resistance	3. List techniques for reducing resistance to change.
1. Education and Communication	
2. Participation	
3. Facilitation and Support	
4. Negotiation	

CHAPTER OUTLINE	CORRESPONDING LEARNING OBJECTIVES
VII. Stimulating Innovation	9. Explain how organizations can stimulate innovation.
A. Creativity versus Innovation	
B. Fostering Innovation	
1. Structural Variables	
2. Cultural Variables	
3. Human Resource Variables	

CHAPTER OVERVIEW

Handling change is an important part of every manager's job. Some external forces that create a need for change include changes in: the marketplace, technology, laws, and the economy. Some internal forces for change are: strategy changes, changes in the work force, new equipment, and employee attitudes. A change agent is a person who assumes the responsibility for managing the change process. The change agent can be a manager, an employee, or an outside consultant. Sometimes it seems logical to hire an outside consultant to manage organizational change because an outside person can be objective. However, there are several disadvantages when an outside change agent is hired. The outside consultant is unfamiliar with the organization's history, culture, operating procedures, and personnel.

Two extremes in views of the change process are the "calm waters" metaphor and the "white-water rapids" metaphor. According to the "calm waters" metaphor, change is a process of unfreezing, attempting a new behavior, and refreezing to develop a new equilibrium for the organization. Change is seen as a routine, easily managed phenomenon. In contrast, the "white-water rapids" metaphor suggests that the environment is dynamic and uncertain. Change is constant, bordering on chaos. In today's complex environment, more companies find themselves in the "white-water rapids" in regard to change.

Most people naturally resist change. People tend to resist change for three reasons:

1. Change brings uncertainty and ambiguity.

2. There is a fear of losing something one already possesses. For example, often people have invested so much in the current system of operation that they fear loss of status, authority, friendships, personal convenience, etc.

3. Often people believe that change is incompatible with the goals and best interests of the organization.

239

Since resistance to change is dysfunctional, managers must find ways to reduce resistance to change. Some ways to reduce resistance to change include the following:

1.   Education and Communication - Sometimes employees do not understand what the change is and why it is needed. Meetings and memos can help to clarify the need for change and lessen resistance.

2.   Participation - It is difficult for employees to resist change if they are part of the decision process for the change.

3.   Facilitation and Support - Sometimes employees resist change because of fear. Employees are less likely to resist change if managers provide support during the change such as counseling, new skills training, or a short paid leave of absence.

4.   Negotiation - If a group or person has power in the organization, negotiation sometimes lessens resistance.

5.   Manipulation and Cooptation - Manipulation is covert attempts to influence employees. For example, a manager might distort facts to make them appear more attractive. Cooptation is a combination of manipulation and participation. This method requires that a person in the organization who resists change be brought into the decision-making process for the change.

6.   Coercion - Sometimes resistance to change is reduced through threats.

Managers must sometimes make changes in structure and changes in technology. Structure is defined in terms of complexity, formalization, and centralization. A manager can change either of these components or can introduce major changes in the actual structural design of the organization. In regard to technology, managers sometimes introduce new equipment, tools, or operating methods. Probably the most visible change in technology in recent years is the expanding use of computers in the workplace.

Organization Development (OD) is a field of management study focusing on techniques to change people and the quality of interpersonal work relationships. There are several popular OD techniques:

1.   Sensitivity Training is a method of changing behavior through unstructured group interaction.

2.   Survey Feedback is a technique for assessing attitudes, identifying discrepancies in them, and resolving the differences by using survey information in feedback groups.

3.   Process Consultation is help given by an outside consultant to a manager in perceiving, understanding, and acting upon process events. The consultant acts as a coach to help the manager determine what processes need improvement. For example, the manager may need to make improvements in formal communication channels, informal relationships among co-workers, or work flow.

4.   Team Building is the interaction among members of work teams to learn how each member thinks and works. This helps work group members to learn to trust others in the work setting.

5.   Intergroup Development is an attempt to change the attitudes, stereotypes, and perceptions that work groups have of each other.

One contemporary issue of importance to managers is changing organizational cultures. The organization culture is made up of relatively permanent characteristics and is difficult to change. However, it is sometimes necessary to change an organization culture over the long-term to ensure continued organization success. Some favorable conditions that might facilitate cultural change include the following:

1.   A dramatic crisis
2.   New leadership
3.   A young and small organization
4.   A weak culture

Another contemporary concern of managers is implementing TQM. TQM focuses on customer needs, team work, and developing a culture where employees continually work to improve quality. TQM programs require the support and leadership of the CEO to be successful. Since some organizations need dramatic, radical shifts in their operations, the incremental change offered by TQM may not be acceptable. In this case, TQM should be the second phase in the change process. After the needed dramatic changes have been implemented, companies can continue improvements incrementally through TQM.

Managers must also deal with stress when changes occur in an organization. Stress is a dynamic condition in which an individual is confronted with an opportunity, constraint, or demand related to what he/she desires and for which the outcome is perceived to be both uncertain and important. Change of any kind can cause stress. An employee's personal life, job, and organization culture can all cause stress. The employee's personality acts to moderate or accentuate the impact of stress. An employee who is a Type A personality is competitive and impatient and a Type B personality is relaxed and easy-going. Symptoms of stress can be physiological, psychological, or behavioral. Some examples of symptoms of stress include high blood pressure, ulcers, irritability, difficulty in making decisions, loss of appetite, accident proneness, etc.

Not all stress is dysfunctional. Often employees perform better and are motivated if they feel a little stress. When the level of stress becomes too much, managers need to try to reduce the stress level so that the employee can continue to be productive. Some ideas for reducing stress include: a performance planning program such as MBO, counseling, time management programs, and physical activity programs.

Innovation becomes a more important issue for managers as global competition continues to increase. An innovative organization can channel creativity to its workers into useful outcomes. When managers change an organization to make it more creative, they want to make it more innovative. Three sets of variables have been found to stimulate innovation.

1.   Structural Variables - Organic structures, frequent communication among work units, and availability of resources all positively influence innovation.

2. Cultural Variables - Innovative organizations tend to reward both successes and failures, encourage experimentation, and celebrate mistakes.

3. Human Resource Variables - Innovative organizations promote training and development, offer high job security to employees, and encourage employees to pursue change.

KEY TERMS AND DEFINITIONS

1. change - An alteration in people, structure, or technology.

2. change agents - People who act as catalysts and manage the change process.

3. organization development (OD) - Techniques to change people and the quality of interpersonal work relationships.

4. sensitivity training - A method of changing behavior through unstructured group interaction.

5. survey feedback - A technique for assessing attitudes, identifying discrepancies in them, and resolving the differences by using survey information in feedback groups.

6. process consultation - Help given by an outside consultant to a manager in perceiving, understanding, and acting upon process events.

7. team building - Interaction among members of work teams to learn how each member thinks and works.

8. intergroup development - Changing the attitudes, stereotypes, and perceptions that work groups have of each other.

9. stress - A dynamic condition in which an individual is confronted with an opportunity, constraint, or demand related to what he or she desires and for which the outcome is perceived to be both uncertain and important.

10. Type A behavior - Behavior marked by a chronic sense of time urgency and an excessive competitive drive.

11. Type B behavior - Behavior that is relaxed, easy-going, and noncompetitive.

12. creativity - The ability to combine ideas in a unique way or to make unusual associations between ideas.

13. innovation - The process of taking a creative idea and turning it into a useful product, service, or method of operation.

TRUE/FALSE QUESTIONS

1. T F Handling change is an integral part of every manager's job.

2. T F Both external and internal factors create a need for change in organizations.

3. T F The change agent in the organization should be the manager of the company.

4. T F According to Kurt Lewin, successful change involves unfreezing the old behavior and attempting a new behavior.

5. T F Computer software manufacturers can safely use the "calm waters" metaphor in regard to change.

6. T F People resist change because of uncertainty, concern over personal loss, and the belief that the change is not in the organization's best interest.

7. T F Negotiation is necessary to reduce resistance to change when there is misinformation.

8. T F Facilitation and support is necessary to reduce resistance to change when there is much anxiety about the change.

9. T F OD is a method of changing behavior through unstructured group interaction.

10. T F Research evidence indicates that sensitivity training has very few disadvantages and is almost always successful.

11. T F The attempt to change the attitudes, stereotypes, and perceptions that members of work groups have about each other is called intergroup development.

12. T F The fact that an organization culture is made of relatively stable and permanent characteristics tends to make the culture very resistant to change.

13. T F When managers talk about changing an organization to make it more creative, they usually mean that they want to stimulate innovation.

14. T F A manager who focuses on the means and methods for accomplishing work and allows communication to follow the organization chart should help to stimulate creativity and innovation in the organization.

15. T F Organizations that foster innovation are intolerant of employee risk taking.

16. T F Organizations that need to make dramatic, radical changes in operations may need to use TQM as the second phase in a two-phase change process, rather than the first phase.

17.   T   F   Stress in itself is undesirable.

18.   T   F   Type B behavior is marked by a chronic sense of time urgency and an excessive competitive drive.

MULTIPLE CHOICE QUESTIONS

19.   Which is not an external force for change?

a.   employee attitudes
b.   laws and regulations
c.   technology
d.   economic changes

20.   Which is not an internal force for change?

a.   work force changes
b.   employee attitudes
c.   strategy changes
d.   economic changes

21.   Outside consultants are sometimes hired as a change agent because:

a.   they do not understand the organization history
b.   they offer an objective perspective
c.   they do not have to live with the repercussions after change is implemented
d.   they do not understand organization culture and operating procedures

22.   An example for this part of Lewin's model of change is a worker who accepts the new equipment he uses as the best approach to his job:

a.   change
b.   refreeze
c.   driving force
d.   unfreeze

23.   An example for this part of Lewin's model of change is a worker who is given a new procedure for her job, and she tries this new procedure:

a.   change
b.   refreeze
c.   driving force
d.   unfreeze

24.   A worker attends a seminar related to the use of computer technology in production. This seminar causes the worker to investigate how the technology could be used in his company:

a.   change
b.   refreeze
c.   driving force
d.   unfreeze

25. An example for this part of Lewin's model of change is a worker who begins to question the use of traditional methods for production that the company has used for thirty years:

    a. change
    b. refreeze
    c. driving force
    d. unfreeze

26. Why do people resist change?

    a. concern over personal loss
    b. uncertainty
    c. belief that the change is not in the organization's best interest
    d. all of the above

27. Counseling, skills training, and therapy used to reduce resistance to change:

    a. education and communication
    b. participation
    c. support
    d. negotiation

28. Meetings and memos are used to explain change so that resistance is reduced:

    a. education and communication
    b. participation
    c. support
    d. negotiation

29. The most important method for reducing resistance to change when there is much fear and anxiety about the change:

    a. education and communication
    b. participation
    c. support
    d. negotiation

30. This is the best approach for lessening the resistance to change when resistance comes from a powerful source:

    a. education and communication
    b. participation
    c. support
    d. negotiation

31. This is the best approach for lessening the resistance to change when there is misinformation about the change:

    a. education and communication
    b. participation
    c. support
    d. negotiation

32. Overcoming resistance to change by threatening the resisters:

   a. coercion
   b. manipulation
   c. negotiation
   d. cooptation

33. This method for overcoming resistance to change is a combination of manipulation and cooptation:

   a. coercion
   b. support
   c. negotiation
   d. cooptation

34. Covert attempts to influence others so that resistance to change is reduced:

   a. coercion
   b. manipulation
   c. negotiation
   d. cooptation

35. Interaction among members of work teams to learn how each member thinks and works:

   a. sensitivity training
   b. team building
   c. survey feedback
   d. process consultation

36. A method of changing behavior through unstructured group interaction:

   a. sensitivity training
   b. team building
   c. survey feedback
   d. process consultation

37. A technique for assessing attitudes, identifying discrepancies in them, and resolving the differences by using information collected through questionnaires in discussions with groups:

   a. sensitivity training
   b. team building
   c. survey feedback
   d. process consultation

38. Help given by outside consultants to a manager in perceiving, understanding, and acting upon organization events:

   a. sensitivity training
   b. team building
   c. survey feedback
   d. process consultation

39. An example for this OD technique is a consultant acting as a coach to help a manager decide what informal relationships among workers need improvement:

    a. sensitivity training
    b. team building
    c. survey feedback
    d. process consultation

40. The use of questionnaires to help managers determine workers' perceptions for decision making practices is an example for this OD technique:

    a. sensitivity training
    b. team building
    c. survey feedback
    d. process consultation

41. Which is not a favorable condition that might facilitate cultural change in an organization?

    a. new leadership
    b. small and young organization
    c. consistent operations over time
    d. weak culture

42. Which of the following should stimulate creativity in an organization?

    a. acceptance of ambiguity
    b. focus on ends rather than means
    c. tolerance of risk
    d. all of the above

43. A process of taking an idea and turning it into a useful product, service, or method or operation:

    a. change
    b. creativity
    c. innovation
    d. intergroup development

44. Changing the attitudes, stereotypes, and perceptions that work groups have of each other:

    a. change
    b. creativity
    c. innovation
    d. intergroup development

45. The ability to combine ideas in a unique way or to make unusual associations between ideas:

    a. change
    b. creativity
    c. innovation
    d. intergroup development

46. Which is not a characteristic of the structure of an organization that expects to implement TQM?

    a. wider span of control
    b. decentralized decision making
    c. increased division of labor
    d. reduced vertical differentiation

47. Which is not a characteristic of the work force that is committed to TQM?

    a. skilled in problem-solving techniques
    b. individual problem solving
    c. team work
    d. commitment to quality and continual improvement

48. A person who is relaxed and noncompetitive:

    a. Type A behavior
    b. Type B behavior
    c. stress
    d. stressor

49. Examples are job dissatisfaction and personal problems:

    a. Type A behavior
    b. Type B behavior
    c. stress
    d. stressor

50. A person who is competitive and impatient:

    a. Type A behavior
    b. Type B behavior
    c. stress
    d. stressor

13 - 1 APPLICATION CASE

REDUCING RESISTANCE TO CHANGE

Top management (Vice-President of Manufacturing) at an automobile manufacturing company has decided to make major improvements in technology. No longer will production workers be required to weld gas tanks by hand. Instead, robots will weld the two parts of the gas tank together. Several individuals who resist this new innovation are listed below. How would you reduce their resistance to change? Explain.

1. The production supervisor (in charge of welders) is afraid he will lose his job because he feels that with robots there will be nothing to supervise.

2. Five production workers who weld gas tanks are unsure if the technology is going to replace them or if they will be given other jobs in the company. They are talking about going on strike or having a work slow down in protest of the new technology.

3. The production manager (of the plant) is concerned that the technology will be very expensive and will cause the company budget to increase. He opposes the move to install robots.

4. A research and development engineer (who must help install and set the controls on the robots) is not happy about the change because no one asked his opinion.

13 - 2 APPLICATION CASE

ORGANIZATION DEVELOPMENT TECHNIQUES

1. Do you think OD techniques are more appropriate for lower level or higher level managers?

2. Do you think OD techniques are more appropriate for well-educated personnel or does this have any affect on success?

3. Do you think the success of OD techniques is tied to a manager's support of and belief in OD activities?

4. Do you think employees' personalities have an impact on the success of OD activities?

5. Can you think of contingency factors in addition to level in the organization, education of employees, support by managers, and employee personality (mentioned above) that might affect the success of OD activities?

13 - 3 APPLICATION CASE

STIMULATING CREATIVITY AND INNOVATION

Mike Miller is the sales manager for a large chemical company that has been in existence for almost one hundred years. The company has a bureaucratic structure and departments are set up according to function. Employees understand that conformity to tradition is rewarded.

Bill is a salesperson who reports directly to Mike. Mike finds that Bill is a very difficult person to supervise. Bill is very innovative and has made a number of suggestions which have proved to be extremely beneficial to the company. Mike believes that Bill is a "little too eccentric" because Bill refuses to wear a tie, works unusual hours, and is very informal in his sales approach. In spite of his different approach to selling, Bill is the top salesperson in the company.

1. Do you think Bill's creativity is a large part of his success? What if he were required to conform to a more traditional sales approach?

2. Bill has presented an idea for a new product to Mike. The product is a revolutionary cleanser that removes stains from materials such as concrete and linoleum. In his spare time, Bill has worked with a friend in Research and Development at the company to develop this product. The two employees continue to work to perfect the cleanser. Do you think the company culture fosters innovation? Explain. (Hint: Use culture innovation variables to answer this question.)

Chapter 14

Foundations of Behavior

CHAPTER OUTLINE	CORRESPONDING LEARNING OBJECTIVES

I. Toward Explaining and Predicting Behavior

   A. Focus of Organizational Behavior

   B. Goals of Organizational Behavior

II. Attitudes

   A. Attitudes and Consistency

   B. Cognitive Dissonance Theory

   C. Attitude Surveys

   D. The Satisfaction-Productivity Controversy

   E. Implications for Managers

III. Personality

   A. Predicting Behavior from Personality Traits

      1. Locus of Control

      2. Authoritarianism

      3. Machiavellianism

      4. Self-Esteem

      5. Self-Monitoring

      6. Risk Taking

Corresponding Learning Objectives:

1. Define the focus and goals of organizational behavior.

2. Identify the role consistency plays in attitudes.

3. Explain the relationship between satisfaction and productivity.

CHAPTER OUTLINE	CORRESPONDING LEARNING OBJECTIVES
B. Matching Personalities and Jobs	
	4. Describe Holland's personality-job fit theory.
C. Implications for Managers	
IV. Perception	
A. Factors Influencing Perception	
B. Attribution Theory	
	5. Describe attribution theory.
C. Frequently Used Shortcuts in Judging Others	
D. Implications for Managers	
V. Learning	
A. Operant Conditioning	
B. Social Learning	
C. Shaping: A Managerial Tool	
	6. Explain how managers can shape employee behavior.
D. Implications for Managers	

CHAPTER OVERVIEW

Organization Behavior (OB) focuses on two major areas: individual behavior and group behavior. The goals of OB are to explain and predict behavior. This knowledge is especially important to managers because it helps them manage their employees' behavior.

The foundation of OB is the individual employee. An employee's attitudes, personality, perceptions, and learning processes influence his/her behavior.

Attitudes are evaluative statements concerning objects, people, or events. Attitudes are made up of three components: cognition, affect, and behavior. Managers are interested in job related attitudes such as job satisfaction, job involvement, and organizational commitment.

1. Research indicates that people seek to reduce inconsistencies among their attitudes and between their attitudes and behavior (cognitive dissonance). If cognitive dissonance is high, employees cannot ignore it and will seek a way to develop consistency. Sometimes employees will not be motivated to reduce dissonance (even if it is high) if they realize their degree of influence is small or if they are rewarded for the status quo.

2. Employees are sometimes given surveys to determine their work attitudes. These surveys are often summarized according to job group, department, division, or organization as a whole.

3. There is still controversy about the relationship of satisfaction and productivity. Research indicates that the positive effect of satisfaction on productivity is fairly small. The more valid conclusion is that productivity leads to satisfaction rather than the other way around. (If the satisfaction-productivity relationship is not strong, results of attitude surveys may produce limited help in improving productivity.)

Personality is a combination of traits that classifies a person. Personality traits related to job behavior include locus of control, authoritarianism, Machiavellianism, self-esteem, self-monitoring, and risk propensity. It makes intuitive sense that both the organization and the individual are better off when personalities and jobs match. John Holland developed a personality-job fit theory. The theory suggests that satisfaction is highest and turnover is lowest when personality and occupation are in agreement. The six job types in Holland's study are realistic, investigative, social, conventional, enterprising, and artistic.

Perception is the process of organizing and interpreting sensory impressions in order to give meaning to the environment. Several factors influence a person's perceptions. These factors can reside in the perceiver, in the object, or in the context of the situation in which the perception is made. Attribution theory is one explanation for how people are judged by others. The theory suggests that people are judged differently depending on what meaning a person attributes to another person's behavior. There tend to be errors or biases in judgment that distort a person's attributions. There is also a tendency for a person to attribute his/her own success to internal factors and blame a failure on an external factor like luck. People tend to take shortcuts in judging others. Since it is impossible to assimilate all a person observes, perceptions are selective. This means that people assimilate certain bits and pieces of what they observe, depending on their own interests, background, and attitudes. One shortcut used for judging other people is stereotyping.

Learning is any relatively permanent change in behavior that occurs as a result of experience. Three ways people learn include: operant conditioning, social learning, and shaping.

1. Operant conditioning is a type of conditioning in which desired voluntary behavior leads to a reward or prevents a punishment. The tendency to repeat a behavior is influenced by the level of reinforcement experienced through the consequences of an action taken.

257

2.   Social learning theory suggests that people learn through observation and direct experience. This theory is an extension of operant conditioning, but it also acknowledges that existence of observational learning and the importance of perception in learning.

3.   Shaping is a way managers mold employees by guiding their learning. There are four ways to shape behavior: positive reinforcement, negative reinforcement, punishment, or extinction.

It is important that managers understand these four components of individual behavior. Managers should follow the suggestions below related to individual behavior.

1.   Managers should do those things that will generate positive job attitudes and reduce job dissonance.

2.   Managers should try to match personality types with jobs so they will have more productive, satisfied workers.

3.   Managers need to recognize that they and their employees react to perceptions, not reality.

4.   Managers should manage learning through the reward they allocate and the examples they set.

KEY TERMS AND DEFINITIONS

1.   behavior - The actions of people.

2.   organizational behavior - The study of the actions of people at work.

3.   attitudes - Evaluative statements concerning objects, people, or events.

4.   cognitive component of an attitude - The beliefs, opinions, knowledge, or information held by a person.

5.   affective component of an attitude - The emotional or feeling segment of an attitude.

6.   behavioral component of an attitude - An intention to behave in a certain way toward someone or something.

7.   job satisfaction - A person's general attitude toward his or her job.

8.   job involvement - The degree to which an employee identifies with his or her job, actively participates in it, and considers his or her performance important to his or her sense of self-worth.

9.   organizational commitment - An employee's orientation toward an organization in terms of his or her loyalty to, identification with, and involvement in the organization.

10. cognitive dissonance - Any incompatibility between two or more attitudes or between behavior and attitudes.

11. attitude surveys - Eliciting responses from employees through questionnaires about how they feel about their jobs, work groups, supervisors, and/or the organizations.

12. personality - A combination of psychological traits that classifies a person.

13. authoritarianism - A measure of a person's belief that there should be status and power differences among people in organizations.

14. Machiavellianism - A measure of the degree to which people are pragmatic, maintain emotional distance, and believe that ends justify means.

15. self-esteem - An individual's degree of like or dislike for him or herself.

16. self-monitoring - A personality trait that measures an individual's ability to adjust his or her behavior to external situational factors.

17. perception - The process of organizing and interpreting sensory impressions in order to give meaning to the environment.

18. attribution theory - A theory used to develop explanations of how we judge people differently depending on the meaning we attribute to a given behavior.

19. fundamental attribution error - A theory used to develop explanations of how we judge people differently depending on the meaning we attribute to a given behavior.

20. self-serving bias - The tendency for individuals to attribute their own successes to internal factors while putting the blame for failures on external factors.

21. selectivity - The process by which people assimilate certain bits and pieces of what they observe, depending on their interests, background, and attitudes.

22. assumed similarity - The belief that others are like oneself.

23. stereotyping - Judging a person on the basis of one's perception of the group to which he or she belongs.

24. halo effect - A general impression of an individual based on a single characteristic.

25. learning - Any relatively permanent change in behavior that occurs as a result of experience.

26. operant conditioning - A type of conditioning in which desired voluntary behavior leads to a reward or prevents a punishment.

27. social learning theory - People can learn through observation and direct experience.

28. shaping behavior - Systematically reinforcing each successive step that moves an individual closer to the desired response.

TRUE/FALSE QUESTIONS

1. T F The goals of OB are to explain and predict behavior.

2. T F High rewards can act to make dissonance less important.

3. T F Satisfaction and productivity have a high and consistent relationship.

4. T F A combination of traits that classifies a person is called his/her attitude.

5. T F People with an internal locus of control believe that their lives are controlled by others.

6. T F Machiavellianism is a measure of the degree to which people are pragmatic, maintain emotional distance, and believe that ends justify means.

7. T F We interpret what we see using our perceptions and call it reality.

8. T F Individuals assimilate all they observe to make assessments of others.

9. T F "Union people expect something for nothing" is an example of stereotyping.

10. T F Operant conditioning argues that behavior is a function of its consequences.

11. T F Managers are interested in every attitude an employee might hold.

12. T F "Learning by mistakes" is an example of modeling.

13. T F Cognitive dissonance is a part of social learning theory.

14. T F When individuals experience dissonance, they will always move toward finding consistency in their attitudes or between behavior and attitudes.

15. T F Machiavellianism is a measure of the degree to which people are pragmatic, maintain emotional distance, and believe that ends justify means.

16. T F People low in self-esteem are less susceptible to external influence than those people high in self-esteem.

17. T F No person actually sees reality.

18. T F When people observe others, they tend to develop explanations of why they behave in certain ways.

MULTIPLE CHOICE QUESTIONS

19. Organizational Behavior is:

    a. a descriptive field of study with goals to explain and predict behavior
    b. concerned with a study of the action of people at work
    c. focuses on individual and group behavior
    d. all of the above

20. Evaluative statements concerning people, objects, or events:

    a. perceptions
    b. attitudes
    c. personality
    d. dissonance

21. A process of organizing and interpreting sensory impressions in order to give meaning to the environment:

    a. perceptions
    b. attitudes
    c. personality
    d. dissonance

22. A combination of traits that classifies a person:

    a. perceptions
    b. attitudes
    c. personality
    d. dissonance

23. Job satisfaction, job involvement, and organization commitment are job related examples for:

    a. perceptions
    b. attitudes
    c. personality
    d. dissonance

24. Inconsistencies that cannot be avoided, but can be rationalized and justified:

    a. perceptions
    b. attitudes
    c. personality
    d. dissonance

25. Locus of control, authoritarianism, Machiavellianism, and risk propensity are organization examples of:

   a. perceptions
   b. attitudes
   c. personality
   d. dissonance

26. A worker who has an attitude that "the ends justify the means" is high in:

   a. authoritarianism
   b. risk propensity
   c. locus of control
   d. Machiavellianism

27. A worker who is not willing to take chances is low in:

   a. authoritarianism
   b. risk propensity
   c. locus of control
   d. Machiavellianism

28. Workers who believe that their lives are controlled by others have external:

   a. authoritarianism
   b. risk propensity
   c. locus of control
   d. Machiavellianism

29. People perceive things differently because of:

   a. past experiences and expectations
   b. attitudes and motives
   c. personality
   d. all of the above

30. Judging people on the basis of our perception of the group to which they belong:

   a. selectivity
   b. stereotyping
   c. assumed similarity
   d. halo effect

31. An intention to act in a certain way toward someone or something:

   a. behavioral component of an attitude
   b. cognitive component of an attitude
   c. affective component of an attitude
   d. cognitive dissonance

32. The beliefs, opinions, knowledge, or information held by a person:

   a. behavioral component of an attitude
   b. cognitive component of an attitude
   c. affective component of an attitude
   d. cognitive dissonance

33. Which is true for the satisfaction-productivity controversy?

   a. The positive relationship between satisfaction and productivity is strong.
   b. The satisfaction-productivity relationship is stronger when the employee behavior is constrained by outside forces.
   c. Satisfaction-productivity correlations are stronger for higher level employees than for lower level employees.
   d. Satisfaction leads to productivity rather than the other way around.

34. Learning by direct observation and by experience:

   a. operant conditioning
   b. selectivity
   c. shaping
   d. social learning theory

35. Molding workers by guiding their learning in graduated steps:

   a. operant conditioning
   b. selectivity
   c. shaping
   d. social learning theory

36. Suspending an employee for two days because he is consistently late to work is an example of this way to shape behavior:

   a. positive reinforcement
   b. extinction
   c. negative reinforcement
   d. punishment

37. Criticizing an employee in front of others for being late to work:

   a. positive reinforcement
   b. extinction
   c. negative reinforcement
   d. punishment

14 - 1 APPLICATION CASE

PERCEPTIONS

1. The way we answer questions is affected by the way we perceive what we hear or read. Answer the following questions based on your first impression of the question.

   a. Do they have a fourth of July in England?

   b. Some months have 30 days, some 31. How many have 28?

   c. If a doctor gave you three pills and told you to take one every half hour, how long would they last?

   d. A farmer had 17 sheep. All but nine died. How many did he have left?

   e. Take two apples from three apples. What do you have?

   f. I have two coins that add up to 55 cents. One is not a nickel. What are the two coins?

   g. A man moors his boat in a harbor at high tide. A ladder is fastened to the boat, with three rungs showing. The rungs are 10 inches apart. At low tide the water level sinks 20 feet. How many rungs of the ladder are now showing?

   h. What word, when you add additional letters becomes smaller?

2. Based on the exercise, how might perceptions affect your managerial decision making?

14 - 2 APPLICATION CASE

PERSONALITY

Discuss your personality in terms of the six characteristics of personality listed in the chapter.

What type of job fits your personality (according to Holland's personality-job fit theory)?

14 - 3 APPLICATION CASE

LEARNING

For the examples below, list the type of learning that a manager has chosen. Select from the following: positive reinforcement, negative reinforcement, punishment, or extinction.

1. The supervisor thanks BJ for working overtime to complete his assignment.

2. Since workers have not been performing to minimum productivity standards, they must work overtime on Saturday.

3. John ignores Mary when she continually tries to ask questions in the staff meeting.

4. The owner of a small firm knows that his brother-in-law (also an employee) takes supplies home from work, The owner has begun to deduct the cost of these supplies from his brother-in-law's pay check.

5. During a staff meeting, a retail manager tells June that she must pay closer attention to her duties or she may lose her job.

Chapter 15

Understanding Groups and Teamwork

CHAPTER OUTLINE	CORRESPONDING LEARNING OBJECTIVES
I. Understanding Group Behavior	
A. What is a Group?	
	1. Contrast formal and informal groups.
B. Why People Join Groups	2. Explain why people join groups.
1. Security	
2. Status	
3. Self-Esteem	
4. Affiliation	
5. Power	
6. Goal Achievement	
C. Stages of Group Development	3. State how roles and norms influence an employee's behavior.
D. Basic Group Concepts	
1. Roles	
2. Norms and Conformity	
3. Status Systems	
4. Group Size	
5. Group Cohesiveness	
E. Toward Understanding Work Group Behavior	4. Describe the key components in the group behavior model.
1. External Conditions Imposed on the Group	
2. Group Member Resources	

CHAPTER OUTLINE	CORRESPONDING LEARNING OBJECTIVES

3. Group Structure

4. Group Processes

5. Group Tasks

II. Turning Groups into Effective Teams

    A. Why Use Teams?

        1. Creates Esprit De Corp

        2. Allows Management to Think Strategically

        3. Speeds Decisions

        4. Facilitates Work Force Diversity

        5. Increases Performance

    B. Characteristics of Effective Teams
        1. Clear Goals

        2. Relevant Skills

        3. Mutual Trust

        4. Unified Commitment

        5. Good Communication

        6. Negotiating Skills

        7. Appropriate Leadership

        8. Internal and External Support

5. Explain the increased popularity of work teams in organizations.

6. Describe the characteristics of effective teams.

7. Identify how managers can build trust.

CHAPTER OUTLINE	CORRESPONDING LEARNING OBJECTIVES
C. Teams and TQM	8. Describe the role of teams in TQM.

CHAPTER OVERVIEW

Individuals tend to act differently in a group than they do when they are alone. Understanding group behavior is important if one is to fully understand OB. People tend to join groups for security, status, self-esteem, affiliation, power, and goal achievement.

Group development is a dynamic process since most groups are constantly changing. Groups usually go through five stages:

1. Forming is characterized by uncertainty about the group's purpose, structure, and leadership.

2. Storming is characterized by intragroup conflict. Members accept the existence of the group, but there is conflict over who will control the group.

3. Norming is the stage when close relationships are formed. The group has a common set of expectations of what defines correct member behavior.

4. Performing is the stage when the group is fully functional. For permanent work groups, performing is the last stage of development.

5. Adjourning is the final stage of development for temporary groups, characterized by concern with wrapping up activities rather than task performance.

To understand the foundation of group behavior, it is important to understand roles, norms and conformity, status systems, group size, and group cohesiveness. A role is the set of expected behavior patterns for people in each position of the organization. All groups establish norms that dictate acceptable standards of behavior in the group. Status is a significant motivator and if not consistent with the group members' perceptions, it will impact their motivation levels. Work group size has both positive and negative impacts on organizations. As groups get larger, the contribution of an individual is lessened. On the other hand, larger groups tend to handle problem-solving issues more effectively than small groups. Generally group cohesiveness is developed because individuals are attracted to one another and share the group's goals.

Determining why some groups are more successful than other groups is complex. This is true because groups do not exist in isolation, but are part of a large organization. The group performance is also affected by group members' abilities and personality characteristics. The structure of the group also shapes members' behavior.

Group processes such as communication patterns, leader behavior, and power dynamics also affect the success of a group. The task itself affects group effectiveness. For example, good performance is difficult when a task is complex and must be coordinated with other groups' tasks.

Work teams are formal work groups who are responsible for the attainment of goals. Organizations use formal work teams for several reasons:

1. Work teams facilitate cooperation and improve employee morale.

2. Work teams allow managers the time to work on strategic planning.

3. Work teams allow the flexibility for faster decision making.

4. Work teams allow diverse groups of people to make decisions that are more innovative and creative than an individual working alone could devise.

5. Work teams usually perform better than individuals working alone.

An effective work team has clear goals, individuals with relevant skills, trust, a unified commitment to the team, good communication skills, negotiating skills, effective leaders, and a supportive work climate.

TQM uses the team work approach. Managers in a TQM environment will encourage workers to share their ideas and will act on these ideas. TQM organizations also often use quality circles. A quality circle is a work group that meets regularly to discuss, investigate, and correct quality problems.

KEY TERMS AND DEFINITIONS

1. group - Two or more interacting and interdependent individuals who come together to achieve particular objectives.

2. forming - The first stage in group development, characterized by much uncertainty.

3. storming - The second stage of group development, characterized by intragroup conflict.

4. norming - The third stage of group development, characterized by close relationships and cohesiveness.

5. performing - The fourth stage in group development, when the group is fully functional.

6. adjourning - The final stage in group development for temporary groups, characterized by concern with wrapping up activities rather than task performance.

7. role - A set of behavior patterns expected of someone occupying a given position in a social unit.

8. norms - Acceptable standards shared by a group's members.

9. status - A prestige grading, position, or rank within a group.

10. group cohesiveness - The degree to which members are attracted to one another and share the group's goals.

11. work teams - Formal groups made up of interdependent individuals responsible for the attainment of a goal.

12. quality circles - Work groups that meet regularly to discuss, investigate, and correct quality problems.

TRUE/FALSE QUESTIONS

1. T F All task groups are also command groups.

2. T F Most people join a group because of needs for security, status, self-esteem, affiliation, power, and goal achievement.

3. T F Storming is a stage of group development characterized by close relationships and cohesiveness.

4. T F Groups proceed through the five stages of group development, in order beginning with forming and ending with adjourning.

5. T F If cohesiveness is low and goals are supported, productivity increases but not as much as when both cohesiveness and goal support are high.

6. T F Every work group is influenced by external conditions imposed from outside the work group.

7. T F The structural variables that shape group members' behavior include roles, norms, and formal leadership.

8. T F Even though each group has its own set of norms, there are common classes of norms that appear in most organizations.

9. T F In his study of group conformity, Asch found that there is pressure in a group for individuals to conform to the group norm.

10. T F The size of a work group has little impact on the group's overall behavior.

11. T F When the results of a group cannot be attributed to any single person, the relationship between an individual input and the group's output is difficult to determine.

12. T F Work teams are informal groups of workers.

13. T F When organizations use work teams, managers have less time for strategic planning because they are busy coordinating the efforts of the work groups.

14. T F The introduction of teams to the workplace does not automatically increase the organization's productivity.

MULTIPLE CHOICE QUESTIONS

15. The group development stage when close relationships develop:

   a. performing
   b. norming
   c. storming
   d. forming

16. Group energy is on performing the task in this group development stage:

   a. performing
   b. norming
   c. storming
   d. forming

17. Intragroup conflict is high in this group development stage:

   a. performing
   b. norming
   c. storming
   d. forming

18. This stage is complete when members have begun to think of themselves as part of a group:

   a. performing
   b. norming
   c. storming
   d. forming

19. This stage is complete when there is a relatively clear hierarchy of leadership within the group:

   a. performing
   b. norming
   c. storming
   d. forming

20. This can be informally conferred on individuals because of their education, age, sex, skill, or experience:

    a. status
    b. norms
    c. group cohesiveness
    d. roles

21. These dictate output levels, absenteeism rates, and promptness or tardiness:

    a. status
    b. norms
    c. group cohesiveness
    d. roles

22. A set of expected behavior patterns attributed to someone who occupies a given position in an organization:

    a. status
    b. norms
    c. group cohesiveness
    d. roles

23. Which is not true for work group behavior?

    a. A group's potential level of performance depends to a large extent on the resources that its members individually bring to the group.
    b. Work groups have a structure that shapes members' behavior.
    c. Attributes that tend to have a positive connotation in our culture tend to be positively related to group productivity and morale.
    d. Effective communication and minimal levels of conflict should be more relevant to group performance when one group's tasks are independent of other unit work units' tasks.

24. Which is not one of the reasons people join groups?

    a. power
    b. status
    c. autonomy
    d. security

25. Which is not a reason work teams are used in organizations?

    a. creates esprit de corp
    b. allows management to think strategically
    c. slows decisions
    d. facilitates work force diversity

15 - 1 APPLICATION CASE

TEAM WORK

Find an article that explains a company's team work approach. Some possible companies include: Chrysler, Ford Motor Company (Taurus), Federal Express, U.S. Steel, General Motors (SATURN).

Discuss the company's reasons for using the team work approach.

Are all of the characteristics of effective teams present in the company's teams? Explain.

15 - 2 APPLICATION CASE

JOINING GROUPS

1. List groups to which you are a member. These can be either informal or formal groups.

2. Why are you a member of these groups? (Discuss your reasoning for joining the groups from the following: security, status, self-esteem, affiliation, power, and goal achievement.)

STAGES OF GROUP DEVELOPMENT

Managers of Automotive Masters have called together workers from several work groups to work on a special project. These workers will develop a plan for implementing new production technology in the plant. Specifically, the group will be concerned with how to communicate the changes to the workers, how to implement usage of the new equipment, how workers should be trained, and how to get workers to accept the new technology. The members of this temporary group include: the production supervisor of production line 1, the production supervisor of production line 2, a quality control supervisor, two production line workers, and one clerical worker.

Discuss what happens in each of the stages of group development for this situation.

(Hint: Be sure to include in your discussion how the group interacts in each stage and what is accomplished in each stage. USE YOUR IMAGINATION!)

FORMING

STORMING

NORMING

PERFORMING

ADJOURNING

Chapter 16

Motivating Employees

CHAPTER OUTLINE	CORRESPONDING LEARNING OBJECTIVES
I. What is Motivation?	1. Define the motivation process.
II. Early Theories of Motivation	
A. Hierarchy of Needs Theory	2. Explain the hierarchy of needs theory.
B. Theory X and Theory Y	3. Differentiate Theory X from Theory Y.
C. Motivation-Hygiene Theory	4. Explain the motivational implications of the motivation-hygiene theory.
III. Contemporary Theories of Motivation	
A. Three-Needs Theory	5. Identify the characteristics that high achievers seek in a job.
B. Goal-Setting Theory	6. Explain how goals motivate people.
C. Reinforcement Theory	7. Differentiate reinforcement theory from goal-setting theory.
D. Equity Theory	8. Describe the motivational implications of equity theory.
E. Expectancy Theory	9. Explain the key relationships in expectancy theory.
F. Integrating Contemporary Theories of Motivation	
IV. Motivating a Diversified Work Force	
V. From Theory to Practice: Suggestions for Motivating Employees	
	10. Identify management practices that are likely to lead to more motivated employees.

A. Recognize Individual
    Differences

B. Match People to Jobs

C. Use Goals

D. Ensure that Goals are
    Perceived as Attainable

E. Individualize Rewards

F. Link Rewards to
    Performance

G. Don't Ignore Money

CHAPTER OVERVIEW

Motivation is the willingness to exert high levels of effort to reach organizational goals conditioned by the employee's ability to satisfy some individual need. Several early motivation theories were based on the satisfaction of needs. Three specific theories formulated in the 1950's include the following:

1. Hierarchy of Needs Theory - According to Abraham Maslow, every person has five needs: physiological, safety, social, esteem, and self-actualization needs. These needs exist in a hierarchy so that when a lower level need is satisfied a person is no longer motivated by that need, but is motivated by the next level need in the hierarchy. The lower-order needs are satisfied externally, while the higher-order needs are satisfied internally. This theory has become very popular and received much attention from practicing managers. However, research does not generally validate the hierarchy of needs theory.

2. Theory X and Theory Y - Douglas McGregor proposed two views on the nature of human beings. He said that a manager's action toward workers is based on a set of assumptions the manager has about workers in general. The Theory X manager views workers as lazy, seeking to avoid responsibility, and disliking work. The Theory Y manager views workers as being creative, seeking responsibility, and exercising self-direction. Theory X assumes that lower-order needs dominate and Theory Y assumes that higher-order needs dominate. McGregor proposed that participation in decision making, responsible and challenging jobs, and good group relations would maximize job motivation.

3. Motivation-Hygiene Theory - According to Frederick Herzberg, eliminating dissatisfaction and motivating employees are different things. He asked a group of people what they dislike about their jobs and what motivates them to work. He discovered the employees are no longer dissatisfied if extrinsic factors such as company policy, supervision, interpersonal relationships, and working conditions are good. However, these hygiene factors do not seem to motivate

employees to work harder. Motivating factors are intrinsic factors such as achievement, recognition, the work itself, responsibility, advancement, and growth. Several researchers criticize the motivation-hygiene theory. Perhaps the greatest criticism is that the theory is "methodology bound". This means that Herzberg found what he did because of the way he conducted his research. Regardless of the criticism, Herzberg's theory has been very popular in management.

Several contemporary theories have been developed for motivation. Some of these include: three-needs theory, goal-setting theory, reinforcement theory, equity theory, and expectancy theory.

1. Three-Needs Theory - According to David McClelland, workers have three needs: need for achievement, need for power, and need for affiliation. Research indicates that people with a high need to achieve prefer job situations with personal responsibility, feedback, and an intermediate degree of risk. A high need to achieve does not necessarily lead to being a good manager. The needs for affiliation and power are closely related to managerial success. The best managers are high in the need for power and low in the need for affiliation. Employees can be trained successfully to stimulate their achievement need.

2. Goal-Setting Theory - Specific goals increase performance and difficult goals, when accepted, result in higher performance than easy goals.

3. Reinforcement Theory - Behavior is a function of its consequences. This means that reinforcers, when immediately given following a response, increase the probability that the behavior will be repeated. The logic of this theory is that people are more likely to continue "good" behavior if they are rewarded and are likely to cease "bad" behavior if they are punished. Research evidence suggests that reinforcement is important, but is not the only explanation for differences in employee motivation.

4. Equity Theory - An employee compares his/her job's input-outcomes ratio to that of relevant others and then corrects any inequity. This means that employees are not concerned with absolute rewards, but with how those rewards compare with other workers' rewards. If an employee perceives that there is an inequity, the employee will adjust his/her work effort so that equity exists.

5. Expectancy Theory - This theory suggests that the tendency to act in a certain way depends on the strength of the expectation that the act will be followed by a given outcome and on the attractiveness of that outcome to the individual. Simply stated, the manager must get the worker to see the connection between effort and being able to perform and the connection between performing and being rewarded. If the employee sees these relationships and the rewards are desirable, the employee will be motivated to work.

There is not one set of guidelines that managers can use that guarantees employees will be motivated. The following recommendations are based on motivation theory:

1. Recognize individual differences.

2. Match people to jobs.

3. Use goals.

4. Ensure that goals are perceived as attainable

5. Individualize rewards.

6. Link rewards to performance.

7. Check the system for equity.

8. Don't ignore money.

KEY TERMS AND DEFINITIONS

1. motivation - The willingness to exert high levels of effort to reach organizational goals conditioned by the effort's ability to satisfy some individual need.

2. need - An internal state that makes certain outcomes appear attractive.

3. hierarchy of needs theory - Maslow's theory that there is a hierarchy of five human needs: physiological, safety, social, esteem, and self-actualization. As each need is substantially satisfied, the next need becomes dominant.

4. physiological needs - Basic food, drink, shelter, and sexual needs.

5. safety needs - A person's needs for security and protection from physical and emotional harm.

6. social needs - A person's needs for affection, belongingness, acceptance, and friendship.

7. esteem needs - Internal factors such as self-respect, autonomy, and achievement; and external factors such as status, recognition, and attention.

8. self-actualization needs - A person's drive to become what he or she is capable of becoming.

9. lower-order needs - Physiological and safety needs.

10. higher-order needs - Social, esteem, and self-actualization needs.

11. Theory X - The assumption that employees dislike work, are lazy, seek to avoid responsibility, and must be coerced to perform.

12. Theory Y - The assumption that employees are creative, seek responsibility, and can exercise self-direction.

13. motivation-hygiene theory - The theory that intrinsic factors are related to job satisfaction, while extrinsic factors are associated with dissatisfaction.

14. hygiene factors - Factors that eliminate dissatisfaction.

15. motivators - Factors that increase job satisfaction.

16. three-needs theory - The needs for achievement, power, and affiliation are major motives in work.

17. need for achievement - The drive to excel, to achieve in relation to a set of standards, to strive to succeed.

18. need for power - The need to make others behave in a way that they would not have behaved otherwise.

19. need for affiliation - The desire for friendly and close interpersonal relationships.

20. goal-setting theory - Specific goals increase performance and difficult goals, when accepted, result in higher performance than easy goals.

21. reinforcement theory - An individual's purposes direct his or her actions; behavior is a function of its consequences.

22. reinforcer - Any consequence immediately following a response that increases the probability that the behavior will be repeated.

23. equity theory - The theory that an employee compares his or her job's inputs-outcomes ratio to that of relevant others and then corrects any inequity.

24. referents - The persons, systems, or selves against which individuals compare themselves to assess equity.

25. expectancy theory - The theory that an individual tends to act in a certain way based on the expectation that the act will be followed by a given outcome and on the attractiveness of that outcome to the individual.

TRUE/FALSE QUESTIONS

1. T   F   Motivation is the result of the interaction between the individual and the situation.

2. T   F   The best known theory of motivation is Douglas McGregor's hierarchy of needs theory.

3. T   F   According to the hierarchy of needs theory, a substantially satisfied need no longer motivates.

4. T   F   Physiological, safety, and social needs are described as lower-order needs.

5. T F Lower-order needs are satisfied externally.

6. T F Research generally validates the hierarchy of needs theory.

7. T F Theory X is the assumption that employees are creative, seek responsibility, and can exercise self-direction.

8. T F In Herzberg's motivation-hygiene theory, intrinsic factors such as recognition, the work itself, responsibility, and advancement were found to be related to job satisfaction.

9. T F According to Herzberg, eliminating dissatisfaction does not necessarily lead to motivation and job satisfaction.

10. T F Need for affiliation is the same as Maslow's esteem needs.

11. T F Reinforcement theory ignores the inner state of the individual and concentrates solely on what happens to a person when he/she takes some action.

12. T F The evidence indicates that reinforcement is not an influence on work behavior.

13. T F In equity theory, individuals are concerned only with the absolute rewards they receive for their efforts.

14. T F Expectancy theory is a contingency approach to motivation.

15. T F According to expectancy theory, money is not a motivator.

16. T F Even though employees have different needs, reinforcers are the same for all employees.

MULTIPLE CHOICE QUESTIONS

17. Which kind of effort must be exerted for motivation?

   a. high level of quality
   b. high level of intensity
   c. high level of quality and intensity
   d. none of the above

18. Which is not true for motivation?

   a. Motivation is related to achieving individual needs.
   b. Motivation is the result of interaction between the individual and the situation.
   c. Motivation is a personal trait that some workers possess and other workers do not possess.
   d. Individuals differ in their motivation drive.

19. Which theory was developed by Douglas McGregor?

    a. hierarchy of needs theory
    b. theory X and theory Y
    c. motivation-hygiene theory
    d. three-needs theory

20. Which theory was developed by Frederick Herzberg?

    a. hierarchy of needs theory
    b. theory X and theory Y
    c. motivation-hygiene theory
    d. three-needs theory

21. Which theory was developed by Abraham Maslow?

    a. hierarchy of needs theory
    b. theory X and theory Y
    c. motivation-hygiene theory
    d. three-needs theory

22. This theory divides needs into those that motivate and those that eliminate dissatisfaction:

    a. hierarchy of needs theory
    b. theory X and theory Y
    c. motivation-hygiene theory
    d. three-needs theory

23. This theory is based on the assumption that when a need is satisfied, it is no longer a motivator:

    a. hierarchy of needs theory
    b. theory X and theory Y
    c. motivation-hygiene theory
    d. three-needs theory

24. Determining if a person enjoys or dislikes work is an important factor for this theory:

    a. hierarchy of needs theory
    b. theory X and theory Y
    c. motivation-hygiene theory
    d. three-needs theory

25. This need might be filled in a person who joins the company soft ball team:

    a. physiological
    b. safety
    c. social
    d. esteem

26. This need is filled when a worker earns enough money to purchase food:

    a. physiological
    b. safety
    c. social
    d. esteem

27. This need is filled when a worker can purchase life and health insurance policies:

    a. physiological
    b. safety
    c. social
    d. esteem

28. Which is a lower-order need?

    a. safety
    b. social
    c. esteem
    d. self-actualization

29. A higher-order need causes people to try to "be all that they can be":

    a. safety
    b. social
    c. esteem
    d. self-actualization

30. A higher-order need that is satisfied when a person is recognized by the boss for doing a good job:

    a. safety
    b. social
    c. esteem
    d. self-actualization

31. Which is not an assumption held by a manager for a Theory X worker?

    a. Employees dislike work.
    b. Since employees dislike work, they must be coerced, controlled, or threatened with punishment to achieve desired goals.
    c. Employees will shirk responsibility and seek formal direction whenever possible.
    d. The ability to make good decisions is widely dispersed throughout the company and is not necessarily the sole province of managers.

32. Theory Y managers assume that:

    a. physiological and social needs dominate the individual
    b. lower-order needs dominate the individual
    c. higher-order needs dominate the individual
    d. none of the above

33. When discussing dissatisfaction, workers in the Herzberg study discussed:

    a. company policy, responsibility, interpersonal relationships, and recognition
    b. company policy, supervision, interpersonal relationships, and working conditions
    c. supervision, working conditions, and recognition
    d. interpersonal relationships, the work itself, power, and advancement

34. When discussing satisfaction, workers in the Herzberg study discussed:

    a. company policy
    b. working conditions
    c. supervision
    d. responsibility and advancement

35. Which of the following is not a criticism of Herzberg's theory?

    a. The results are inconsistent with previous research.
    b. Reliability of the methodology is in question.
    c. Herzberg assumed a relationship between satisfaction and productivity.
    d. One overall measure of satisfaction was utilized.

36. A desire for friendly and close interpersonal relationships:

    a. need for achievement
    b. need for affiliation
    c. need for power
    d. all of the above

37. A drive to excel or need to succeed:

    a. need for achievement
    b. need for affiliation
    c. need for power
    d. all of the above

38. Individuals high on this need prefer cooperative situations and desire relationships involving a high degree of mutual understanding:

    a. need for achievement
    b. need for affiliation
    c. need for power
    d. all of the above

39. A desire to have impact:

    a. need for achievement
    b. need for affiliation
    c. need for power
    d. all of the above

40. According to reinforcement theory, this controls behavior:

   a. reinforcers
   b. norms
   c. needs
   d. roles

41. Which of the following explains differences in employee motivation levels?

   a. differences in goals
   b. differences in expectations
   c. differences in reinforcement
   d. all of the above

42. Which is true for equity theory?

   a. It is a reinforcement theory.
   b. Individuals are concerned with absolute rewards.
   c. Given payment by time, overrewarded employees will produce more than equitably paid employees.
   d. Given payment by quantity of production, underrewarded employees will produce a large number of high quality units in comparison with equitably paid employees.

43. An example of this expectancy relationship is an individual's perception that exerting a given amount of effort will lead to successful performance of a job task:

   a. attractiveness
   b. referent
   c. performance-reward linkage
   d. effort-performance linkage

44. Answering the question for expectancy theory "What perceived outcomes does the job offer the employees?" is:

   a. attractiveness
   b. referent
   c. performance-reward linkage
   d. effort-performance linkage

45. Which is not true for expectancy theory?

   a. The emphasis is on what is realistic for employees to achieve.
   b. The theory is based on self-interest.
   c. The emphasis is on expected behaviors and expectations.
   d. The theory emphasizes payoffs or rewards.

16 - 1 APPLICATION CASE

MASLOW'S HIERARCHY OF NEEDS

Classify each of the needs below according to Maslow's hierarchy.

1. Wanting to be recognized as a good singer.

2. Hoping that other people will accept you.

3. Wanting a loving family.

4. Feeling comfort knowing other people have the same problems that you do.

5. Purchasing an insurance policy.

6. Achieving your career goals.

7. Being recognized by your boss for getting a new company account.

8. Setting and attaining challenging goals.

9. Being called a nickname that you like.

10. Getting a job promotion.

11. Wanting a raise so you can better provide for your family.

12. Being selected as group leader at work.

16 - 2 APPLICATION CASE

NEEDS AND MOTIVATION

Larry is a young man who had a rough childhood. His father left his mother when he was very young. His mother went to work trying to support him and three older sisters. Often there was little food to eat.

Since he was the youngest, Larry did not get much attention. He often had to entertain himself. At school, Larry was very shy and withdrawn. Teachers tended to ignore him. Since he was short for his age, other boys did not often choose him for sports. Other kids would poke fun at his old clothes.

Larry knew that there was no way he could go to college. When he graduated from high school, Larry joined the Marines. Larry is now a successful sergeant. After six years as a Marine, Larry has decided to make this his career.

1. Identify specific needs that Larry probably feels are important because of his disadvantaged childhood.

2. How does the Marines satisfy Larry's needs for achievement, power, and affiliation? What about safety and self-actualization?

16 - 3 APPLICATION CASE

THE ROLE OF MONEY AS A MOTIVATOR

Explain the role of money as a motivator (if there is one) for the following theories that were discussed in this chapter:

1. Maslow's Hierarchy of Needs

2. Motivation-Hygiene Theory

3. Three-Needs Theory

4. Equity Theory

5. Expectancy Theory

Chapter 17

Leadership

CHAPTER OUTLINE	CORRESPONDING LEARNING OBJECTIVES
I. Managers versus Leaders	1. Explain the difference between managers and leaders.
II. Trait Theories	2. Summarize the conclusions of trait theories.
III. Behavioral Theories	3. Identify the two underlying behaviors in the behavioral leadership studies.
A. The Ohio State Studies	
B. The University of Michigan Studies	
C. The Managerial Grid	
D. Summary of Behavioral Theories	
IV. Contingency Theories	
A. The Fiedler Model	4. Describe the Fiedler Contingency Model.
B. The Hersey-Blanchard Situational Theory	5. Explain the Hersey-Blanchard Situational Theory.
C. Path-Goal Theory	6. Summarize the Path-Goal Model.
D. Vroom-Yetton Leader-Participation Model	
E. Sometimes Leadership is Irrelevant!	7. Explain when leaders may not be that important.
V. Emerging Approaches to Leadership	
A. Attribution Theory of Leadership	
B. Charismatic Leadership Theory	8. Identify the key characteristics of charismatic leaders.

CHAPTER OVERVIEW

Managers and leaders are not necessarily the same. Managers are appointed and they have legitimate power. Many times leaders are appointed and have legitimate power, but leaders can also lead informally without legitimate power in the situation. Ideally all managers should be leaders. For discussion purposes in this chapter, leaders are defined as those who are able to influence others and who possess managerial authority.

Researchers who studied trait theories of leadership searched for characteristics that differentiate leaders from nonleaders. For example, some traits often associated with good leaders are: intelligence, charisma, decisiveness, enthusiasm, self-confidence, and integrity. Research efforts at isolating these traits resulted in a number of dead ends. A major movement away from trait theories began as early as the 1940's.

Leadership research from the late 1940's to the mid-1960's emphasized the preferred behavioral styles that leaders demonstrated. If behavioral theories could determine critical behaviors needed by good leaders, leaders could be trained in those behaviors. Three examples of behavioral theories of leadership include: The Ohio State Studies, The University of Michigan Studies, and The Managerial Grid.

1. The Ohio State Studies - Researchers sought to identify independent dimensions of leader behavior. Two dimensions used in the research were initiating structure and consideration. Initiating structure refers to the extent to which a leader is likely to define and structure his/her role and those of workers in the search for goal attainment. Consideration is the extent to which a person has job relationships characterized by mutual trust, respect for workers' ideas, and regard for their feelings. Results indicated that a leader is more effective if he/she is a high-high leader (high in both initiating structure and consideration).

302

2. The University of Michigan Studies - Two dimensions of leadership researched at the University of Michigan were: employee-oriented behavior and production-oriented behavior. Leaders who are employee-oriented emphasize interpersonal relationships and production-oriented leaders emphasize technical aspects of the job. Results indicated that employee-oriented leaders are associated with higher group productivity and higher job satisfaction.

3. The Managerial Grid - Blake and Mouton developed a grid with two dimensions for leader style: concern for people and concern for production. Five key leader behaviors were identified. The 1,1 leader (impoverished) scored low on both behaviors. The 5,5 leader (middle-of-the-road) desired adequate mix of some of each behavior. The 9,1 (task) and the 1,9 (country club) leaders emphasized only one of the leader dimensions. Results indicated that the 9,9 leader (team) is the most appropriate. However, critics suggest that evidence does not support a conclusion that a 9,9 style is most effective in all situations.

It became clear that situational influences must be considered when determining appropriate leader styles. Several contingency theories of leadership have been developed.

1. The Fiedler Model - This model proposes that effective group performance depends on the proper match of leader-member relations, task structure, and leader position power. Fiedler then developed a continuum of leader styles from relationship-oriented to task-oriented. Using the three contingency factors, Fiedler suggested appropriate leader behaviors for eight different situations. Fiedler assumes that a leader style is fixed. This means that there are two ways to improve leader effectiveness: change the leader to fit the situation and change the situation to fit the leader.

2. Hersey-Blanchard Situational Theory - Maturity is the contingency factor used for this research. Maturity is defined as the ability and willingness of people to take responsibility for directing their own behavior. Two variations of leader behaviors were suggested in this research: task and relationship behaviors. These two leader behaviors provide for four specific leader styles including telling, selling, participating, and delegating. Results of the research indicate that as workers become mature, a leader should move through these four styles. He/she should begin by using authoritative behavior and move toward participative behavior.

3. Path-Goal Theory - According to Robert House, the leader's job is to assist his/her followers in attaining their goals and to provide the necessary direction and/or support to ensure that their goals are compatible with the overall objectives of the group or organization. The leader's behavior is acceptable to workers if they view the behavior as an immediate source of satisfaction or as a means of future satisfaction. In addition, a leader's behavior is motivational to the degree that it makes worker need satisfaction contingent on effective performance and provides the coaching, guidance, and rewards necessary for effective performance. House identified four leader behaviors: directive, supportive, participative, and achievement-oriented. House assumes that a leader is flexible and can display any or all of these four leader behaviors. Two contingency factors that affect the leader's behavior choice are environmental factors and characteristics of the worker. According to this research, employee performance and satisfaction are likely to be positively influenced when the

leader compensates for things lacking in either the employee or the work setting.

4. Leader-Participation Model - In this research, Vroom and Yetton related leadership behavior and participation to decision making. Five leader behaviors discussed include: Autocratic I, Autocratic II, Consultative I, Consultative II, and Group II. A leader can answer a series of seven contingency questions to determine his/her correct decision making behavior.

Three emerging approaches to leadership include the following:

1. Attribution Theory of Leadership - Leadership is one of the attributions that people make about other individuals. Generally, people characterize leaders as intelligent, outgoing, good at verbal communication, aggressive, understanding, and industrious.

2. Charismatic Leadership Theory - Charismatic leaders tend to have self-confidence, a vision, strong convictions in that vision, behave out of the ordinary, and be perceived as change agents. This leader style may not always be desirable. These leaders tend to be self-possessed, autocratic, and given to thinking that their opinions have a greater degree of certainty than they merit. Charismatic leaders can be valuable when the company has a crisis and when the firm is making radical changes in operations.

3. Transactional versus Transformational Leadership - Most of the leadership theories discuss transactional leaders. These leaders guide or motivate their followers in the direction of established goals by clarifying role and task requirements. Another type of leader is the transformational leader. Transformational leaders inspire followers to transcend their own self-interests for the good of the organization and are capable of having a profound effect on their followers. Research shows that transformational leaders tend to be evaluated as more effective than transactional leaders.

KEY TERMS AND DEFINITIONS

1. leaders - Those who are able to influence others and who possess managerial authority.

2. trait theories - Theories isolating characteristics that differentiate leaders from nonleaders.

3. behavioral theories - Theories identifying behaviors that differentiate effective from ineffective leaders.

4. initiating structure - The extent to which a leader defines and structures his or her role and those of subordinates to attain goals.

5. consideration - The extent to which a person has job relationships characterized by mutual trust, respect for subordinates' ideas, and regard for their feelings.

6. high-high leader - A leader high in both initiating structure and consideration.

7. managerial grid - A two-dimensional portrayal of leadership based on concern for people and concern for production.

8. Fiedler Contingency Model - The theory that effective groups depend on a proper match between a leader's style of interacting with subordinates and the degree to which the situation gives control and influence to the leader.

9. least-preferred co-worker (LPC) questionnaire - A questionnaire that measures whether a person is task or relationship oriented.

10. leader-member relations - The degree of confidence, trust, and respect subordinates have in their leader.

11. task structure - The degree to which the job assignments are procedurized.

12. position power - The degree of influence a leader has over power variables such as hiring, firing, discipline, promotions, and salary increases.

13. situational leadership theory - A contingency theory that focuses on followers' maturity.

14. maturity - The ability and willingness of people to take responsibility for directing their own behavior.

15. path-goal theory - The theory that a leader's behavior is acceptable to subordinates insofar as they view it as a source of either immediate or future satisfaction.

16. leader-participation model - A leadership theory that provides a set of rules to determine the form and amount of participative decision making in different situations.

17. attribution theory of leadership - Proposes that leadership is merely an attribution that people make about other individuals.

18. charismatic leadership - Followers make attributions of heroic or extraordinary leadership abilities when they observe certain behaviors.

19. transactional leaders - Leaders who guide or motivate their followers in the direction of established goals by clarifying role and task requirements.

20. transformational leaders - Leaders who provide individualized consideration, intellectual stimulation, and possess charisma.

TRUE/FALSE QUESTIONS

1. T F Manager and leader are synonymous terms.

2. T F All managers should ideally be leaders.

3. T F Trait theory is valid because there are specific characteristics all leaders possess.

4. T F According to researchers, if the behavioral theory of leadership could determine critical behavior determinants of leadership, then it would be possible to train people to be leaders.

5. T F Two popular behavioral leadership theories are the Ohio State Studies and the University of Michigan Studies.

6. T F Two dimensions of leader behavior discussed in the Ohio State Studies were employee-oriented behavior and production-oriented behavior.

7. T F Initiating structure from the Ohio State Studies and production oriented behavior from the University of Michigan Studies are essentially the same.

8. T F From their research findings, Blake and Mouton concluded that managers perform best using the 5,5 leader style.

9. T F The Fiedler Contingency Model proposes that effective group performance depends on the proper match between the leader's style of interacting with his/her subordinates and the degree to which the situation gives control and influence to the leader.

10. T F The Fiedler Model proposes matching an individual's LPC and an assessment of the three contingency variables to achieve maximum leadership effectiveness.

11. T F According to Fiedler, to improve leader effectiveness a manager can change his/her leader style.

12. T F The Hersey-Blanchard Model is a behavioral theory of leadership.

13. T F Maturity is the important component in the Path-Goal Theory.

14. T F The leader-participation model relates leader behavior and participation in decision making by providing a set of rules to determine the form and amount of participative decision making needed in different situations.

15. T F Leadership may not always be important.

16. T F Transformational leaders guide or motivate their followers in the direction of established goals by clarifying role and task requirements.

MULTIPLE CHOICE QUESTIONS

17. Which is not true for leaders?

    a. All leaders are managers.
    b. Ideally all managers should be leaders.
    c. Leaders are identified in the text as those who are able to influence others and possess managerial authority.
    d. All of the above are true.

18. Theories isolating characteristics that differentiate leaders from nonleaders:

    a. behavioral theories
    b. trait theories
    c. contingency theories
    d. none of the above

19. Theories that identify behaviors that differentiate effective from ineffective leaders:

    a. behavioral theories
    b. trait theories
    c. contingency theories
    d. none of the above

20. Theories identifying situational influences on leader effectiveness:

    a. behavioral theories
    b. trait theories
    c. contingency theories
    d. none of the above

21. Research conducted from the late 1940's to the mid-1960's was categorized as:

    a. behavioral theories
    b. trait theories
    c. contingency theories
    d. none of the above

22. "Leaders are born and not made" illustrates:

    a. behavioral theories
    b. trait theories
    c. contingency theories
    d. none of the above

23. Which of the following is a contingency model of leadership?

    a. University of Michigan Studies
    b. Ohio State Studies
    c. Managerial Grid
    d. Hersey-Blanchard Model

24. Two dimensions used in this theory are initiating structure and consideration behavior:

    a. University of Michigan Studies
    b. Ohio State Studies
    c. Managerial Grid
    d. Hersey-Blanchard Model

25. Two dimensions used in this theory are employee oriented and production oriented behavior:

    a. University of Michigan Studies
    b. Ohio State Studies
    c. Managerial Grid
    d. Hersey-Blanchard Model

26. Country-club, team, and impoverished are leader styles for this theory:

    a. University of Michigan Studies
    b. Ohio State Studies
    c. Managerial Grid
    d. Hersey-Blanchard Model

27. Results of this research suggest that leaders perform best with maximum concern for production and maximum concern for people:

    a. University of Michigan Studies
    b. Ohio State Studies
    c. Managerial Grid
    d. Hersey-Blanchard Model

28. The leader style from the Managerial Grid when a leader concentrates on job efficiency, but has little concern for developing the morale of workers:

    a. task
    b. country-club
    c. middle-of-the-road
    d. team

29. The leader style from the Managerial Grid when a leader is concerned with adequate task efficiency and adequate satisfaction and morale:

    a. task
    b. country-club
    c. middle-of-the-road
    d. team

30. The LPC questionnaire was used to develop situational aspects important to leaders:

    a. Path-Goal Theory
    b. Leader-Participation Model
    c. Fiedler Contingency Model
    d. Hersey-Blanchard Situational Theory

31. Maturity is an important situational factor for this theory:

    a. Path-Goal Theory
    b. Leader-Participation Model
    c. Fiedler Contingency Model
    d. Hersey-Blanchard Situational Theory

32. This theory provides a sequential set of rules that should be followed in determining the form and amount of participation needed in decision making:

    a. Path-Goal Theory
    b. Leader-Participation Model
    c. Fiedler Contingency Model
    d. Hersey-Blanchard Situational Theory

33. A leader's behavior is acceptable to workers insofar as they view it as a source of either immediate or future satisfaction:

    a. Path-Goal Theory
    b. Leader-Participation Model
    c. Fiedler Contingency Model
    d. Hersey-Blanchard Situational Theory

34. The three situational factors in this theory are leader-member relations, task structure, and leader position power:

    a. Path-Goal Theory
    b. Leader-Participation Model
    c. Fiedler Contingency Model
    d. Hersey-Blanchard Situational Theory

35. This theory proposes that leader behavior will be ineffective when it is redundant with sources of environment structure or incongruent with worker characteristics:

    a. Path-Goal Theory
    b. Leader-Participation Model
    c. Fiedler Contingency Model
    d. Hersey-Blanchard Situational Theory

36. The emphasis of this theory is on characteristics of the followers, not characteristics of the leader:

    a. Path-Goal Theory
    b. Leader-Participation Model
    c. Fiedler Contingency Model
    d. Hersey-Blanchard Situational Theory

37. This theory assumes that the leader style is fixed:

    a. Path-Goal Theory
    b. Leader-Participation Model
    c. Fiedler Contingency Model
    d. Hersey-Blanchard Situational Theory

38. This theory includes five leader behaviors (Autocratic I, Autocratic II, Consultative I, Consultative II, and Group II):

    a. Path-Goal Theory
    b. Leader-Participation Model
    c. Fiedler Contingency Theory
    d. Hersey-Blanchard Situational Theory

39. Possible leader behaviors for this theory include supportive, directive, achievement-oriented, and participative leaders:

    a. Path-Goal Theory
    b. Leader-Participation Model
    c. Fiedler Contingency Theory
    d. Hersey-Blanchard Situational Theory

40. Ted Turner and Lee Iacocca are examples of this type of leader:

    a. transactional leader
    b. authoritative leader
    c. transformational leader
    d. none of the above

41. A leader who guides or motivates followers in the direction of established goals by clarifying role and task requirements:

    a. transactional leader
    b. consultative leader
    c. transformational leader
    d. participative leader

42. Which is not true for a charismatic leader?

    a. A charismatic leader is usually participative and is willing to listen to the opinions of others.
    b. A charismatic leader might not always be needed to achieve high levels of employee performance.
    c. It is not unusual for a charismatic leader to pull an organization through a crisis, but perform poorly after the crisis subsides.
    d. It is more important to have a charismatic leader when the followers' task has an ideological component.

43. The Hersey-Blanchard leader style associated with high task and high relationship behavior:

   a. telling
   b. participating
   c. delegating
   d. selling

44. This leader style from the Hersey-Blanchard Situational Theory is concerned with facilitating and communicating:

   a. telling
   b. participating
   c. delegating
   d. selling

45. This leader style from the Hersey-Blanchard Situational Theory gives little direction or support to workers:

   a. telling
   b. participating
   c. delegating
   d. selling

46. The Hersey-Blanchard leader style associated with high task and low relationship behavior:

   a. telling
   b. participating
   c. delegating
   d. selling

47. According to Hersey and Blanchard, people who are unable but willing to do necessary job tasks need this type of leader:

   a. telling
   b. participating
   c. delegating
   d. selling

48. According to Hersey and Blanchard, people who are able but unwilling to do what the leader wants need this type of leader:

   a. telling
   b. participating
   c. delegating
   d. selling

17 - 1 APPLICATION CASE

TRAIT THEORIES OF LEADERSHIP

1. Rate the well known leaders who are listed below according to traits they possess(ed). 1 = the most outstanding leadership trait for the person, 11 = the least outstanding leadership trait for the person.

	Martin Luther King, Jr.	John F. Kennedy	Adolf Hitler	Abraham Lincoln	Ronald Reagan
Intelligence					
Charisma					
Good Communication Skills					
Empathy					
Patience					
Self-Awareness					
Goal-Oriented					
Emotional Stability					
Attractiveness					
Dominance					
Self-Confidence					

2. What do you consider to be the most important characteristics of an effective leader?

3. Do your ratings suggest that trait theories are useful or not very useful in determining the effectiveness of leaders?

17 - 2 APPLICATION CASE

LEADERSHIP CONTINGENCY FACTORS

You are the manager of a large toy store chain. In your job, you supervise 50 workers and you are responsible for ordering merchandise, taking inventory, and monitoring general store operations. The following contingencies apply to your setting:

1. relationship with workers - You get along with the workers and have an informal relationship with most of the workers.
2. leader position power - You have legitimate power over all personnel in the store. This includes the authority to hire and fire personnel.
3. task structure - Job tasks are very structured.
4. worker maturity - About half of the employees are new workers hired for the Christmas season; one-fourth have been with the company for about a year; one-fourth have been with the company for more than two years.
5. characteristics of workers - Most workers have an external locus of control and much perceived ability to do their jobs.

Based on this information, determine if your leader style should be more participative or more authoritative. (Hint: Determine the appropriate leader behavior for each contingency and then decide how the leader can best manage all of the workers.)

17 - 3 APPLICATION CASE

CHARISMATIC LEADERS

Choose a well known leader that you believe is a charismatic leader. Find articles or books in the library that explain the leader's style and answer the following questions.

1. What positive traits does the leader possess?

2. What negative traits does the leader possess?

3. Was the leader hired to get the company out of a crisis or did the leader have some positive impact on a company crisis that happened after he/she was hired? Discuss.

Chapter 18

Communication and Interpersonal Skills

CHAPTER OUTLINE	CORRESPONDING LEARNING OBJECTIVES
I. Understanding Communication	
A. What is Communication?	1. Define communication and explain why it is important to managers.
B. The Communication Process	2. Describe the communication process.
C. Methods of Communicating	
1. Oral	
2. Written	
3. Nonverbal	
4. Electronic Media	
D. Barriers to Effective Communication	
1. Filtering	
2. Selective Perception	
3. Emotions	
4. Language	
5. Nonverbal Cues	
E. Overcoming the Barriers	3. List techniques for overcoming communication barriers.
1. Use Feedback	
2. Simplify Language	
3. Listen Actively	

CHAPTER OUTLINE	CORRESPONDING LEARNING OBJECTIVES
4. Constrain Emotions	
5. Watch Nonverbal Cues	
II. Developing Interpersonal Skills	
III. Active Listening Skills	
A. Active versus Passive Listening	4. Identify behaviors related to effective active listening.
B. Developing Effective Active Listening Skills	
1. Make Eye Contact	
2. Exhibit Affirmative Nods and Appropriate Expressions	
3. Avoid Distracting Actions or Gestures	
4. Ask Questions	
5. Paraphrase	
6. Avoid Interrupting the Speaker	
7. Don't Overtalk	
8. Make Smooth Transitions Between the Roles of Speaker and Listener	
IV. Feedback Skills	
A. Positive versus Negative Feedback	
B. Developing Effective Feedback Skills	5. Identify behaviors related to providing effective feedback.
1. Focus on Specific Behaviors	
2. Keep Feedback Impersonal	

CHAPTER OUTLINE	CORRESPONDING LEARNING OBJECTIVES
3. Keep Feedback Goal-Oriented	
4. Make Feedback Well-Timed	
5. Ensure Understanding	
6. Direct Negative Feedback Toward Behavior that the Recipient Can Control	
V. Delegation Skills	
A. What is Delegation?	
B. Is Delegation Abdication?	
C. Contingency Factors in Delegation	6. Describe the contingency factors in delegation.
1. The Size of the Organization	
2. The Importance of the Duty or Decision	
3. Task Complexity	
4. Organizational Culture	
5. Qualities of Subordinates	
D. Developing Effective Delegating Skills	7. Identify behaviors related to effective delegating.
1. Clarify the Assignment	
2. Specify the Subordinate's Range of Discretion	
3. Allow the Subordinate to Participate	

CHAPTER OUTLINE	CORRESPONDING LEARNING OBJECTIVES
4. Inform Others that Delegation has Occurred	
5. Establish Feedback Controls	
VI. Discipline Skills	
A. The "Hot Stove" Rule	8. Explain the "hot stove" rule.
1. Immediacy	
2. Advance Warning	
3. Consistency	
4. Impersonal Nature	9. Identify behaviors related to effective disciplining.
B. Developing Effective Discipline Skills	
1. Confront the Employee in a Calm, Objective, and Serious Manner	
2. State the Problem Specifically	
3. Keep the Discussion Impersonal	
4. Allow the Employee to Explain His or Her Position	
5. Maintain Control of the Discussion	
6. Obtain Agreement on How Mistakes Can Be Prevented	
7. Select Disciplinary Action Progressively, Considering Mitigating Circumstances	
VII. Conflict Management Skills	

CHAPTER OUTLINE	CORRESPONDING LEARNING OBJECTIVES
A. What is Conflict?	
1. The Traditional View	
2. The Human Relations View	
3. The Interactionist View	
B. Functional versus Dysfunctional Conflict	
C. Developing Effective Conflict Resolution Skills	10. Describe the steps in analyzing and resolving conflict situations.
1. What is Your Underlying Conflict-Handling Style?	
2. Be Judicious in Selecting the Conflicts that You Want to Handle	
3. Evaluate the Conflict Players	
4. Assess the Source of the Conflict	
5. Know Your Options	
D. What About Conflict Stimulation?	
	11. Explain when a manager might want to stimulate conflict.
1. Change the Organization's Culture	
2. Use Communication	
3. Bring in Outsiders	
4. Restructure the Organization	
5. Appoint a Devil's Advocate	

CHAPTER OUTLINE	CORRESPONDING LEARNING OBJECTIVES
VII. Negotiation Skills	12. Contrast distributive and integrative bargaining.
A. Bargaining Strategies	
1. Distributive Bargaining	
2. Integrative Bargaining	
B. Decision-Making Biases That Hinder Effective Negotiations	
1. Irrational Escalation of Commitment	
2. The Mythical Fixed Pie	
3. Anchoring and Adjustments	
4. Framing Negotiations	
5. Availability of Information	
C. Developing Effective Negotiation	
1. Research Your Opponent	
2. Begin with a Positive Overture	
3. Address Problems Not Personalities	
4. Pay Little Attention to Initial Offers	
5. Emphasize Win-Win Solutions	
6. Be Open to Accepting Third-Party Assistance	

CHAPTER OVERVIEW

Communication is defined as the transference and understanding of meaning. The communication process consists of a message that passes through a source to a receiver. This message must be encoded by the sender, sent through a communication channel, and decoded by the receiver. Feedback is then used to make sure that the message has been understood. The source begins the communication process by encoding a thought. Four conditions affect the encoded message: skill, attitudes, knowledge, and social-cultural systems. These same four conditions affect the decoded message. Often there is noise in the transmission of the message that interferes with the communication process.

Communication can be oral, written, and nonverbal. Popular forms of oral communication include speeches, formal one-on-one and group discussions, and informal rumors. Sometimes oral communication is difficult because the more people who are involved in the communication, the more distorted the message becomes. Written communications include memos, letters, organizational periodicals, and bulletin boards. A disadvantage of written communication is that there is no built-in feedback mechanism. Nonverbal communication is transmitted without words. Two forms of nonverbal communication include: body language and verbal intonations. Body language is gestures, facial configurations, and other movements of the body that convey meaning. Verbal intonations refers to the emphasis in someone's voice that conveys a certain meaning. Sometimes nonverbal communication is the only method of communicating in a certain situation, but often nonverbal messages are part of verbal communication. Electronic media is an instantaneous transmission of written messages on computers that are linked together. This is a fast growing method of communicating.

Several factors in the communication process may make communication difficult or may even cause communication to breakdown. Some possible communication barriers are listed below.

1. Filtering (deliberate manipulation of information to make it appear more favorable to the receiver)

2. Selective Perception (interpretation of messages by the receiver based on his/her needs, motivations, experience, background, and other personal characteristics)

3. Emotions

4. Language

5. Nonverbal Cues

Managers can learn to overcome these barriers to communication. Some methods for overcoming communication barriers are listed below.

1. Use feedback. If managers use feedback, it is less likely that misunderstandings will occur in communicating.

2. Simplify language.

3. Listen actively. This means that managers should listen for full meaning without making premature judgments or interpretations.

4.   Constrain emotions.

5.   Watch nonverbal cues.

Managers can develop other key skills in addition to communication skills. These skills will allow the manager to be more proficient at his/her job. These skills include: active listening, providing feedback, delegating, disciplining, managing conflict, and negotiating.

Active listening has four requirements: intensity, empathy, acceptance, and a willingness to take responsibility for completeness. A good active listener can concentrate on what the speaker is saying, put himself/herself in the speaker's shoes, be objective, and use feedback to be sure that communication has occurred. Some specific techniques for becoming a better active listener include the following:

1.   Make eye contact.

2.   Exhibit affirmative nods and appropriate facial expressions.

3.   Avoid distracting actions or gestures.

4.   Ask questions.

5.   Paraphrase what the speaker has said.

6.   Avoid interrupting the speaker.

7.   Don't overtalk.

8.   Make smooth transitions between the roles of speaker and listener.

The way managers give feedback is an important interpersonal skill that should help managers in their job performance. Positive feedback is almost always accepted and negative feedback often meets resistance. This means that managers must be careful to use negative feedback in situations where it will be constructive. For example, research suggests that negative feedback is most likely to be accepted when it comes from a credible source or it is objective in form. Six specific suggestions can help managers become more effective in providing feedback.

1.   Focus on specific behaviors.

2.   Keep feedback impersonal.

3.   Keep feedback goal-oriented.

4.   Make feedback well-timed.

5.   Ensure understanding.

6.   Direct negative feedback toward behavior that the recipient can control.

Delegation is the assignment of authority and responsibility to another person so that he/she can carry out specific activities. Delegation does not mean that a manager directs all of his/her work to be done by someone else. Instead, the manager should delegate some tasks by clarifying what is to be done, the range of discretion the worker has in the situation, and the expected level of performance. Several contingency factors can help a manager decide if he/she should use centralization or decentralization:

1. Size - Larger organizations tend to delegate more than smaller organizations.

2. Importance of the Duty of Decision - The more important the decision, the less delegation.

3. Task Complexity - As tasks become more complex, it is more necessary to delegate, but managers must be sure the worker who is given authority has the specialized knowledge that is required.

4. Organizational Culture - The more managers trust workers, the more they will delegate.

5. Qualities of Subordinates - When workers are skilled, motivated, and knowledgeable, managers are more likely to delegate.

Several actions differentiate the effective from the ineffective delegator. An effective delegator will:

1. Clarify the assignment.

2. Specify the subordinate's range of discretion.

3. Allow the subordinate to participate.

4. Inform others that delegation has occurred.

5. Establish feedback controls.

Discipline refers to actions taken by a manager to enforce the organization's standards and regulations. The most frequent discipline problems include: attendance, on-the-job behaviors, dishonesty, and outside activities. Most managers use the "hot stove" rule in their disciplining of employees. This means that the discipline is immediate, consistent, impersonal, and the employee has advance warning before formal disciplinary action is taken. Seven behaviors explain effective disciplining of employees:

1. Confront the employee in a calm, objective, and serious manner.

2. State the problem specifically.

3. Keep the discussion impersonal.

4. Allow the employee to explain his/her actions.

5. Maintain control of the discussion.

6. Obtain agreement on how mistakes can be prevented in the future.

7. Select disciplinary action progressively, considering mitigating circumstances.

Handling conflict is another important interpersonal skill needed by managers. Conflict is incompatible differences that result in interference or opposition. The traditional view of conflict is that conflict is "bad", but the human relations view suggests that conflict is inevitable and natural. According to the interactionist view of conflict, some conflict is even necessary for the organization to perform effectively. Those conflicts that support the goals of the organization are called functional, while conflicts that prevent the organization from achieving its goals are dysfunctional conflicts. Some guidelines for handling conflict include the following:

1. Determine your conflict resolution style. It is important for a manager to understand his/her natural reaction to conflict.

2. Be judicious in selecting the conflicts that you want to handle.

3. Evaluate the conflict players.

4. Assess the source of the conflict.

5. Know your options. The manager has five techniques for reducing conflict. These include avoidance, accommodation, forcing, compromise, and collaboration. Each of these options has advantages and disadvantages. The manager should choose the best option for a particular situation. It has been suggested that sometimes conflict is good for an organization. Some ways that managers might stimulate conflict include:

   1. Change the organization culture.

   2. Use communication to "plant" possible decisions so that employees will take a stand on the issue.

   3. Bring in outsiders with different backgrounds, values, and managerial styles.

   4. Restructure the organization.

   5. Appoint a devil's advocate to purposely present arguments that run counter to those proposed by the majority.

Negotiations (bargaining) is a process in which two or more parties exchange goods or services and attempt to agree on the exchange rate for them. Distributive bargaining is a win-lose approach where there is an attempt to divide a fixed amount of resources. Integrative bargaining is a win-win approach where there is an attempt to determine a settlement where all parties get what they desire. Six recommendations for effective negotiation include the following:

1. Research your opponent.

2. Begin with a positive overture.

3. Address problems not personalities.

4. Pay little attention to initial offers.

5.   Emphasize win-win solutions.

6.   Be open to accepting third-party assistance.

Negotiations must be objective and unbiased if managers want to take advantage of opportunities and achieve the best results from their negotiations.

KEY TERMS AND DEFINITIONS

1.   communication - The transferring and understanding of meaning.

2.   interpersonal communication - Communication between two or more people in which the parties are treated as individuals rather than objects.

3.   message - A purpose to be conveyed.

4.   encoding - Converting a message into symbols.

5.   channel - The medium by which a message travels.

6.   decoding - Retranslating a sender's message.

7.   communication process - The seven stages in which meaning is transmitted and understood.

8.   noise - Disturbances that interfere with the transmission of a message.

9.   nonverbal communication - Communication transmitted without words.

10.   body language - Gestures, facial configurations, and other movements of the body that convey meaning.

11.   verbal intonation - An emphasis given to words or phrases that conveys meaning.

12.   electronic mail - Instantaneous transmission of written messages on computers that are linked together.

13.   filtering - The deliberate manipulation of information to make it appear more favorable to the receiver.

14.   active listening - Listening for full meaning without making premature judgments or interpretations.

15.   paraphrasing - Restating what a speaker has said but in your own words.

16.   delegation - The assignment to another person of authority and responsibility to carry out specific activities.

17.   discipline - Actions taken by a manager to enforce the organization's standards and regulations.

18. "hot stove" rule - Discipline should immediately follow an infraction, provide ample warning, be consistent, and impersonal.

19. conflict - Perceived incompatible differences that result in interference or opposition.

20. traditional view of conflict - The view that all conflict is bad and must be avoided.

21. human relations view of conflict - The view that conflict is a natural and inevitable outcome in any organization.

22. interactionist view of conflict - The view that some conflict is necessary for an organization to perform effectively.

23. functional conflicts - Conflicts that support an organization's goals.

24. dysfunctional conflicts - Conflicts that prevent an organization from achieving its goals.

25. avoidance - Withdrawal from or suppression of conflict.

26. accommodation - Resolving conflicts by placing another's needs and concerns above one's own.

27. forcing - Satisfying one's own needs at the expense of another.

28. compromise - A solution to conflict in which each party gives up something of value.

29. collaboration - Resolving conflict by seeking a solution advantageous to all parties.

30. devil's advocate - A person who purposely presents arguments that run counter to those proposed by the majority.

31. negotiation - A process in which two or more parties exchange goods or services and attempt to agree upon the exchange rate for them.

32. distributive bargaining - Negotiations that seek to divide up a fixed amount of resources: a win-lose situation.

33. integrative bargaining - Negotiation that seeks one or more settlements that can create a win-win solution.

TRUE/FALSE QUESTIONS

1. T   F   Everything a manager does involves communication.

2. T   F   Communication is telling another person some information.

3.   T   F   A receiver, who retranslates the sender's message, is encoding.

4.   T   F   Noise in communication is disturbances that interfere with the transmission of the message.

5.   T   F   Examples of communication channels include spoken words, memos, and reports.

6.   T   F   The major disadvantage of oral communication is that the more people who are involved, the greater the potential for distortion.

7.   T   F   A major disadvantage of written communication is that there is no built-in feedback mechanism.

8.   T   F   Nonverbal communication includes body language and verbal intonation.

9.   T   F   A barrier to communication is something that causes a breakdown in communication.

10.   T   F   Selective perception is the deliberate manipulation of information to make it appear more favorable to the receiver.

11.   T   F   Communication problems attributed to misunderstandings occur just as frequently if a manager uses a feedback loop in the communication process.

12.   T   F   Contingency factors in delegation include company size, importance of the duty or decision, job complexity, organization culture, and skill/ability of workers.

13.   T   F   According to the "hot stove" rule, the best channel for organization communication is written communication.

14.   T   F   In administering discipline, managers should be loose, informal, and relaxed.

15.   T   F   The traditional view of conflict is that conflict is a natural and inevitable outcome in any organization.

16.   T   F   Dysfunctional conflicts prevent an organization from achieving its goals.

17.   T   F   Every conflict is worth a manager's time and effort.

18.   T   F   Distributive bargaining is a win-win approach to negotiation.

MULTIPLE CHOICE QUESTIONS

19. Which is not true for communication?

    a. Communication involves the transfer of meaning.
    b. Understanding communication means that there is agreement about the message.
    c. To have communication, meaning must be imparted and understood.
    d. Communication can be verbal, written, or nonverbal.

20. An example for this part of the communication process is a manager writing a memo to an employee about a new company policy:

    a. message
    b. encoding
    c. channel
    d. noise

21. The sender perceives that certain information is important and he spends much time deciding just how the information should be communicated. This is an example of which part of the communication process?

    a. message
    b. encoding
    c. channel
    d. noise

22. An example of this part of the communication process is a manager telling a worker "You're fired!"

    a. message
    b. encoding
    c. channel
    d. noise

23. Illegible print, telephone static, and sounds of machinery are examples:

    a. message
    b. encoding
    c. channel
    d. noise

24. The perception of the receiver in determining the meaning of a message:

    a. feedback
    b. noise
    c. channel
    d. decoding

25. Making sure that a message has been understood is:

    a. feedback
    b. noise
    c. channel
    d. decoding

26. Which is a disadvantage of written communication?

    a. The more people involved, the more likely there is to be distortion in the message.
    b. There is no built-in feedback mechanism.
    c. It is less time consuming than other methods of communication.
    d. none of the above

27. Body language is:

    a. gestures
    b. facial configurations
    c. movements of the body
    d. all of the above

28. Nonverbal communication is:

    a. gestures
    b. facial configurations and other body movements
    c. emphasis on words and phrases
    d. all of the above

29. Every oral communication also has:

    a. nonverbal communication
    b. filtering
    c. active listening
    d. conflict

30. A barrier to communication when a receiver sees and hears communication depending on his/her needs, motivations, experiences, and other personal characteristics:

    a. emotions
    b. language
    c. selective perception
    d. filtering

31. Deliberate manipulation of information to make it appeal more favorable to the receiver:

    a. emotions
    b. language
    c. selective perception
    d. filtering

32. This barrier to communication sometimes causes the receiver or sender to disregard rational and objective thinking:

a. emotions
b. language
c. selective perception
d. filtering

33. Which is not a requirement for active listening?

a. empathy
b. acceptance and willingness to take responsibility for completeness
c. manager keeps control in the discussion
d. intensity

34. Which is not true for paraphrasing in active listening?

a. Paraphrasing is not important for good active listening.
b. Paraphrasing is a control device that a listener uses to be sure he/she is listening carefully.
c. Paraphrasing is a feedback mechanism.
d. Paraphrasing is a control device a listener uses to be sure he/she is listening accurately.

35. This part of the "hot stove" rule is illustrated when a manager disciplines a worker as soon as possible after the rules infraction has occurred:

a. advance warning
b. impersonal nature
c. immediacy
d. consistency

36. An example that illustrates this part of the "hot stove" rule is a policy manual that states company rules and punishments:

a. advance warning
b. impersonal nature
c. immediacy
d. consistency

37. This part of the "hot stove" rule is illustrated when a manager treats all violators of a work rule in the same manner:

a. advance warning
b. impersonal nature
c. immediacy
d. consistency

38. The human relations view of conflict is:

   a. the view that all conflict is bad and must be avoided
   b. the view that some conflict is necessary for the organization to perform effectively
   c. the view that conflict is a natural and inevitable outcome in any organization
   d. the view that conflict should support an organization's goals.

39. The interactionist view of conflict is:

   a. the view that all conflict is bad and must be avoided.
   b. the view that some conflict is necessary for the organization to perform effectively
   c. the view that conflict is a natural and inevitable outcome in any organization
   d. the view that conflict should support an organization's goals

40. Resolving conflict by placing another's needs and concerns above one's own:

   a. collaboration
   b. accommodation
   c. compromise
   d. avoidance

41. A method for resolving conflict that requires each person to give up something:

   a. collaboration
   b. accommodation
   c. compromise
   d. avoidance

42. Resolving conflict by withdrawing from the conflict:

   a. collaboration
   b. accommodation
   c. compromise
   d. avoidance

43. Resolving conflict by seeking a solution that is advantageous to all parties:

   a. collaboration
   b. accommodation
   c. compromise
   d. avoidance

44. Two parties have interests that are convergent or congruent:

   a. integrative bargaining
   b. forcing
   c. distributive bargaining
   d. negotiation

18 - 1 APPLICATION CASE

COMMUNICATION BARRIERS

Mary is a sales representative for a large consumer goods company. As part of her job, Mary travels to major supermarket chain stores and negotiates with managers to stock her products in their stores. Mary is about 25 years old, but looks much younger (about 18). Mary recognizes that her youthful looks may cause some managers not to take her seriously so she tries to compensate in several ways:

--Mary dresses very professionally (always in a dark suit).
--Mary uses as many marketing terms as possible and tries to talk formally in her
        presentations.
--She tries not to show her sense of humor because she feel the managers will not
        respect her.
--She carries herself in a very proper, almost haughty manner.

1.   What are the likely barriers to communication for this situation? Explain.

2.   How can Mary overcome these communication barriers?

18 - 2 APPLICATION CASE

CONTINGENCY FACTORS IN DELEGATION

For each of the situations below, decide if the manager should delegate authority or centralize authority. Explain your reasoning. (Hint: Identify the important contingency factors for each situation to make your decision about the appropriateness of delegation.)

1. A large organization makes and sells complex electronic equipment. Should the engineering manager delegate product design improvements for an existing product to product engineers? (The product engineers are already familiar with the product.)

2. A small advertising agency has workers who have good relationships and special expertise in advertising techniques. Should the company president delegate authority over projects to lower level advertising specialists?

3. A small manufacturing company has workers who are unskilled, and work at routine jobs. Should the manufacturing director delegate decision-making authority?

4. A large sports equipment company must decide if it wants to invest in development of a new type of weight training equipment. The initial investment is $400,000. Should the Research and Development Director delegate this decision to staff members in R & D?

5. A large finance service firm has a group of well-trained workers who complete relatively simple tasks. However, the managers do not have much confidence in the worker's abilities to direct themselves. Should the manager delegate decision-making authority that will allow lower level managers to make loan application approval decisions?

18 - 3 APPLICATION CASE

RESOLVING CONFLICT

It was George's first day on the job. George was critical of his work group after just a few short hours of working with them. He considered his fellow workers lazy and inefficient. Being a hard worker, George found their frequent breaks in production, their practical jokes, and their lack of concern for quality to be annoying. On the third day of George's employment, Tom, a fellow worker, came to him and in a friendly manner said, "Look buddy, you keep working your head off and it will make it tough for every one. Slow down. The work will be here tomorrow. You don't want management to raise our production quotas." Tom insisted that he was speaking for the whole group who felt that George looked down on them, and that George was making it hard on everyone. After this discussion, George noticed that the work group seemed to be giving him the cold shoulder. That began a feud that lasted for months. Tom became the target of George's anger and Tom responded in kind. In time, George's performance began to slip and his absence record became unfavorable. This conflict seemed to have a negative effect on the entire production group.

1.   How might the supervisor solve the conflict between Tom and George? (Choose 3 methods for resolving conflict and explain how they would be implemented and the likely consequences that would result.)

2. Which method do you think is most appropriate for solving this conflict? Explain.

Chapter 19

Foundations of Control

CHAPTER OUTLINE	CORRESPONDING LEARNING OBJECTIVES
I. What is Control?	1. Define control.
II. The Importance of Control	2. Explain why control is important.
III. The Control Process	3. Describe the control process.
A. Measuring	
1. How We Measure	
2. What We Measure	
B. Comparing	
C. Taking Managerial Action	
1. Correct Actual Performance	
2. Revise the Standard	
D. Summary	
IV. Types of Control	4. Distinguish between the three types of control.
A. Feedforward Control	
B. Concurrent Control	
C. Feedback Control	
V. The Focus of Control	5. Define the factors that managers can control.
A. People	
B. Finances	
C. Operations	

CHAPTER OUTLINE	CORRESPONDING LEARNING OBJECTIVES

D. Information

E. Organization Performance

6. Contrast the organizational goals approach and the systems approach to organizational effectiveness.

    1. The Organizational Goals Approach

    2. The Systems Approach

    3. The Strategic Constituencies Approach

7. Explain the strategic constituencies approach to organizational effectiveness.

VI. Qualities of an Effective Control System

8. Describe the qualities of an effective control system.

VII. The Dysfunctional Side of Controls

9. Explain how controls can become dysfunctional.

CHAPTER OVERVIEW

Control is the process of monitoring activities to ensure they are being accomplished as planned and correcting any significant deviations in planned versus actual performance. The control process consists of three distinct steps:

1. Measuring actual performance - Managers usually measure actual performance using a combination of the following sources of information: personal observation, statistical reports, oral reports, and written reports. Some criteria that are used by most organizations to assess performance include employee satisfaction, turnover, absenteeism, and budgets. However, it is difficult to measure some job activities in quantifiable terms. In this case, managers can break the job down into objective segments that allow for measurement.

2. Comparing actual performance against a standard - A manager must determine the acceptable range of variation in performance because it is highly unlikely that performance meets the standard exactly. The manager must decide how much of a deviation from the standard is cause for concern.

3. Taking managerial action to correct deviations or inadequate standards - A manager has three options in regard to corrective action. He/she can do nothing, correct actual performance, or revise the standard. If a manager determines that action is needed to allow for better performance, he/she can take immediate corrective action or basic corrective action. Immediate corrective action is correcting an activity right now in order to get things back on track.

Basic corrective action is determining how and why performance has deviated and correcting the source of deviation. Immediate corrective action is a short-term approach, while basic corrective action is a more permanent approach to solving the performance problem. Sometimes performance is not up to standards because a standard was incorrectly set. If this is the case, managers would choose to take corrective action by changing the standard.

Three types of controls that managers might use include the following:

1. Feedforward control is control that prevents anticipated problems. This approach to control is desired by managers because it allows for correction before a mistake has occurred. However, these controls require timely and accurate information that is often difficult to develop.

2. Concurrent control is control that occurs while an activity is in progress. The best known form of concurrent control is direct supervision.

3. Feedback control is control imposed after an action has occurred. The major problem with this method of control is that when the manager finds out there is a problem, the damage is already done. Feedback has two advantages over the other methods of control: it provides managers with information on how effective its planning effort was and it can enhance an employee's motivation.

Most control efforts are directed at one of five areas in the organization: people, finances, operations, information, and organizational performance. Example performance measures for each of the areas of control are listed below.

1. People - performance evaluation process

2. Finances - profits, budgets, financial ratios, and financial statements

3. Operations - efficiency, quality, well-maintained equipment

4. Information - management information system that provides the right data to the right person when he/she needs it

5. Organization Performance - Three approaches to measuring organizational effectiveness are the organizational goals approach, the systems approach, and the strategic constituencies approach. The goal approach is appraising an organization's effectiveness according to whether it accomplished its goals. The systems approach is appraising an organization's effectiveness in terms of both means and ends. The strategic constituencies approach is appraising an organization's effectiveness according to how well the organization satisfies the demands of its key constituencies.

The following characteristics should make a control system more effective:

1. accuracy
2. timeliness
3. economy
4. flexibility
5. understandability
6. reasonable criteria
7. strategic placement

8. emphasis on the exception
9. multiple criteria
10. corrective action

No control system is perfect. If controls become too inflexible or too unreasonable, the performance of the organization can suffer. If this happens, instead of the organization running the controls, the controls run the organization. Managers must be careful in development and implementation of controls to design in flexibility.

KEY TERMS AND DEFINITIONS

1. control - The process of monitoring activities to ensure they are being accomplished as planned and of correcting any significant deviations.

2. control process - The process of measuring actual performance, comparing it against a standard, and taking managerial action to correct deviations or inadequate standards.

3. range of variation - The acceptable parameters of variance between actual performance and the standard.

4. immediate corrective action - Correcting an activity at once in order to get performance back on track.

5. basic corrective action - Determining how and why performance has deviated and correcting the source of deviation.

6. feedforward control - Control that prevents anticipated problems.

7. concurrent control - Control that occurs while an activity is in progress.

8. feedback control - Control imposed after an action has occurred.

9. organizational goals approach - Appraising an organization's effectiveness according to whether it accomplishes its goals.

10. systems approach to organizational effectiveness - Appraising an organization's effectiveness in terms of both means and ends.

11. strategic constituencies approach - Appraising an organization's effectiveness according to how well the organization satisfies the demands of its key constituencies.

TRUE/FALSE QUESTIONS

1. T F All managers should be involved in the control function even if their units are performing as planned.

2.   T   F   Managers can effectively carry out most control activities in the organization by personally observing the activity.

3.   T   F   A disadvantage of statistical reports as a method of control measurement is that these reports provide limited information about an activity.

4.   T   F   The performance of some activities is difficult to measure in quantifiable terms.

5.   T   F   Subjective measures of performance are limited, but they are better than having no standards for control.

6.   T   F   Any deviation from the plan needs corrective attention.

7.   T   F   A manager takes basic corrective action by determining how and why the performance deviation occurred and correcting the source of the deviation.

8.   T   F   "Putting out fires" describes the basic corrective action approach to control.

9.   T   F   Feedback controls are desirable because they allow management to prevent problems rather than cure them later.

10.   T   F   Direct supervision is the best known form of concurrent control.

11.   T   F   Feedforward control provides information that will help employees know how well they have performed.

12.   T   F   Assessing effectiveness by determining if goals have been achieved is the systems approach.

13.   T   F   The main advantage of the goal approach for measuring effectiveness is that it discourages management from looking for immediate results at the expense of future success.

14.   T   F   The strategic constituencies approach for measuring effectiveness is fairly easy for managers to implement.

15.   T   F   An effective control system not only indicates when a significant deviation from standard occurs, but also suggests what action should be taken to correct the deviation.

16.   T   F   The greater the degree of decentralization, the more managers need feedback on the performance of subordinates' decision making.

17.   T   F   Extensive controls are likely to be implemented if an error would be highly damaging to the organization.

MULTIPLE CHOICE QUESTIONS

18. Which is not true for control?

    a. Control is the final link in the functional chain of activities.
    b. All managers should be involved in control activities.
    c. Control is not important if plans are well conceived.
    d. Control is a process of measuring actual performance, comparing actual against a standard, and taking corrective action.

19. This method for measuring performance allows managers to pick up nonverbal cues:

    a. statistical reports
    b. personal observation
    c. written reports
    d. oral reports

20. Having documents available for later reference is no longer a disadvantage of this method for measuring performance:

    a. statistical reports
    b. personal observation
    c. written reports
    d. oral reports

21. Graphs, bar charts, and nonverbal displays are examples for this method of measuring performance:

    a. statistical reports
    b. personal observation
    c. written reports
    d. oral reports

22. Which is not true for subjective measures of performance?

    a. Subjective measures have significant limitations.
    b. Subjective measures are preferable to objective measures for performance.
    c. Subjective measures are better than having no standard at all.
    d. Often subjective measures can be broken down into objective parts.

23. A manager changes the planned sales level for the work group from 10,000 to 8,000 units. This is an example of:

    a. basic corrective action
    b. do nothing
    c. immediate corrective action
    d. revising the standard

24. Since salespersons are not achieving expectations, a manager cuts the price by 30 % hoping to increase sales:

   a. basic corrective action
   b. do nothing
   c. immediate corrective action
   d. revising the standard

25. A manager finds that salespersons are not achieving their quotas, but the quotas are within the range of deviation:

   a. basic corrective action
   b. do nothing
   c. immediate corrective action
   d. revising the standard

26. Since salespersons are not achieving expectations, a manager traces the problem to use of incorrect distribution channels and the manager changes the distribution channel:

   a. basic corrective action
   b. do nothing
   c. immediate corrective action
   d. revising the standard

27. This type of control is used to prevent anticipated problems:

   a. feedforward control
   b. basic control
   c. concurrent control
   d. feedback control

28. This type of control occurs while an activity is in progress:

   a. feedforward control
   b. basic control
   c. concurrent control
   d. feedback control

29. This type of control is imposed after an action has occurred:

   a. feedforward control
   b. basic control
   c. concurrent control
   d. feedback control

30. This is the most desirable type of control:

   a. feedforward control
   b. basic control
   c. concurrent control
   d. feedback control

31. The major disadvantage of this type of control is that by the time managers know there is a deviation, the damage has been done:

    a. feedforward control
    b. basic control
    c. concurrent control
    d. feedback control

32. Direct supervision is an example for this type of control:

    a. feedforward control
    b. basic control
    c. concurrent control
    d. feedback control

33. This type of control has two advantages over the other types of control-- managers have meaningful information on how effective planning was and employee motivation usually improves:

    a. feedforward control
    b. basic control
    c. concurrent control
    d. feedback control

34. What do managers control?

    a. people and information
    b. finances
    c. operations
    d. all of the above

35. If an organization achieves desired sales and profit levels it is effective. This is an example for which approach to measuring effectiveness?

    a. systems approach
    b. strategic constituencies approach
    c. organizational goals approach
    d. none of the above

36. If an organization satisfies managers, workers, stockholders, customers, and suppliers, the organization is effective. This is an example for which approach to measuring effectiveness?

    a. systems approach
    b. strategic constituencies approach
    c. organizational goals approach
    d. none of the above

37. An advantage of this approach is that management is discouraged from looking for immediate results at the expense of future success:

   a. systems approach
   b. strategic constituencies approach
   c. organizational goals approach
   d. none of the above

38. A disadvantage of this approach is that managers may tend to overlook the long-term health of the organization:

   a. systems approach
   b. strategic constituencies approach
   c. organizational goals approach
   d. none of the above

19 - 1 APPLICATION CASE

TYPES OF CONTROLS

Wilson's is an independent grocery store that operates in a large midwestern city. Because it cannot compete with national chains such as Kroger and Safeway, Wilson's has developed its own unique marketing niche. Wilson's prides itself on its "local home-town friendliness" and personal service to customers.

Recently, the owner of the store has had problems with his utility workers. These workers bag groceries, take groceries to customers cars, and stock shelves. Most of these utility workers are high school students who work part-time. Some specific problems with the utility workers include the following:

1. Many customers have reported that the utility workers are rude or discourteous.
2. Customers have also reported that utility workers have damaged items while depositing them in their vehicles.
3. There is a "no tipping" policy, but some utility workers have been encouraging customers to tip.
4. When there is slack time, utility workers are supposed to collect grocery carts from the parking lot and clean the store. Instead, these workers spend their slack time loafing.

According to the organization chart, the utility workers report directly to the store owner or the assistant manager, depending on the shift and day of the week. Since both the store owner and his assistant manager have broad responsibilities, it is impossible for them to closely observe the utility workers in action. The store owner believes that there must be a way to assure that the utility workers' behave in an appropriate manner.

1. List some specific FEEDFORWARD CONTROLS the store owner should use to control the utility workers.

2. List some specific CONCURRENT CONTROLS the store owner should use to control the utility workers.

3. List some specific FEEDBACK CONTROLS the store owner should use to control the utility workers.

19 - 2 APPLICATION CASE

DESIGNING AN EFFECTIVE CONTROL SYSTEM

Ten characteristics are listed in the textbook that make a control system more effective.

1.   Which of the ten characteristics are you using to effectively control your college degree process? Explain how you are using these characteristics. (Hint: Think about your plans to follow your degree plan and how you control scheduling, study time, work time, etc. so that you can achieve your plans.)

2. Which of the characteristics should you be using that you are not using? Explain how use of these characteristics would make your control of your college degree process more effective.

19 - 3 APPLICATION CASE

CONTROL PROCESS

A production manager for a large consumer product company is concerned about the productivity of his production line workers. He feels he needs to set up some controls to make sure that enough products are produced to fill orders. In addition, there is a problem with excessive absences of the production workers.

What advice would you give the production manager in regard to developing controls for productivity and for absenteeism? (Hint: Use the Control Process shown in Figure 19-2 in the text to answer this question.)

Chapter 20

Information Control Systems

CHAPTER OUTLINE	CORRESPONDING LEARNING OBJECTIVES
I. What is a Management Information System?	1. Explain the purpose of a management information system (MIS).
	2. Differentiate between data and information.
II. Linking Information and Organizational Communication	
A. Formal versus Informal Communication	
B. Direction of Communication Flow	3. Contrast the four directions in which communication can flow.
1. Downward	
2. Upward	
3. Lateral	
4. Diagonal	
C. Communication Networks	
1. Five Communication Networks	4. Identify five common communication networks.
2. Evaluation of Network Effectiveness	
3. An Informal Network: The Grapevine	
III. The Evolution of Management Information Systems	
A. Stage 1: Centralized Data Processing	
B. Stage 2: Management-Focused Data Processing	

CHAPTER OUTLINE	CORRESPONDING LEARNING OBJECTIVES
C. Stage 3: Decentralized End-User Computing	5. Compare centralized and end-user systems.
D. Stage 4: Interactive Networks	6. Explain the value of networking.
E. The Next Stage: Expert Systems and Cellular Communications	
IV. Debunking a Few Myths About MIS	
A. The Replacement Myth	
B. The "More is Better" Myth	7. Explain why more information is not always better.
C. The "New is Better" Myth	
V. Designing the MIS	8. Outline the key elements in designing an MIS.
A. Analyze the Decision System	
B. Analyze Information Requirements	
C. Aggregate the Decisions	
D. Design Information Processing	
VI. Implementing the MIS	
A. Pretest the System Before Installation	
B. Prepare Users with Proper Training	
C. Prepare for Resistance	
D. Get Users Involved	
E. Check for Security	
F. Build in Regular Reviews	

CHAPTER OUTLINE	CORRESPONDING LEARNING OBJECTIVES
VII. Using Information Systems to Gain a Competitive Advantage	9. Explain how an MIS can relate to an organization's strategy.
VIII. How MIS is Changing the Manager's Job	
A. Hands-On Involvement	
B. Decision-Making Capability	
C. Organization Design	
D. Power	10. Describe how an MIS changes power relationships in an organization.
IX. Organizational Communication: An MIS Update	11. Explain how MIS's are changing communication in organizations.
A. Patterns of Communication Flow Will Change	
B. Communication Overload Should Be Lessened	
C. Face-to-Face Communication Will Take on a More Symbolic Role	

CHAPTER OVERVIEW

A management information system (MIS) is a system that provides management with needed information on a regular basis. An information system can be manual or computer-based. The focus in this chapter is on computer-based information systems. An MIS system provides information to managers, not merely data. Information is analyzed and processed while data is defined as raw, unanalyzed facts.

Management Information Systems and communication are closely linked since communication of important information is the primary concern of MIS. Formal communication is communication that follows the authority chain of command or that is necessary to do a job. Informal communication is not approved by management and not defined by any structural hierarchy. Organizational communication can flow several ways in the organization:

1. Downward communication flows from a manager down the authority hierarchy. Communication can flow downward through face-to-face contact or through memos and other written correspondence.

2. Upward communication flows from subordinates to higher-level managers. The extent of upward communication depends on the culture and the amount of participation in decision-making.

3. Lateral communication is communication among members of work groups, among managers, or among any horizontally equivalent personnel. Lateral communication is sometimes needed to save time and to facilitate coordination. Sometimes these lateral relationships are formally sanctioned and sometimes they are informal.

4. Diagonal communication cuts across functions and levels in an organization. This method for communicating is sometimes necessary for speed and efficiency.

Organizational communications can be more fully explained by considering the networks or patterns of communication. There are five basic patterns of communication:

1. Chain network - Communication can move only upward and downward along the chain of command with one person answering to one other person.

2. Y network - Communication patterns follow the formal chain of command with more than one person answering to the manager.

3. Wheel network - Several workers report to a manager and there is no contact among the workers. All communication is channeled through the manager.

4. Circle network - Workers are allowed to interact with adjoining members, but no further.

5. All-channel network - Each member of the workgroup can communicate freely with other workers.

A manager should choose the network that will allow him/her to achieve the company's goals. No single network is best for all situations. If speed is important, the wheel and all-channel network are preferred. The chain, Y , and wheel score high on accuracy. The circle and all-channel networks promote high employee satisfaction. In addition to these formal networks, there is also an informal network for communication. There are several patterns for communicating informally. The cluster is the most popular pattern. The cluster pattern involves a few people who act as communicators on the grapevine. Managers can make use of the grapevine to send messages that are useful for achieving motivation or other work goals.

The evolution of MIS can be explained in four distinct stages.

1. Stage 1: Centralized Data Processing - 1954, the date when computers were first used in business, marks the beginning of MIS. During this time the MIS was generally involved in processing routine data for billing, payroll, and other clerical functions. Batch processing was used to process data. This means that data were stored and processed all at the same time.

2. Stage 2: Management-Focused Data Processing - The period between 1965 and 1979 saw centralized data processing expand by providing support information for management and operational activities. Organizations began to use real-time processing. This means that MIS was able to continuously update data as transactions occurred. Remote terminals were also introduced during this time.

3. Stage 3: Decentralized End-User Computing - During this stage, managers became the end-users and were responsible for information control. Personal computers became popular. Data systems departments evolved into information support centers. Instead of generating information for managers, MIS managers began helping managers become more effective end-users.

4. Stage 4: Interactive Networks - Networking is linking computers so that they can communicate with each other. The emphasis in this stage is on creating and implementing mechanisms to integrate end-users.

5. The Next Stage: Expert Systems and Cellular Communications - One important development for future MIS is expert systems. Expert systems are software programs that encode the relevant experience of a human expert. For example, managers are working on fully integrating production systems by using expert systems. Cellular modems are expanding the reach of computer networks. Wireless communications will make it possible to link people and their computers around the world.

There are several myths related to the use of computers and MIS:

1. The Replacement Myth - Computer systems do not replace other forms of communication.

2. The "More is Better" Myth - An increased quantity of information will not necessarily lead to improved decision-making. The manager can become overwhelmed with information. The value of the information is also important, not just information quantity. A manager who has the relevant data might not understand how it fits together. In short, too much information can hinder decision-making.

3. The "New is Better" Myth - It is not necessary to have the latest in technology in order to be an effective organization.

In designing an MIS system, several steps must be taken. Management should analyze the decision system. This means that they should make sure that decisions are made by the right person, at the right level, and in the right department of the organization. Information requirements must also be analyzed. Management must determine the exact information required to effectively make management decisions. After needs for information have been determined, management should locate "overlap" in the decision processes of the functional departments. At this point, outside consultants are usually brought in to develop the actual system for collecting, storing, transmitting, and retrieving information.

After the MIS plan has been designed, it must be implemented by managers. The following steps are important in the implementation of MIS:

1. Pretest the system before installation.
2. Prepare users with proper training.
3. Prepare for resistance.
4. Get users involved.
5. Check for security.
6. Build in regular reviews.

The use of MIS has changed the manager's job. Today's managers cannot avoid using computers. Decisions can be made more quickly and more information is available for making decisions. Managers can often handle more subordinates because computer control substitutes for some personal control. MIS changes the status hierarchy in an organization. For example, middle managers do not have as much power now because they no longer have to communicate the information from top managers to lower level managers.

MIS has also changed the way people in organizations communicate. MIS permits more lateral and diagonal communication on a formal basis. Communication overload should become less of a problem because information systems can filter information for importance. In addition, face-to-face communication becomes important for symbolic significance, not for communication of job assignments.

KEY TERMS AND DEFINITIONS

1. management information systems (MIS) - A system that provides management with needed information on a regular basis.

2. data - Raw, unanalyzed facts.

3. information - Analyzed and processed data.

4. formal communication - Communication that follows the authority chain of command or that is necessary to do a job.

5. informal communication - Communication that is not approved by management and not defined by any structural hierarchy.

6. downward communication - Communication that flows from a manager down the authority hierarchy.

7. upward communication - Communication that flows from subordinates to higher-level managers.

8. lateral communication - Communication among any horizontally equivalent personnel.

9. diagonal communication - Communication that cuts across functions and levels in an organization.

10. communication networks - Vertical and horizontal communication patterns.

11. grapevine - The informal communication network.

12. batch processing - Storing data and processing them all at the same time.

13. real-time processing - The continuous updating of data as transactions occur.

14. end-user - The person who uses information and assumes responsibility for its control.

15. data base management - A computerized system that allows the user to organize, get at easily, ad select and review a precise set of data from a larger base of data.

16. word processing - Software packages that allow users to write, change, edit, revise, delete, or print letters, reports, and manuscripts.

17. spreadsheets - Software packages that allow users to turn a computer's memory into a large worksheet in which data and formulas can be entered to perform a variety of calculations.

18. networking - Linking computers so that they can communicate with each other.

19. expert systems - Software programs that encode the relevant experience of a human expert.

TRUE/FALSE QUESTIONS

1. T F The term "system" in MIS implies order, arrangement, and purpose.

2. T F Information is raw, unanalyzed facts.

3. T F The MIS system must be regularly modified and updated if it is to give the organization a sustainable, competitive advantage.

4. T F Lateral communication is used to inform, direct, coordinate, and evaluate subordinates.

5. T F In a highly authoritative environment, upward communication still takes place, but it is limited to the managerial ranks and to providing control information to upper management.

6. T F The circle network does not allow work group members to interact.

7. T F If speed of communication is important, the circle and chain networks are preferred.

8. T F The grapevine is an informal network for communication.

9. T F The first computer was installed for business application in 1954.

10. T F It wasn't until stage two of the evolution of MIS that batch processing was used in organizations.

11. T F Since managers have become end-users, data processing professionals have had to switch from providing managers with information to helping them get their own information.

12. T F Expert systems are computer links that allow managers to communicate through two or more computers.

13. T F More information is always better.

14. T F An MIS will not replace other, less formal means of gaining information about organizational activities.

15. T F The MIS must be tailored to meet the varying needs of different functional managers.

16. T F MIS does not impact the decision making process.

MULTIPLE CHOICE QUESTIONS

17. Which is not true for an MIS?

    a. MIS is a system that provides management with needed information on a regular basis.
    b. The MIS provides a system of order, arrangement, and purpose.
    c. MIS is a computer based system.
    d. MIS focuses on providing management with information, not just data.

18. Informal communication is:

    a. not defined by a structural hierarchy
    b. another term for the "grapevine"
    c. is communication that is not approved by management
    d. all of the above

19. Communication among members of work groups, among managers, or among any horizontally equivalent persons:

    a. downward communication
    b. upward communication
    c. lateral communication
    d. diagonal communication

20. Communication that flows from a manager through the chain of command to lower level workers:

    a. downward communication
    b. upward communication
    c. lateral communication
    d. diagonal communication

21. Communication that cuts across functions and levels in the organization:

    a. downward communication
    b. upward communication
    c. lateral communication
    d. diagonal communication

22. Communication that flows from subordinates to higher level managers:

    a. downward communication
    b. upward communication
    c. lateral communication
    d. diagonal communication

23. A communication network that allows members to interact with an adjoining member, but no further:

    a. chain
    b. Y
    c. wheel
    d. circle

24. A communication network that has direct line authority relationships with no deviation:

    a. chain
    b. Y
    c. wheel
    d. circle

25. This communication network is used when fast communication is needed and there is a definite leader:

    a. chain
    b. Y
    c. wheel
    d. circle

26. This communication network is used when high accuracy and moderate speed are needed and there is a leader with some power:

    a. chain
    b. Y
    c. wheel
    d. circle

27. This communication network promotes high employee satisfaction:

    a. chain
    b. Y
    c. wheel
    d. circle

28. The most popular grapevine pattern:

   a. single strand
   b. cluster
   c. gossip
   d. probability

29. Introduction of remote terminals that provided access to a computer's central processing unit from external locations occurred during this stage:

   a. Stage 1: Centralized Data Processing
   b. Stage 2: Management-Focused Data Processing
   c. Stage 3: Decentralized End-User Computing
   d. Stage 4: Interactive Networks

30. During this stage of MIS evolution, managers became end-users and personal computers became popular:

   a. Stage 1: Centralized Data Processing
   b. Stage 2: Management-Focused Data Processing
   c. Stage 3: Decentralized End-User Computing
   d. Stage 4: Interactive Networks

31. During this stage of MIS evolution, the first computer was installed for business use:

   a. Stage 1: Centralize Data Processing
   b. Stage 2: Management-Focused Data Processing
   c. Stage 3: Decentralized End-User Computing
   d. Stage 4: Interactive Networks

32. During this stage of MIS evolution, the emphasis was creating and implementing mechanisms to integrate end-users:

   a. Stage 1: Centralized Data Processing
   b. Stage 2: Management-Focused Data Processing
   c. Stage 3: Decentralized End-User Computing
   d. Stage 4: Interactive Networks

33. During this stage of MIS evolution, data systems departments evolved into information support centers:

   a. Stage 1: Centralized Data Processing
   b. Stage 2: Management-Focused Data Processing
   c. Stage 3: Decentralized End-User Computing
   d. Stage 4: Interactive Networks

34. During this stage of MIS evolution, the computer was used primarily for payroll and billing functions:

   a. Stage 1: Centralized Data Processing
   b. Stage 2: Management-Focused Data Processing
   c. Stage 3: Decentralized End-User Computing
   d. Stage 4: Interactive Networks

35. This stage of MIS evolution is characterized by the use of batch systems:

    a. Stage 1: Centralized Data Processing
    b. Stage 2: Management-Focused Data Processing
    c. Stage 3: Decentralized End-User Computing
    d. Stage 4: Interactive Networks

36. During this stage of MIS evolution, networks were developed so that managers could communicate with each other through computers:

    a. Stage 1: Centralized Data Processing
    b. Stage 2: Management-Focused Data Processing
    c. Stage 3: Decentralized End-User Computing
    d. Stage 4: Interactive Networks

37. During this stage of MIS evolution, real-time processing was first used:

    a. Stage 1: Centralized Data Processing
    b. Stage 2: Management-Focused Data Processing
    c. Stage 3: Decentralized End-User Computing
    d. Stage 4: Interactive Networks

38. A type of software package that allows managers to transfer data to and from each other; messages are transferred through computer instead of telephone:

    a. spreadsheets
    b. data base management
    c. communication
    d. graphics

39. A type of software package that allows the end-user to organize, get at easily, and select and review a precise set of data from a larger base of data:

    a. spreadsheets
    b. data base management
    c. communication
    d. graphics

40. A type of software package that allows the user to turn computer memory into a large worksheet and to develop a method for asking "what-if" questions and seeing results through calculations made by computer:

    a. spreadsheets
    b. data base management
    c. communication
    d. graphics

41. Which is not true for expert systems?

    a. Expert systems are based on quantitative reasoning.
    b. An expert system is the application of artificial intelligence to managerial decision-making.
    c. An expert system is a software program that is used to encode the relevant experience of a human expert and allow a system to act like that expert in analyzing and solving unstructured problems.
    d. Expert systems are based on qualitative reasoning.

42. Which is a myth about MIS?

    a. More information is not always better.
    b. Managers do not necessarily need the latest technology.
    c. Managers need the latest technology.
    d. Formal MIS will not replace other information sources.

20 - 1 APPLICATION CASE

DESIGNING THE MANAGEMENT INFORMATION SYSTEM

You are the owner of a small advertising firm. Recently you purchased computer equipment for the company with hopes that you can improve your company's management of information.

The company employs fifteen workers: 6 are artists, 3 are salespersons, 2 are managers, 2 are secretaries, and 2 are print shop workers. The advertising company solicits work from major advertisers (retail, manufacturing, and service organizations). Generally, the advertising firm develops print ads for newspapers and magazines and sometimes for billboards. New business is generated in two ways: salespersons solicit new business and sometimes new clients phone the company themselves. In addition to new customers, the company maintains a continuing client list of 75 advertisers. Most of these current clients have ads that were developed from scratch by the firm and are then used over a period of time.

The two secretaries try to keep up with billing, client information, addresses for possible clients, deadlines for advertising campaign completions, schedules for printing, examples of past work done by the company for each client, etc.

1.   Identify the management decisions for which information is needed.

2.   What information is needed to make the decisions listed in question 1 above?

3. Identify areas where there is overlap in the decisions that are being made so that you can help the company reduce duplication.

4. What information did you learn from your analysis that you want to make sure the consultants who develop the MIS know?

5. Do you think an MIS will help the advertising firm better manage its information? Explain.

20 - 2 APPLICATION CASE

HOW MIS IS CHANGING THE MANAGER'S JOB

Use the situation for the advertising firm discussed in Application Case 20 - 1 to answer these questions. (USE YOUR IMAGINATION!!)

1.   Do you think the structure of the company will change as a result of an MIS? Explain.

2.   Do you think the supervisor's job will change as a result of the MIS? Explain.

3. Do you think the decision-making capabilities of the company will change as a result of the MIS? Explain.

20 - 3 APPLICATION CASE

NEW ISSUES RELATED TO COMPUTER USE

The widespread use of computers has opened up new controversial areas that will have a definite impact on our lives. What are the advantages and disadvantages of the use of the new technology developments listed below?

1.   The home doubling as a workplace (electronic mail and interactive computers)

2.   The increasing availability of networks

3. Expert systems (artificial intelligence)

4. Cellular Technology (wireless communication)

Chapter 21

Operations Management

CHAPTER OUTLINE	CORRESPONDING LEARNING OBJECTIVES
B. Purchasing Control	
1. Building Close Links with Suppliers	
2. Economic Order Quantity Model	6. Explain how to determine the most economic order quantity.
3. Inventory Ordering Systems	
C. Maintenance Control	
	7. Identify the three approaches to maintenance control.
D. Quality Control	
VII. Current Issues in Operations Management	
A. Technology and Product Development	
B. Implementing TQM Successfully	8. Explain how contingency factors affect the implementation of TQM.
C. Reducing Inventories	9. Discuss the advantages and potential problems of just-in-time inventory systems.
D. Flexibility as a Competitive Advantage	10. Explain how flexible manufacturing systems could give an organization a competitive advantage.
E. Speed as a Competitive Advantage	

CHAPTER OVERVIEW

Operations management refers to the design, operation, and control of the transformation process that converts resources into finished goods and services. Every organization produces something and even every functional area in the organization produces something. For example, hospitals produce medical services, airlines produce transportation services, manufacturing companies produce products, and accounting produces effective accounting procedures.

378

Productivity is a major goal for most organizations. Productivity is the overall output of goods and services produced, divided by the inputs needed to generate that output. Organizations can improve their productivity by focusing on people and on operations variables. To improve through people, managers can focus on participative decision making, management by objectives, team-based work groups, and equitable pay systems. Some operational variables that managers work with to improve productivity include: capacity planning, process planning, facilities location planning, and facilities layout planning.

Operations management includes both manufacturing and service organizations. The number of service organizations in the U.S. continues to increase. Service organizations produce nonphysical outputs such as educational, medical, and transportation services that are intangible, cannot be stored in inventory, and incorporate the customer or client in the actual production process. Deindustrialization is taking place among advanced economies. Deindustrialization is the conversion of an economy from dominance by manufacturing to dominance by service-oriented businesses. Productivity is an important issue for services, but making productivity improvements in service organizations is more difficult than making productivity improvements in manufacturing. This is true because fewer factors in services are under management's control.

Some management scholars argue that strategy should have more of a "manufacturing focus". According to Wickham Skinner, too many important operations decisions have been relegated to lower-level managers in the past. He suggests that the organization's overall strategy should reflect its manufacturing capabilities and limitations and should include operations objectives and strategies.

Four key planning decisions for operations include: capacity, location, process, and layout.

1. Capacity Planning is assessing an operating system's ability to produce a desired number of output units for each type of product during a given time period. The first step in capacity planning is to forecast sales demand.

2. Facilities Location Planning is the design and location of an operations facility. Several factors will influence the location decision: availability of labor skills, labor costs, energy costs, proximity to suppliers or customers, etc.

3. Process Planning is determining how a product or service will be produced. Deciding on the best combinations of processes in terms of costs, quality, labor efficiency, and similar considerations is difficult because the decisions are intertwined.

4. Facilities Layout Planning is assessing and selecting among alternative layout options for equipment and work stations. The objective of layout planning is to find a physical arrangement that will best facilitate production efficiency and that is also appealing to employees. Options for layout include: process layout, product layout, and fixed-position layout. A process layout is arranging manufacturing components together according to similarity of function. A product layout is arranging manufacturing components according to the progressive steps by which a product is made. Fixed-position layout is a manufacturing layout in which the product stays in place while tools, equipment, and human skills are brought to it.

After design decisions have been made, managers are concerned with tactical operations decisions. Tactical operations decisions include the following:

1. Aggregate Planning is planning overall production activities and their associated operating resources. The aggregate plan sets inventory levels and production rates and estimates the size of the total operation's labor force on a monthly basis.

2. Master Scheduling is a schedule that specifies quantity and type of items to be produced; how, when, and where they should be produced; labor force levels; and inventory. The master schedule breaks the aggregate plan into detailed plans for each of the products or services provided by the company.

3. Material Requirements Planning is a system that dissects products into the materials and parts necessary for purchasing, inventorying, and priority-planning purposes.

The elements of the operations system must be monitored. Control is important for costs, purchasing, maintenance, and quality.

1. Cost Control - Many companies use a cost center approach. A cost center is a unit in which managers are held responsible for all associated costs. Generally, the costs for organizations are direct costs (incurred in proportion to the output of a particular good or service). Sometimes a company also incurs indirect costs (costs that are largely unaffected by changes in output). Top managers must identify where the control lies and hold lower-level managers accountable for costs under their control.

2. Purchasing Control - One method for controlling purchasing is to build close links with suppliers. Math models can also be used to determine the "best" number of units to order. The Economic Order Quantity (EOQ) Model is a technique for balancing purchasing, ordering, carrying, and stockout costs to derive the optimum quantity for a purchase order. In addition the these methods, managers must choose a reorder schedule such as fixed-point, fixed-interval, or ABC system. The fixed-point reordering system is a system that "flags" the fact that inventory needs to be replenished when it reaches a certain level. The fixed-interval reordering system is a system that uses time as the determining factor for reviewing and reordering inventory items. The ABC system is a priority system for monitoring inventory items.

3. Maintenance Control - If an organization is to provide products and services when they are needed, consideration must be given to maintaining equipment. There are three approaches to maintenance control. Preventive maintenance is maintenance performed before a breakdown occurs. Remedial maintenance is maintenance that calls for the overhaul, replacement, or repair of equipment when it breaks down. Conditional maintenance is maintenance that calls for an overhaul or repair in response to an inspection. Maintenance control should also be considered when equipment is acquired for the company. For example, equipment that has fewer parts will have fewer things that can go wrong.

4. Quality Control - There are two categories of statistical tests that are used for monitoring quality. Acceptance sampling is a procedure in which a sample is taken and a decision to accept or reject a whole lot is based on a calculation of sample risk error. Process control refers to sampling that is done during the

transformation process to determine whether the process itself is under control. The examination of items will be either a count (attribute sampling) or a measure (variable sampling).

Several current issues are of concern to the operations manager. Some of these are explained below.

1. Computer-integrated Manufacturing (CIM) combines the organization's strategic business plan and manufacturing plan with state-of-the-art computer applications. The technologies of computer-aided design (CAD) and computer-aided manufacturing (CAM) are typically the basis for CIM. CIM is not fully operational, but in the future a CIM should allow for a single change in a computer program to immediately realign the manufacturing process.

2. Total Quality Management (TQM) concepts such as teams, benchmarking, training, and employee empowerment can be used by companies to improve overall service to customers.

3. Just-in-Time (JIT) is a system in which inventory items arrive at the time they are needed in the production process instead of being stored in stock. In Japan, these JIT systems are called kanban. JIT is not appropriate for every company. In those companies that can use JIT, it can help management reduce inventory costs.

4. Flexible Manufacturing Systems are systems in which custom-made products can be mass produced by means of computer-aided design, engineering, and manufacturing. By integrating these operations activities, management can produce low-volume, custom products at a cost comparable to what had been possible only through mass production.

KEY TERMS AND DEFINITIONS

1. operations management - The design, operation, and control of the transformation process that converts resources into finished goods and services.

2. productivity - The overall output of goods and services produced, divided by the inputs needed to generate that output.

3. manufacturing organizations - Organizations that produce physical goods such as steel, automobiles, textiles, and farm machinery.

4. service organizations - Organizations that produce non-physical outputs such as educational, medical, and transportation services that are intangible, can't be stored in inventory, and incorporate the customer or client in the actual production process.

5. deindustrialization - The conversion of an economy from dominance by manufacturing to dominance by service-oriented businesses.

6. capacity planning - Assessing an operating system's ability to produce a desired number of output units for each type of product during a given time period.

7. facilities location planning - The design and location of an operations facility.

8. process planning - Determining how a product or service will be produced.

9. facilities layout planning - Assessing and selecting among alternative layout options for equipment and work stations.

10. process layout - Arranging manufacturing components together according to similarity of function.

11. product layout - Arranging manufacturing components according to the progressive steps by which a product is made.

12. fixed-position layout - A manufacturing layout in which the product stays in place while tools, equipment, and human skills are brought to it.

13. aggregate planning - Planning overall production activities and their associated operating resources.

14. master schedule - A schedule that specifies quantity and type of items to be produced; how, when, and where they should be produced; labor force levels; and inventory.

15. material requirements planning (MRP) - A system that dissects products into the materials and parts necessary for purchasing, inventorying, and priority-planning purposes.

16. cost center - A unit in which managers are held responsible for all associated costs.

17. direct costs - Costs incurred in proportion to the output of a particular good or service.

18. indirect costs - Costs that are largely unaffected by changes in output.

19. economic order quantity model (EOQ) - A technique for balancing purchases, ordering, carrying, and stockout costs to derive the optimum quantity for a purchase order.

20. fixed-point reordering system - A system that "flags" the fact that inventory needs to be replenished when it reaches a certain level.

21. fixed-interval reordering - A system that uses time as the determining factor for reviewing and reordering inventory items.

22. ABC system - A priority system for monitoring inventory items.

23. preventive maintenance - Maintenance performed before a breakdown occurs.

24. remedial maintenance - Maintenance that calls for the overhaul, replacement, or repair of equipment when it breaks down.

25. conditional maintenance - Maintenance that calls for an overhaul or repair in response to an inspection.

26. acceptance sampling - A quality control procedure in which a sample is taken and a decision to accept or reject a whole lot is based on a calculation of sample risk error.

27. process control - A quality control procedure in which sampling is done during the transformation process to determine whether the process itself is under control.

28. attribute sampling - A quality control technique that classifies items as acceptable or unacceptable on the basis of some variable.

29. variable sampling - A quality control technique in which a measurement is taken to determine how much an item varies from the standard.

30. computer-integrated manufacturing (CIM) - Combines the organization's strategic business plan and manufacturing plan with state-of-the-art computer applications.

31. Just-in-Time inventory system (JIT) - A system in which inventory items arrive when they are needed in the production process instead of being stored in stock.

32. kanban - The Japanese name for a just-in-time inventory system.

33. flexible manufacturing systems - Systems in which custom-made products can be mass produced by means of computer-aided design, engineering, and manufacturing.

TRUE/FALSE QUESTIONS

1. T F Every organization has an operations system that creates value by transforming inputs into outputs.

2. T F To improve productivity, management needs to focus on operations variables, not people.

3. T F Today in the U.S. manufacturing organizations dominate.

4. T F Deindustrialization is the conversion of an economy from dominance by manufacturing to dominance by service-oriented businesses.

5. T F It is harder to improve productivity in a manufacturing organization than a service organization because fewer factors are under management's control.

6. T F Four key decisions (capacity, location, process, and layout) provide the long-term strategic direction for operations planning.

7. T F A master schedule is a type of long-term plan.

8. T F Capacity planning is determining how a product or service will be produced.

9. T F A process layout is arranging manufacturing components according to the progressive steps by which a product is made.

10. T F Fixed-position layout is the logical layout choice for airplane production.

11. T F Material requirements planning is planning overall production activities and their associated operating resources.

12. T F A rapidly growing trend in manufacturing is turning suppliers into partners.

13. T F The objective of EOQ is to balance the costs associated with inventories: carrying costs, purchasing costs, stockout costs, and ordering costs.

14. T F A fixed-interval reordering system is a system that "flags" the fact that inventory needs to be replenished when it reaches a certain level.

15. T F Quality should be designed into the product in the manufacturing process.

16. T F Computer-aided manufacturing (CAM) and computer-aided design (CAD) are typically the basis for computer integrated manufacturing (CIM).

MULTIPLE CHOICE QUESTIONS

17. Which is not true for operations management?

    a. Inputs in operations systems include people, capital, equipment, and materials.
    b. Every organization needs an operations management system.
    c. Operations management refers to the design, operation, and control of raw materials into finished goods and services.
    d. Service organizations are not concerned with operations management.

18. Which is not true for productivity?

    a. Productivity is outputs divided by inputs needed to generate the output.
    b. Productivity can be improved by dealing with larger numbers of suppliers.
    c. For individual companies, increased productivity means a more competitive cost structure.
    d. Productivity is a composite of people and operations variables.

19. These organizations dominate the United States:

    a. manufacturing
    b. service
    c. industrialization
    d. operations

20. An example is a company that produces consumer products:

    a. manufacturing
    b. service
    c. deindustrialization
    d. operations management

21. According to Wickham Skinner, too many production decisions have been relegated to lower-level managers because:

    a. people who work in day-to-day activities should be in control
    b. there has not been a manufacturing focus to strategy for several years
    c. top managers do not understand production
    d. strategic planning is not that important

22. This type of planning begins with a forecast of sales demand:

    a. capacity planning
    b. facilities location planning
    c. process planning
    d. facilities layout planning

23. Some options for this type of planning are process, product, and fixed-position:

    a. capacity planning
    b. facilities location planning
    c. process planning
    d. facilities layout planning

24. Considerations for this type of planning include shipping costs, availability of labor skills, and energy costs:

    a. capacity planning
    b. facilities location planning
    c. process planning
    d. facilities layout planning

25. Companies that build ships usually use this type of layout:

    a. process layout
    b. product layout
    c. fixed-position layout
    d. none of the above

26. A company makes shirts and has departments for cutting, sewing sleeves, sewing fronts/backs, buttons, and pressing. Each department works on batches of items so that the shirts are not made in any particular order, but each department is kept busy each day producing its component part of the shirt. What kind of layout does the company use?

    a. process layout
    b. product layout
    c. fixed-position layout
    d. none of the above

27. An example for this layout is an assembly line production of cassette players:

    a. process layout
    b. product layout
    c. fixed-position layout
    d. none of the above

28. This plan specifies the quantity and type of each item to be produced for a period of time:

    a. aggregate planning
    b. master scheduling
    c. material requirements planning
    d. capacity planning

29. A system that dissects products into the materials and parts necessary for purchasing, inventory, and priority planning purposes:

    a. aggregate planning
    b. master scheduling
    c. material requirements planning
    d. capacity planning

30. During this type of planning, the best overall production rate to adopt and the overall number of workers needed for a specific time period are determined:

    a. aggregate planning
    b. master scheduling
    c. material requirements planning
    d. capacity planning

31. Cost center managers are held responsible for these costs in their units:

    a. direct costs
    b. indirect costs
    c. both direct and indirect costs
    d. neither direct nor indirect costs

32. What can managers do to facilitate control of inputs?

    a. Managers can gather data about quality of supplies and their compatibility with operations processes.
    b. Managers can gather information on dates that supplies arrive and their condition on arrival.
    c. Managers can obtain data on supplier price performance.
    d. All of the above activities will help managers control inputs.

33. A system that uses time as the determining factor for ordering inventory items:

    a. EOQ
    b. fixed-interval reordering system
    c. ABC system
    d. fixed-point reordering system

34. A priority system for monitoring inventory items:

    a. EOQ
    b. fixed-interval reordering system
    c. ABC system
    d. fixed-point reordering system

35. A technique for balancing purchasing, ordering, carrying, and stockout costs to derive the optimum quantity for a purchase order:

    a. EOQ
    b. fixed-interval reordering system
    c. ABC system
    d. fixed-point reordering system

36. A system that "flags" the fact that inventory needs to be replenished when it reaches a certain level:

    a. EOQ
    b. fixed-interval reordering system
    c. ABC system
    d. fixed-point reordering system

37. Profits foregone from orders lost because of lack of inventory:

    a. purchase cost
    b. ordering cost
    c. stockout cost
    d. carrying cost

38. Some examples of this cost include paperwork and follow up inspection when orders arrive:

    a. purchase cost
    b. ordering cost
    c. stockout cost
    d. carrying cost

39. Examples of this cost include money tied up in inventory storage, insurance, and taxes:

a. purchase cost
b. ordering cost
c. stockout cost
d. carrying cost

40. An example for this type of maintenance is oiling equipment daily:

a. conditional maintenance
b. preventive maintenance
c. remedial maintenance
d. none of the above

41. An example for this type of maintenance is when a belt breaks and it is being repaired, workers notice that some saws need to be sharpened:

a. conditional maintenance
b. preventive maintenance
c. remedial maintenance
d. none of the above

42. An example for this type of maintenance is a production line is suddenly shut down because a belt is broken and must be replaced:

a. conditional maintenance
b. preventive maintenance
c. remedial maintenance
d. none of the above

43. Sampling items during the transformation process to see if the transfer process is under control:

a. acceptance sampling
b. variable sampling
c. attribute sampling
d. process control

44. A quality control technique where items are accepted or rejected based on some measurement:

a. acceptance sampling
b. variable sampling
c. attribute sampling
d. process control

45. An examination of some number of materials or products to determine if a lot should be accepted or rejected based on the calculation of sample risk error:

   a. acceptance sampling
   b. variable sampling
   c. attribute sampling
   d. process control

46. The use of computers to visually display product designs:

   a. CAD
   b. CIM
   c. CAM
   d. JIT

47. A computer is used to guide and control the actual production of a product:

   a. CAD
   b. CIM
   c. CAM
   d. JIT

48. The entire manufacturing process from order entry to order shipping is computerized:

   a. CAD
   b. CIM
   c. CAM
   d. JIT

21 - 1 APPLICATION CASE

IMPROVING PRODUCTIVITY

1. Write down the steps you use when making a sandwich. (You choose the kind of sandwich and the ingredients that are needed.)

2. What would you do differently in the production of sandwiches if you need to improve your productivity so that you can make several dozen sandwiches for a party? (Hint: Think of steps that can be combined.)

21 - 2 APPLICATION CASE

FACILITIES LAYOUT PLANNING

1. Are you using a process or product layout in the production of sandwiches for the party (See Application Case 21 - 1 above)? Explain.

2. Which approach is better for this situation? Why?

21 - 3 APPLICATION CASE

INVENTORY ORDERING SYSTEMS

A small production company needs to determine if it should use a fixed-point reorder system or a fixed-interval reorder system for several items (Two of these items are explained below). The company makes three kinds of wood tables: dining tables, sofa end tables, and computer tables.

1. Which inventory reorder system should be used for each component? Why?

    -- screws for final assembly of tables (The tables are produced on an assembly line and about 200 tables are produced each work day. Each kind of table produced by the company requires the same number and size of screws.)

    -- glue that is purchased in gallon cans (The company uses different amounts of glue per day depending on the kind/size of table being produced.)

2. What contingency factors related to inventory will affect your inventory ordering philosophy?

21 - 4 APPLICATION CASE

QUALITY CONTROL

Use the scenario for wood table manufacturing from Application Case 21 - 3 above.

1. How can you "build in quality" for the production of the product?

2. What kind of quality control process will you select for monitoring production of the tables?

ANSWERS TO OBJECTIVE QUESTIONS

Chapter 1

1.	T	11.	T	21.	a
2.	T	12.	T	22.	b
3.	F	13.	c	23.	a
4.	T	14.	d	24.	d
5.	F	15.	a	25.	a
6.	F	16.	b	26.	a
7.	F	17.	c	27.	c
8.	T	18.	d	28.	b
9.	F	19.	a	29.	c
10.	F	20.	c	30.	d

Chapter 2

1.	T	12.	T	23.	a	34.	c	45.	c
2.	F	13.	T	24.	d	35.	d	46.	b
3.	F	14.	T	25.	b	36.	a	47.	a
4.	T	15.	F	26.	c	37.	c	48.	b
5.	F	16.	T	27.	b	38.	a	49.	d
6.	F	17.	T	28.	b	39.	a	50.	d
7.	T	18.	T	29.	d	40.	a	51.	d
8.	T	19.	F	30.	c	41.	c	52.	d
9.	T	20.	T	31.	c	42.	d	53.	b
10.	F	21.	b	32.	a	43.	b	54.	a
11.	F	22.	c	33.	c	44.	d		

Chapter 3

1.	F	13.	F	25.	c	37.	b
2.	T	14.	F	26.	b	38.	a
3.	T	15.	T	27.	a	39.	c
4.	T	16.	T	28.	c	40.	d
5.	F	17.	F	29.	d	41.	d
6.	F	18.	T	30.	b	42.	d
7.	T	19.	T	31.	c	43.	a
8.	F	20.	F	32.	a	44.	d
9.	T	21.	b	33.	a	45.	b
10.	F	22.	c	34.	d	46.	c
11.	T	23.	a	35.	c		
12.	T	24.	b	36.	a		

Chapter 4

1.	F	11.	T	21.	d	31.	b	41.	d
2.	T	12.	F	22.	a	32.	d	42.	d
3.	F	13.	F	23.	c	33.	b	53.	c
4.	T	14.	F	24.	a	34.	c		
5.	T	15.	T	25.	b	35.	b		
6.	T	16.	T	26.	c	36.	c		
7.	F	17.	F	27.	d	37.	d		
8.	F	18.	T	28.	a	38.	d		
9.	F	19.	c	29.	b	39.	a		
10.	T	20.	a	30.	d	40.	c		

Chapter 5

1.	F	13.	F	25.	c	37.	d
2.	T	14.	T	26.	b	38.	c
3.	T	15.	F	27.	d	39.	b
4.	F	16.	F	28.	c	40.	a
5.	F	17.	T	29.	a	41.	b
6.	F	18.	T	30.	b	42.	a
7.	F	19.	F	37.	c	43.	d
8.	T	20.	F	32.	a	44.	d
9.	T	21.	b	33.	d	45.	c
10.	T	22.	d	34.	a	46.	d
11.	F	23.	a	35.	b	47.	d
12.	F	24.	a	36.	d		

Chapter 6

1.	F	11.	T	21.	c	31.	a	41.	b
2.	T	12.	T	22.	b	32.	c	42.	a
3.	T	13.	T	23.	d	33.	b	43.	c
4.	F	14.	F	24.	d	34.	a	44.	b
5.	T	15.	T	25.	a	35.	b	45.	d
6.	F	16.	F	26.	c	36.	d	46.	a
7.	T	17.	F	27.	a	37.	c	47.	b
8.	T	18.	F	28.	c	38.	a	48.	c
9.	F	19.	T	29.	b	39.	a	49.	a
10.	T	20.	F	30.	c	40.	c	50.	d

Chapter 7

1.	F	11.	F	21.	b	31.	b	41.	c
2.	T	12.	T	22.	a	32.	a	42.	d
3.	T	13.	F	23.	d	33.	b	43.	d
4.	F	14.	T	24.	b	34.	a	44.	d
5.	T	15.	T	25.	c	35.	d		
6.	F	16.	F	26.	d	36.	c		
7.	F	17.	F	27.	b	37.	d		
8.	F	18.	T	28.	c	38.	a		
9.	T	19.	d	29.	a	39.	b		
10.	T	20.	b	30.	a	40.	d		

Chapter 8

1.	F	12.	T	23.	a	34.	c	45.	a
2.	T	13.	T	24.	a	35.	b	46.	a
3.	F	14.	F	25.	c	36.	c	47.	b
4.	T	15.	F	26.	b	37.	b	48.	c
5.	T	16.	F	27.	d	38.	a	49.	d
6.	F	17.	T	28.	a	39.	d	50.	a
7.	F	18.	F	29.	c	40.	c	51.	c
8.	T	19.	b	30.	d	41.	b	52.	b
9.	F	20.	c	31.	d	42.	d		
10.	F	21.	d	32.	a	43.	a		
11.	F	22.	d	33.	b	44.	b		

Chapter 9

1.	T	11.	F	21.	b	31.	a	41.	c
2.	T	12.	T	22.	d	32.	b	42.	a
3.	F	13.	F	23.	b	33.	b	43.	b
4.	T	14.	T	24.	d	34.	b	44.	c
5.	F	15.	F	25.	a	35.	d	45.	b
6.	T	16.	F	26.	a	36.	a		
7.	F	17.	T	27.	c	37.	c		
8.	F	18.	b	28.	c	37.	a		
9.	F	19.	d	29.	a	39.	b		
10.	T	20.	c	30.	b	40.	d		

Chapter 10

1.	F	13.	T	25.	c	37.	b	49.	a
2.	T	14.	F	26.	a	38.	d	50.	b
3.	F	15.	T	27.	d	39.	b	51.	c
4.	T	16.	F	28.	a	40.	d	52.	b
5.	T	17.	F	29.	c	41.	c	53.	d
6.	T	18.	F	30.	b	42.	a	54.	a
7.	F	19.	b	31.	b	43.	b	55.	d
8.	F	20.	c	32.	a	44.	d	56.	c
9.	T	21.	d	33.	c	45.	c		
10.	F	22.	b	34.	b	46.	c		
11.	F	23.	c	35.	a	47.	b		
12.	T	24.	a	36.	c	48.	d		

Chapter 11

1.	T	12.	F	23.	a	34.	c	45.	c
2.	F	13.	T	24.	b	35.	b	46.	b
3.	F	14.	T	25.	b	36.	b	47.	d
4.	T	15.	F	26.	a	37.	a	48.	a
5.	T	16.	F	27.	c	38.	d	49.	c
6.	F	17.	T	28.	a	39.	c	50.	b
7.	T	18.	T	29.	b	40.	a	51.	a
8.	T	19.	F	30.	c	41.	d	52.	d
9.	F	20.	F	31.	b	42.	b		
10.	T	21.	c	32.	c	43.	d		
11.	F	22.	b	33.	d	44.	d		

Chapter 12

1.	T	14.	F	27.	a	40.	a	53.	a
2.	F	15.	F	28.	d	41.	d	54.	b
3.	F	16.	F	29.	a	42.	c	55.	d
4.	F	17.	T	30.	c	43.	d	56.	c
5.	T	18.	T	31.	b	44.	c	57.	d
6.	F	19.	T	32.	d	45.	b	58.	b
7.	T	20.	d	33.	c	46.	d	59.	c
8.	T	21.	a	34.	a	47.	c	60.	d
9.	F	22.	c	35.	d	48.	c		
10.	F	23.	d	36.	b	49.	c		
11.	T	24.	b	37.	d	50.	b		
12.	F	25.	c	38.	c	51.	c		
13.	T	26.	d	39.	b	52.	d		

Chapter 13

1.	T	11.	T	21.	b	31.	a	41.	c
2.	T	12.	T	22.	b	32.	a	42.	d
3.	F	13.	T	23.	a	33.	d	43.	c
4.	F	14.	F	24.	c	34.	b	44.	d
5.	F	15.	F	25.	d	35.	b	45.	b
6.	T	16.	T	26.	d	36.	a	46.	c
7.	F	17.	F	27.	c	37.	c	47.	b
8.	T	18.	F	28.	a	38.	d	48.	b
9.	F	19.	a	29.	c	39.	d	49.	d
10.	F	20.	d	30.	d	40.	c	50.	a

Chapter 14

1.	T	10.	T	19.	d	28.	c
2.	T	11.	F	20.	b	29.	d
3.	F	12.	F	21.	a	30.	b
4.	F	13.	F	22.	c	31.	a
5.	F	14.	F	23.	b	32.	b
6.	T	15.	T	24.	d	33.	c
7.	T	16.	F	25.	c	34.	d
8.	F	17.	T	26.	d	35.	c
9.	T	18.	T	27.	b	36.	d
						37.	c

Chapter 15

1.	F	9.	T	17.	c
2.	T	10.	F	18.	d
3.	F	11.	T	19.	c
4.	F	12.	F	20.	a
5.	T	13.	F	21.	b
6.	T	14.	T	22.	d
7.	T	15.	b	23.	d
8.	T	16.	a	24.	c
				25.	c

Chapter 16

1.	T	11.	T	21.	a	31.	d	41.	d
2.	F	12.	F	22.	c	32.	c	42.	c
3.	T	13.	F	23.	a	33.	b	43.	d
4.	F	14.	T	24.	b	34.	d	44.	a
5.	T	15.	F	25.	c	35.	d	45.	a
6.	F	16.	F	26.	a	36.	b		
7.	F	17.	c	27.	b	37.	a		
8.	T	18.	c	28.	a	38.	b		
9.	T	19.	b	29.	d	39.	c		
10.	F	20.	c	30.	c	40.	a		

Chapter 17

1.	F	11.	F	21.	a	31.	d	41.	a
2.	T	12.	F	22.	b	32.	b	42.	a
3.	F	13.	F	23.	d	33.	a	43.	d
4.	T	14.	T	24.	b	34.	c	44.	b
5.	T	15.	T	25.	a	35.	a	45.	c
6.	F	16.	F	26.	c	36.	d	46.	a
7.	T	17.	a	27.	c	37.	c	47.	d
8.	F	18.	b	28.	a	38.	b	48.	b
9.	T	19.	a	29.	c	39.	a		
10.	T	20.	c	30.	c	40.	c		

Chapter 18

1.	T	13.	F	25.	a	37.	b
2.	F	14.	F	26.	b	38.	c
3.	F	15.	F	27.	d	39.	b
4.	T	16.	T	28.	d	40.	b
5.	T	17.	F	29.	a	41.	c
6.	F	18.	F	30.	c	42.	d
7.	T	19.	b	31.	d	43.	a
8.	T	20.	c	32.	a	44.	a
9.	T	21.	b	33.	c		
10.	F	22.	a	34.	a		
11.	F	23.	d	35.	c		
12.	T	24.	d	36.	a		

Chapter 19

1.	T	10.	T	19.	b	28.	c
2.	F	11.	F	20.	d	29.	d
3.	T	12.	F	21.	a	30.	d
4.	T	13.	F	22.	b	31.	d
5.	T	14.	F	23.	d	32.	c
6.	F	15.	T	24.	c	33.	d
7.	T	16.	T	25.	b	34.	d
8.	F	17.	T	26.	a	35.	c
9.	F	18.	c	27.	a	36.	b
						37.	a
						38.	c

Chapter 20

1.	T	12.	F	23.	d	34.	a
2.	F	13.	F	24.	a	35.	a
3.	T	14.	T	25.	c	36.	d
4.	F	15.	T	26.	b	37.	b
5.	T	16.	F	27.	d	38.	c
6.	F	17.	c	28.	b	39.	b
7.	F	18.	d	29.	b	40.	a
8.	T	19.	c	30.	c	41.	a
9.	T	20.	a	31.	a	42.	c
10.	F	21.	d	32.	d		
11.	T	22.	b	33.	c		

Chapter 21

1.	T	12.	T	23.	d	34.	c	45.	a
2.	F	13.	T	24.	b	35.	a	46.	a
3.	F	14.	F	25.	c	36.	d	47.	c
4.	T	15.	T	26.	a	37.	c	48.	b
5.	F	16.	T	27.	b	38.	b		
6.	T	17.	d	28.	b	39.	d		
7.	F	18.	b	29.	c	40.	b		
8.	F	19.	b	30.	a	41.	a		
9.	F	20.	a	31.	a	42.	c		
10.	T	21.	b	32.	d	43.	d		
11.	F	22.	a	33.	b	44.	b		